FOREIGN LANGUAGES IN THE ELEMENTARY SCHOOL

THEODORE ANDERSSON:

Foreign Languages in the Elementary School

A STRUGGLE AGAINST MEDIOCRITY

❖•❖

UNIVERSITY OF TEXAS PRESS
AUSTIN & LONDON

Standard Book Number 292-78402-3
Library of Congress Catalog Card Number 71-82531
Copyright © 1969 by Theodore Andersson
All Rights Reserved
Type set by G&S Typesetters, Austin
Printed by The Steck-Warlick Company, Austin
Bound by Universal Bookbindery, Inc., San Antonio

PERMISSIONS

I wish to thank the following for permission to print extracts from the books, articles, and papers included below:

From "Languages and Education—A Criticism," *The Graduate Journal*, Vol. IV, No. 2 (Fall, 1961), and "The Faces of Language: Tool—Communication—Culture—Style," *The Graduate Journal*, Vol. VI, No. 2 (Fall, 1964), both by Theodore Andersson. Reprinted by permission of *The Graduate Journal* of The University of Texas.

From *Foreign Languages in the Elementary School*, published by the Cincinnati Public Schools and reprinted by their permission.

From "Historical Account of German Instruction in the Public Schools of Indianapolis, 1869–1919," by Frances Ellis, published in *The Indiana Magazine of History*. Vol. L, No. 2 (June, 1954). Reprinted by permission of the *Indiana Magazine of History*.

From *The Silent Language*, by Edward T. Hall. Copyright © 1959 by Edward T. Hall. Reprinted by permission of Doubleday & Company, Inc.

From "Language Study and World Affairs," by Earl McGrath, published in *The Modern Language Journal*, Vol. XXXVI, No. 5 (May, 1952); and from "Report on the Status and Practices in the Teaching of Foreign Language in the Public Elementary Schools of the United States," by Emilie Margaret White and others, published in *The Modern Language Journal*, Vol. XXXVII, No. 3 (March, 1953). Both reprinted by permission of *The Modern Language Journal*.

From *Foreign-Language Programs in Elementary Schools*, Educational Research Service Circular No. 6, published by National Education Association, American Association of School Administrators, and Research Division. Reprinted by permission of National Education Association.

From "Learning Theory as it Influences Instructional Materials and Resources," by Donald Snygg. Reprinted by permission of Carlita L. Snygg.

From *Evaluation of the Effect of Foreign Language Study in Elementary School Upon Achievement in the High School,* published by the Somerville Public Schools and reprinted by their permission.

From "Foreign-Language Teaching and Intercultural Understanding," by Wilmarth Starr, published in *School and Society,* March 19, 1955, and reprinted by permission of *School and Society.*

From "A Foreign Language in the Primary School," by H. H. Stern, reprinted by his permission.

From "Some Psychological Aspects of the Teaching and Learning of Languages," by James E. Wicker, reprinted by his permission.

From "The Non-Specialist Teacher of FLES," *The Modern Language Journal,* Vol. LI, No. 2, by Charles E. Johnson, Joseph S. Flores, Fred P. Ellison, and Miguel A. Riestra, reprinted by their permission.

TO HARRIET

PREFACE

This study is the outgrowth of a tentative little book written in 1953, entitled *The Teaching of Foreign Languages in the Elementary School* and published by D. C. Heath and Company. The optimistic thesis of that book was that by beginning language instruction in the early elementary grades, when children are of an age to learn easily and well, foreign-language teachers could contribute more efficiently to the education of our youth.

In the decade and a half that have elapsed since then, foreign-language instruction has improved conspicuously, thanks first to the efforts of the Modern Language Association and secondly to the powerful boost given by the National Defense Education Act of 1958. However, close observation of foreign-language teaching in the elementary school—commonly called FLES—has revealed two weaknesses in my earlier reasoning: (1) The achievement of efficiency, which is essential to success, continues to elude us because of an all-pervading mediocrity, not only within the ranks of foreign-language teachers but throughout the educational system; and (2), implausible as it may seem, fellow educators in other fields do not *want* languages taught more efficiently, not if this efficiency would mean more curricular hours spent on language instruction, not even if it would only entail a more effective distribution of instructional time.

The present book has been written, therefore, in a considerably more somber mood than was its forerunner, but not entirely without hope for the future. My aim is to place FLES in context by tracing its history back for a century and a quarter; by relating it to language teaching in general, both here and abroad; and by trying to establish for it a fitting place in our educational structure.

ACKNOWLEDGMENTS

Clearly, though I accept responsibility for the points of view presented and for the marshaling of data to support them, I could not have written this book without assistance from many sources, only a few of which can I indicate here.

My potential interest in educational problems was crystallized by the late President A. Whitney Griswold of Yale, when in 1951 he offered me the opportunity to direct Yale's new Master of Arts in Teaching program. When the late Edward S. Noyes, long-time director of admissions at Yale, succeeded me in 1954 as director of an expanded Master of Arts in Teaching program, he gave me continued support in my study of language-teaching problems. He it was also who, while acting president of the College Entrance Examination Board, asked me to direct the first of the board's Colloquia on Curricular Change—Curricular Change in the Foreign Languages, 1963—thus enabling me to extend and update my knowledge. Of the many other helpful colleagues at Yale, two deserve special thanks. Henri Peyre, my chairman in the Department of French, whose interests are all-encompassing, gave me unfailing support for my ideas on teaching. Nelson Brooks was throughout our close collaboration in the Yale M.A.T. program and has continued to this day to be a friendly but discerning critic.

My two years of association with the Modern Language Association Foreign Language Program added enormously to my professional education. This opportunity I owe to the late William Riley Parker, executive secretary and later president of the Modern Language Association, architect and first director of its Foreign Language Program, and distinguished Milton biographer. To have lived through those exciting times of self-examination and reform in close association with a real scholar and professional and, over many a nightcap, to have shared in a discussion of Bill Parker's most imaginative ideas is a privilege that I treasure. Inspiring, too, were the leadership of George Winchester (Win) Stone, who succeeded Bill Parker as executive secretary and also later became president of the association, and the collaboration of Kenneth W. Mildenberger. To the latter I owe many an opportunity to follow at close range developments in the field of foreign languages. In particular, his invitation to me, when he became director of language development in the United States Office of Education, to direct the Foggy Bottom Conference (A Research Study Conference on Problems of State Level Supervision of Instruction in Modern Foreign Language, August 1–13, 1960, George Washington University) provided me with a mass of invaluable information on federal and state involvement in foreign-language education. To John Hurt Fisher, presently executive secretary of the Modern Language Association, and Donald D. Walsh, retired director of its Foreign Language Program and presently secretary-treasurer of the Northeast Conference on the Teaching of Foreign Languages, I am indebted for a close professional association from which I have profited greatly.

Though not staff members of the Modern Language Association, Stephen A. Freeman, director of the Middlebury Summer Language Schools and vice-president emeritus of the college; Howard Lee Nostrand, long-time chairman of the Department of Romance Languages of the University of Washington; and Wilmarth H. Starr, head, All-University Department of Romance and Slavic Languages and Literatures, New York University, have made outstanding contributions to the Foreign Language Program. Their particular brand of imaginative and constructive criticism has taught me much, and I pay them grateful tribute.

To James Bryant Conant I am indebted for an invitation to the International Congress on Modern Language Teaching, which he helped organize in Berlin in August and September 1964; for this Congress brought us all up to date on the theory and practice of modern-language teaching.

I am thankful also to many of the foreign-language specialists in the United States Office of Education but in particular to the following: to Marjorie C. Johnston, now retired, who since 1945 has provided me with both counsel and information; to A. Bruce Gaarder, who has generously shared with me his special knowledge of bilingual education and other subjects; to Joseph C. Hutchinson, now of the Defense Language Institute, East Coast; to Elizabeth Keesee; to Esther M. Eaton, now retired; and to Mary E. Hays, also retired, all of whom have responded promptly to my many calls for help.

I am also deeply obligated to The University of Texas: to the University Research Institute for a summer research grant that enabled me to prepare the first complete draft of the present book; to the Administrative Officers—to Chancellor Harry Ransom, to President Norman Hackerman, to the late Dean J. Alton Burdine, to Dean W. Gordon Whaley, and to Dean Wayne Holtzman—for their unswerving support of my pedagogical interests and for granting me a joint appointment in the College of Education; to the reference librarians, especially Miss Kathleen Blow, chief reference librarian, and Miss Mary Louise Nelson, who have helped sleuth many an elusive reference; to Mrs. Graham Blackstock, formerly of the University Press, now with the Bureau of Business Research, for her comprehensive criticism of an earlier version of this book; and finally to my long-suffering secretaries, who, one after another, have had to suffer through great parts of the typescript. Within my own Department of Romance Languages I have encountered a more than generous indulgence for my concern with teaching problems. Especially helpful have been Ernest F. Haden, who among other generous gestures, yielded to me his course on "The Teaching of Modern Languages" when I first arrived in Austin in 1957; and Mildred V. Boyer, whose help since her arrival in 1959 has been so constant as to amount almost to a collaboration. Among several friendly colleagues in the College of Education I want especially to mention gratefully Thomas D. Horn, chairman of the Department of Curriculum and Instruction, a stalwart colleague; John Pierce-Jones, director of the Child Development Education and Research Center, and Edward Cervenka, formerly research associate, and now instructor at Teacher's College, Columbia University, for their contributions to the evaluation of bilingual programs; and Joseph Michel, director of the Foreign Language Education Center, on whose help I have always been able to count.

I wish it were possible to name all of the many school administrators and teachers whose warm receptions have added to my pleasure in visiting FLES programs in many parts of the country or who have provided me with valuable information concerning their programs, but unfortunately it is not. However, I do wish to mention a few fellow educators in Texas from whom I have learned a great deal, especially about bilingual education. They are: W. R. Goodson, associate director, Commission on Secondary Education, Southern Association of Colleges and Schools; Harold C. Brantley, superintendent, United Consolidated Public Schools, Laredo, and Víctor Cruz-Aedo, formerly elementary supervisor in the same system and now an appointee of the Texas Education Agency; Mrs. Marie Esman Barker, first special project director for Title III, and now instructor in education at The University of Texas at El Paso, and Carlos Rivera, coordinator of Spanish in the elementary grades, El Paso Public Schools; Al Ramírez, former mayor of Edinburg and director of instruction in the Edinburg Schools, and now assistant director for curriculum, Region I Education Service Center in Edinburg; Nick Garza, formerly principal of the J. T. Brackenridge Elementary School, and now principal of Lanier High School, San Antonio Independent School District; P. A. Tanskley, superintendent of the Del Rio Independent School District, and R. J. Waddell, supervisor of elementary education, Del Rio; and Marshel Ashley, former superintendent, Pete Williams, former director of instruction, and Miss Patricia Rogers, former director of special projects, of the Del Valle Independent School District in 1967–1968.

Finally let me express my great debt of gratitude to my wife, Harriet Murdock Andersson, who long ago taught me to write acceptably and who despairs of ever doing more. She has read the whole of every draft and has removed many of the worst blemishes. To her I dedicate this book. I wish it were more worthy of her.

Austin, Texas

CONTENTS

TABLES

INTRODUCTION

The teaching of foreign languages in the elementary schools has stirred much popular interest and some professional controversy. The common knowledge that young children who are placed in a foreign environment "pick up" the local language faster and more accurately than adolescents or adults and the observation that children in elementary-school language classes usually excel high-school students in acquiring basic language skills—though not in learning formal grammar—account for parents' enthusiasm for this recent educational development. Many school administrators are also favorably disposed toward this trend because of the positive educational values they find in it, but there are still, especially among professional educators,[1] some sincere skeptics and a few outspoken opponents. The most frequently stated reasons for this opposition are: (1) doubt concerning the appropriateness of including foreign languages in our public-school curriculum, especially in the elementary grades, (2) the already crowded elementary-school curriculum, (3) the cost of adding a new subject, and (4) the scarcity of qualified teachers. An early chapter examines the cogency of these questioning points of view and establishes a perspective by viewing foreign-language teaching in the elementary school against the background of modern-foreign-language teaching today.

[1] I use this term to refer to educators concerned primarily with the subject "Education." In Great Britain and to a limited extent in the United States the term "educationist" is used as a synonym. Contrasting with the term "professional educator" I use the term "academic educator"—to avoid the misnomer "academician"—to designate educators concerned primarily with subjects other than Education, especially with those subjects included in the humanities, the social sciences, and the natural sciences.

The teaching of foreign languages in the elementary grades has grown steadily during the last decade. A survey completed by the Modern Language Association of America in 1961—the latest as this book goes to press—revealed 3,863 communities with some kind of program in 1959–1960. This figure represents a forty-fold increase over the figure for 1952–1953, when eighty-nine communities had some language classes in the grades.

This rapid growth has given rise to the widespread belief that the teaching of foreign languages in the elementary school is only a recent phenomenon in American education. At the same time many considered it to be a traditional practice in European education. Neither of these beliefs is accurate. A review of its history and present status will help place foreign-language teaching in the elementary school in its proper setting and will increase understanding of the conflicting conceptions that prevail concerning it. My analysis will also touch upon the nature of language and the process of language learning and upon the relation of language to the other humanities and the other social sciences, for it is my contention that language belongs to both of these fields.

The foregoing topics have to do mainly with theory, but this book is meant also to be of practical interest, linking good practice to sound theory. A school board that is intent on establishing a foreign-language program in its elementary schools wants to know how other successful programs were launched; what language or languages to select; in what grade to begin; how to assure a continuous and cumulative program; how to guarantee the use of resourceful methods and up-to-date materials and equipment; how to measure achievement and compare it with that obtained in the secondary schools; and how to solve the troublesome problems of teacher recruitment, training, and certification. Chapters on these subjects will form the core of the book.

Many educators agree that unless sound principles prevail in an effective majority of our programs this promising movement is threatened with failure. It will, therefore, be useful, in a concluding chapter, to analyze the forces in our society which favor such principles and those which militate against them. A prediction of the probable success or failure of foreign-language instruction in the elementary school completes the story.

FOREIGN LANGUAGES IN THE ELEMENTARY SCHOOL

1. Modern-Foreign-Language Teaching Today: A Perspective[1]

❖❖

ONE OF THE MARKS of our century is competition. Competition there has always been, among individuals, groups, and nations; but it seems more intense, more pervasive today than it has been in the past. The rapid growth of populations, the consequent reduction of available living space, the increased mobility resulting from speedier travel, the unabated development of industry, the terrifying advances in technical warfare, all of these and many other factors account for our impression that the struggle for natural and human resources, for markets, and for men's mind and hearts is fiercer than it has ever been.

Like every other aspect of American life, education reflects this intensified competition. There was a time when a son's ambition was limited by social custom to learning his father's trade. The principle of equal educational opportunity for all, recognized since our birth as a nation, has loosened the restrictions of class, but not until the beginning of our century did large numbers from all social strata take advantage of the opportunity for a free high-school education. And now there are proportionately over four times as many students in college as there were in high school in 1900.[2]

[1] A version of this chapter has been published separately under the title "Languages and Education—A Criticism" in *The Graduate Journal of The University of Texas*, Vol. IV, No. 2 (Fall, 1961), pp. 406–421.

[2] U.S., Department of Commerce, Bureau of the Census and in collaboration with Social Science Research Council, *The Statistical History of the United*

Statistics mirror an educational transformation that has resulted in a steadily increasing struggle for entrance into our best schools and colleges. Good medical schools take one out of two applicants, good independent secondary schools one out of three, and good liberal arts colleges one out of four. The University of California only admits high-school graduates ranking in the top tenth of their class. In an article entitled "The Graduate-School Squeeze," *Time* reported that "Out of 5,246 applicants, Harvard took 1,853. Yale's Law School got two thousand requests for 165 openings. Michigan's graduate office mailed out twenty thousand [forms], got twelve thousand back, accepted half [this number], enrolled two thousand. Chicago enrolls only 1,500 of six thousand applicants. Seventy-five percent of graduate applicants fail to land their first choice."[3]

Just as significant as the statistical trends are the changes that have taken place in our thinking about education. Time was when the primary purpose of education was the cultivation and refinement of the individual as a member of a privileged social or professional class. With the extension of universal free schooling, education came to be associated with economic and social opportunity for able and industrious members of any class. And finally, our experience in World War II, in the Korean War, in the "Cold War," and in the Vietnamese conflict has made us aware that education is not only of cultural and economic advantage to the individual but is urgently needed for national security. At first this need was thought of as technical. The National Defense Education Act of 1958 was designed to help repair our deficiencies in the teaching of science, mathematics, and modern foreign languages. Especially significant is the fact that this was our first recognition in peacetime that ability to communicate with other peoples in their languages is a matter of national self-interest and security. The amendment of this act affords federal support for most of the rest of the curriculum in secondary

States from Colonial Times to the Present. The high-school enrollment in 1900 (age 15–19) was 519,251 (p. 207) out of a high-school–age population of 6,543,189 (p. 10).

U. S., Department of Commerce, Bureau of the Census, *Statistical Abstracts of the United States.* The college enrollment in 1960 (public and private) was 3,610,000 (p. 129) out of a college-age population (20–24) of 11,112,000, including armed forces abroad (p. 6).

3 "The Graduate-School Squeeze," *Time,* April 15, 1966, p. 82.

education. The passage of the Economic Opportunity Act in 1964; of the Elementary and Secondary Education Act and of the Higher Education Act in 1965; of the International Education Act in 1966; of the Education Professions Development Act of 1967, and of the Elementary and Secondary Education Amendments and the Bilingual Education Act of 1968 all move us closer to a full recognition of the interrelationship of education and national well-being. The teaching of languages is subject to as much confusion as any aspect of our education; but this book will attempt to elucidate prevailing theory and practice of foreign-language instruction in our public elementary schools (commonly abbreviated FLES).

What is the present state of language instruction in the United States? This may be described summarily by stating that if we were to set out to teach modern languages as INefficiently as possible we would invent a system very much like the one which, even now in this second half of the twentieth century, continues to prevail in many of our schools and colleges.

Lest some readers, accustomed to consider criticisms of education as "attacks," think I am unduly severe, let me assure them that the language-teaching profession has during the last few years subjected itself to thorough self-criticism. Having found this process salutary, language teachers are now better able to welcome criticism from those outside the profession, regarding it as a sure sign of public interest and as a necessary condition of tax support. Like other teachers, they want to do the best job possible. If individually they fall short of this goal, they want to know it. And when obstacles beyond their control stand in their way, their frustration is proportionate to their high aims. The following paragraphs are not a criticism of teachers and certainly not an "attack" on them. Being a faithful description of much of our language teaching of the past and even of the present, they imply constructive criticism of our society, that is, of ourselves.

If then, INefficiency were the goal, language teaching would be organized somewhat as follows:

Despite our avowed belief in the principle of equal educational opportunity for all, we would fail to make language instruction available in many of the high schools in the United States.[4]

[4] In 1954, 56.4 per cent of high schools provided no modern-foreign-language instruction. By 1959 this percentage had been reduced to 40.0, by 1964 to 23.4,

We would in most communities delay the opportunity to begin the learning of a second language until the age of fourteen or fifteen, when the student has lost his early language-learning ability and is least well motivated for this kind of learning.

Having begun too late, we would then provide an average sequence of study of two years as compared with four to nine years in Europe and other parts of the world. This two-year sequence we would place in grades nine and ten or ten and eleven so that the student who wishes to continue his language study in college would forget much of it in the interval and would have to start over or at least repeat a part of the basic course, with a consequent blunting of his interest.

If despite these handicaps a student should develop in the learning of a second language the kind of interest teachers hope for and if he should wish to pursue his study into a third and fourth year, we would discourage him from such a plan. Our guidance counselors would inform him that only some 30 per cent of colleges granting the bachelor's degree require a foreign language for admission and most of these require only two years of one language—which is true. They would therefore urge him to drop his language and to explore other fields. If a student should be sufficiently determined on his course to appeal to the principal, the latter would in many cases tell him that for budgetary reasons it is impossible to organize an "advanced" class for fewer than a specific number of students—ten or fifteen or twenty or twenty-five. The prior questions of educational value for the individual student or of the national need for language specialists would generally not be considered. Nor would provision regularly be made for highly motivated students to study independently, with occasional help and supervision, though it is feasible to put a whole course on tape or discs. By this simple device of substituting administrative and budgetary expediency for educational values we have reduced the study of Latin and the modern foreign languages to an ineffectual two years and have practically eliminated classical Greek from our public-school programs; thus we sever our links with the sources of our cultural heritage in Greece and Rome and weaken our communications with modern Europe.

and by 1965 to 22.3 (see Glen Willbern, "Foreign Language Enrollments in Public Secondary Schools, 1965," *Foreign Language Annals*, Vol. I, No. 3 (March, 1968), p. 244).

To continue with the sad listing of our misguided efforts, we would prepare language courses as nearly as possible proof against adolescent interest. Though students make no secret of their primary interest in the speech and way of life of other peoples, we would from the beginning place ahead of these interests other objectives, such as grammar, translation, reading, and writing—all of which are appropriate goals later but not at the outset.

Our methods and materials would be no more successful. Having noted that in learning our own language we first learn to understand the spoken word, then to speak, then to read and write, and finally to understand grammar, we would reverse this process and begin with grammar, then introduce reading and writing, and finally, if at all, speaking and understanding the spoken word. In selecting reading materials we would choose what had been chosen for us by a previous generation of teachers or what we as sophisticated adults like or what we think ought to be good for our youth. If students did not thrill at the sight of sentences consisting of words laid end to end in illustration of some "rule," or of paragraphs of information about "civilization" written without charm, or of a French classical tragedy written in impeccable alexandrines, we would be surprised and a little hurt.

We would seal off the classroom from the outside world. We would not so much talk the second language as talk about it. We would not invite native speakers to come and speak to us about life in another part of the world. We would not arrange to have our students meet native speakers outside or correspond by letter or tape with youngsters abroad; or, if we did initiate such correspondence, we would allow it to languish for lack of guidance in how to make it interesting. We would not show pictures or, if we did, we would choose pictures of monuments, not of people in action. In a word, we would make the experience as academic and as little lively as possible.

Knowing that one of our principal objectives should be the preservation of our multiple language and cultural resources, we would nevertheless stand by idly and allow them to wither away because of our failure to explain to our taxpayers how the proper cultivation of these resources can contribute to our national economy and security as well as to our intellectual growth.

How does it happen that in the second half of the twentieth century a professional group, which has for decades been organized to improve its educational processes, can do no better than to follow such a course? Only a partial answer can be attempted. (1) The faculty and administration of liberal arts colleges and universities which train the best scholarly minds have been unwilling to reward adequately researchers in the field of teaching and have thus declined any real responsibility for preparing qualified teachers. (2) Some teachers and administrators in these colleges and universities have been guilty of academic snobbishness toward their colleagues in teachers' colleges and secondary and elementary schools instead of cooperating with them in what is, after all, a continuous and indivisible educational process. (3) Language teachers have not conceived of languages broadly enough and have, therefore, not sought the collaboration of their colleagues in other fields, especially in the social sciences, or the support of those in business, diplomacy, and government who now increasingly need personnel skilled in the use of foreign languages. (4) Language teachers, particularly in high schools, often have no choice but to accept teaching conditions that make professional growth difficult at best—classes both too many and too large, assignments outside their field of major competence, clerical and other routine duties. Many teachers who have hitherto been able and willing to reject these unprofessional conditions might even now be available to our schools if their services were invited under flexible conditions, for example, on a part-time basis. To acquire professional stature a teacher needs an opportunity for research and time to think, read, write, travel, and in other ways possess his soul and cultivate his mind.

The crowded events of our times—the obliteration of space, the commingling of peoples, wars and the menace of more horrible wars —have served to sharpen our focus. As a result, the general public —not only educators, government officials, international businessmen, travelers, and parents of children learning a second language in the grades—is beginning to understand both the need for more and better language instruction and the possibility that our children may receive a kind of instruction which is a far cry from the unhappy memory of their own two-year grammar-translation experience.

The main features of a language program that gives at once hope of meeting the needs of the individual learner and of contributing to our national interest and cultural maturity are sketched below.

Since it is known that the younger the learner of a second language is, the better he learns it, such a program should begin, ideally, in the nursery school, in kindergarten, or in the first grade—at the latest. Evidence supports the assumption that unless a child is exposed to another language under favorable conditions before the age of ten he is not likely to learn to speak it without accent. It can be done by some, but it takes time and a grim determination.

The language or languages selected should depend on a combination of local resources and national need. In addition to the usual Western European languages, especially those which are commonly spoken in the United States, provision should be made for Russian, Chinese, Japanese, and Arabic, to begin with.

Once begun early, such a program should continue *and progress* throughout the elementary and secondary grades as long as it is educationally rewarding to the individual learner.

In the nursery school, kindergarten, and primary grades (grades one through three), learning should be by ear principally, in the way the child learns his own language, and should be as informal as possible, though of course carefully planned.

In the intermediate grades (grades four through six), while continuing to hear and speak, the children should see what the second language looks like in print; they should begin to read, write, and spell what they have learned to understand and say and should then extend their practice in reading and writing, emphasizing the imaginative and the artistic. Literary tastes and cultural insights can best be developed if they are included among the teaching objectives from the earliest grades on.

In the junior high school (grades seven through nine) the learners should continue, always in a more mature and challenging way, to hear, speak, read, and write. Having learned proper usage by direct imitation of good models, the students should now study systematically the structure or grammar of the language—at least those students who are academically talented.

In the senior high school, students should be able to understand, speak, read, and write a second language well enough to enjoy reasonably mature literature and appreciate the way of life of the people whose language they are studying.

The Advanced Placement Program of the College Entrance Examination Board is well adapted to such a sequence.[5] By following

[5] College Entrance Examination Board, *Advanced Placement Program: 1966–1968 Course Descriptions*, ($1.50, Box 592, Princeton, New Jersey 08540) con-

a systematic course of readings in a foreign literature in the tenth, eleventh, and twelfth grades and by taking an examination in his senior year, a student may receive advanced standing and credit toward graduation in the college of his choice. Such a course, often comparable to a good college literature course, can well serve as a worthy climax to both literary and cultural studies in the secondary school.

Language is not merely communication with vocal sounds and the stuff of which literature is made; it is at the same time an important part of the characteristic behavior of a people bound together in one culture. It is intimately related to a particular way of feeling, thinking, and acting. It is rooted in and reflects a commonly accepted set of values. In a word it is not only one of the humanities; it is also a social science, closely related to linguistics, cultural anthropology, sociology, and social psychology. Unfortunately the teaching of these subjects is now restricted almost entirely to the university level, whereas many of their concepts should be conveyed to secondary-school students throughout a properly oriented foreign-language course. This need to extend the teaching of social-science concepts to the high school underlines the urgent demand for a closer collaboration among language teachers, social scientists, and curriculum planners at all educational levels.

One of the rare social scientists to investigate this important interdisciplinary area, Joshua A. Fishman of Yeshiva University, observes, "It is anomalous that a country that has been a haven for immigrants for several centuries should be faced by a dearth of individuals proficient in the languages of the world. The foreign-language knowledge and creativity of America's numerous ethnic groups has largely been overlooked in this connection. A utilization and furtherance of this resource could redound to the benefit of America's relation with the rest of the world. It could also enrich our cultural scene and enable the minority ethnic groups to maintain themselves at a cultur-

---

tains course descriptions and sample examination questions in the following subjects: American history, biology, chemistry, English, European history, French, German, Latin, mathematics, physics, and Spanish. Separate reprints for each subject may be ordered at $.25 per copy. *A Guide to the Advanced Placement Program,* which discusses objectives, offerings, and activities of the program, is available on request: CEEB, Box 592, Princeton, New Jersey 08540.

ally creative level."[6] Social scientists and language teachers working together with curriculum specialists have it within their reach to tap this resource of language skill and intercultural understanding and to apply to our education the results of research in these fields.

While planning and developing such a long-range course of language study, it is important to strengthen the present program in the secondary schools. Opportunity for the study of at least one foreign language should be extended to the high schools that still have no such instruction. The widely prevalent two-year sequence should be extended first to three years, in grades ten to twelve; then to four, in grades nine to twelve; then to six, in grades seven to twelve; and should finally be articulated completely with a program in the elementary school.

Of course it will not do merely to increase the amount of *un*satisfactory language instruction. The old-fashioned grammar and translation approach should be discarded and replaced by instruction that conforms to present requirements. This involves an initial emphasis on hearing and speaking, preferably without the use of books but with a plentiful use of tape or disc recordings. In the words of Nelson Brooks of Yale,

The program of an institute must be built upon the premise that we are turning away from one thing towards something else. What we are turning away from—explanation of grammar, translation, word lists, foreign phrases that are hobbled to English and to a book—must first be made clear. Then what we are turning towards must be made equally clear— some mastery of a foreign language as it is used by those who speak it, without written script, without English, without analysis, and with reference to the world in which they live, that is, their culture. When the skills of hearing and speaking are learned, the teacher must know how to teach the new language in its written form but in such a way that the ability to hear and speak will not be blunted and the ability to carry on the processes of thought in the new language will not be hampered by intrusions from the mother tongue.[7]

Effective language teaching will of course require qualified teachers. The Modern Language Association has defined the subject-mat-

[6] Joshua A. Fishman, letter to author.

[7] Nelson Brooks, unpublished paper contributed to a Modern Language Association Conference on Foreign Language Teachers, December 6–7, 1958.

ter competencies and, in cooperation with the Educational Testing Service, has developed the Modern Language Association Foreign Language Proficiency Tests for Teachers and Advanced Students to measure these competencies as objectively as possible.[8] The American Association of Colleges for Teacher Education is engaged in a three-year study of standards and evaluative criteria for accreditation of teacher education and expects to have an important revision of standards ready by late 1969.[9] It remains for professional educators to define the *professional* qualifications of teachers—foreign-language teachers among others. Then academic and professional educators working together should translate these definitions into flexible programs for the training of new language teachers or the retraining of language teachers already in service. Useful "Guidelines for Teacher Education Programs in Modern Foreign Languages" have been prepared by the Modern Language Association in cooperation with the National Association of State Directors of Teacher Education and Certification with the support of the Carnegie Corporation of New York.[10] Finally, as Earl Armstrong has suggested,[11] current certification procedures will need to be completely revised. Such a revision should make it possible for teachers to be licensed on the basis of demonstrated proficiency, however acquired, rather than on the basis of course credits. In order to facilitate this process we shall need to develop tests and other evaluative techniques to appraise as objectively as possible the various professional or technical—as distinguished from subject-matter—competencies

[8] For a description of these tests see Wilmarth H. Starr, "MLA Foreign Language Proficiency Tests for Teachers and Advanced Students," *PMLA*, Vol. LXXVII, No. 4, Part 2 (September, 1962), pp. 31–42.

[9] See The American Association of Colleges for Teacher Education, *Standards and Evaluative Criteria for the Accreditation of Teacher Education: A Draft of the Proposed New Standards, With Study Guide,* December, 1967. See also *A Summary of Revisions of Standards and Evaluative Criteria for the Accreditation of Teacher Education: April 1968 Revisions of the Draft of Proposed New Standards,* May, 1968. For information write: AACTE, 1201 Sixteenth St., N.W., Washington, D.C. 20036.

[10] See The Modern Language Association of America, "Guidelines for Teacher Education Programs in Modern Foreign Languages," *PMLA*, Vol. LXXXI, No. 2 (May, 1966), pp. A-2, A-3. See also Appendix F.

[11] Earl Armstrong, "The Teaching Profession: Retrospect and Prospect," in Lindley J. Stiles, ed., *The Teacher's Role in American Society,* Fourteenth Yearbook of the John Dewey Society, pp. 285-287.

of teachers. By this means it will be feasible to identify wholly or partially qualified teachers and, after a minimum of training, to induct them into service, under supervision and on trial for a time, if necessary.

Colleges and universities have a key role to play, but state departments of education and local school systems can also supply urgently needed new services. (1) If the latter do not already have them, they can appoint qualified foreign-language coordinators or consultants to assist teachers or schools that desire a more effective program. (2) They can gather and maintain up-to-date information on language teaching. (3) They can maintain a complete, up-to-date library of textbooks and of audio-visual and other teaching aids, as well as of full information on recent advances in language teaching. (4) They can provide recordings on tape or discs for use by teachers or for rental by individual learners, whether or not enrolled in school. (5) They can cooperate with the state foreign-language teachers association in facilitating meetings, conferences, workshops, visits, and travel. (6) They can survey language resources, revise courses of study and textbook lists, prepare new teaching materials, and make periodic surveys of the state of language teaching.

The Modern Language Association, the American Council on the Teaching of Foreign Languages, the United States Office of Education with its staff of competent foreign-language specialists—now unfortunately reduced—the National Education Association Department of Foreign Languages—now regrettably inactive—state and local departments of education, colleges and universities, can all do much to assist teachers in learning to use modern methods and materials. But most important of all, the individual teacher has it in his power to become a real professional. He can work in solitude with discs or tape. He can collaborate with other teachers in his school, community, or state on experimentation, research, or other professional work. He can increase his effectiveness by adding his efforts to those of other language teachers in order to create a powerful and effective association. Or he can, if he is talented and ambitious, collaborate in the work of one or more of the national associations.

None of this can really be effective without adequate support by taxpayers and voters, but the latter cannot be expected to support what they do not understand. In fact, if they think they are supporting the kind of language teaching most of them experienced in school and college, they will be most unenthusiastic. Therefore, it is the language educator's responsibility to keep colleagues, administrators, parents, school-board members, and the general public fully informed concerning the facts, trends, and problems of language instruction.[12]

I have outlined two language programs, one a long-range program beginning in the nursery school, kindergarten, or early grades of the elementary school and progressing through the elementary and secondary grades, and the other a transitional program gradually lengthening and strengthening the sequence of study in the secondary school. It may well be that the long-range program here envisaged is itself only transitional. We may perhaps look forward to the day when our children will learn more language and culture out of school than in. In fact, those who are lucky enough to live in a bilingual area often do. Why in this fast shrinking world may we not anticipate that many of our children—not only our high-school and college students—will be spending long periods abroad, perhaps in exchange for visits by foreign children living in our own families? Already this is being done in Europe and in parts of our country. The time may not be distant when, finding our foreign-language programs in the elementary school too inefficient and too modest in their objectives, we shall want to organize international nursery schools in which preschool children may learn the elements of several languages at once.

12 An invaluable aid in this is William Riley Parker's *The National Interest and Foreign Languages* ($1.00).

2. Why Foreign Languages?[1]

❖❖

WHAT, IF ANY, are the theoretical and practical justifications for foreign-language learning in the elementary school? In these days of mounting enrollments, crowded curricula, and budgetary strain, every addition to the course of study must be carefully scrutinized. An added subject should be expected to give value proportionate to its cost. However, the proper test is not: Will it add to the cost? Of course it will. Rather the test should be: Is it worth the added expense? The philosophical and practical questions of value need to be considered before deciding whether the introduction of a modern foreign language is or is not justifiable.

As a teacher interested in the improvement of language teaching,[2] I had always assumed that it was "a good thing" for more Americans to know languages, whether they were born to them, had acquired them through travel or residence in a non-English-speaking community, or had learned them in school. It was something of a shock for me to realize that not everyone shares this assumption. Some educators have even said in print that the fact that children can learn foreign languages more easily than older persons is no justification

[1] A version of this chapter has been published separately under the title "The Faces of Language: Tool—Communication—Culture—Style" in *The Graduate Journal of The University of Texas*, Vol. VI, No. 2 (Fall, 1964), pp. 304–321.

[2] Nelson Brooks (*Language and Language Learning*, p. 232) proposes the term "languist" for a specialist in the theory and practice of language teaching.

for including them in the elementary-school program.[3] The advocate
of languages in the elementary school is, therefore, forced to decide
whether or not such an opinion is serious enough to merit consideration. The truth seems to be that, though not based on rigorous reasoning, this point of view does represent an honest conviction and that
its dissemination by a few educators has raised doubts in the minds
of others. For this reason the chief values of foreign language in
instructional programs at any level will be discussed in this chapter,
whereas not until the following chapter will the specific advantages
of foreign languages in the elementary school be studied.

Skepticism about foreign languages is of course not confined to
educators. Throughout our history we have as a people betrayed the
fact that we do not universally prize knowledge of other languages
and that we do not honor those citizens who possess such knowledge.[4] A classic example of our undervaluation of foreign languages
—caused, to be sure, by war hysteria—was our outlawing of German
instruction during and following World War I, thus destroying a
specialized skill, which in time of war is even more urgently needed
than in peacetime. And it went further than this: German music and
literature were denigrated and denied.

For the sake of convenience and despite a certain overlapping of
discussion, the values of modern foreign languages will be grouped

[3] See, for example, Martin Haberman, "FLES: A Right Practice for Wrong
Reasons," *The National Elementary Principal*, Vol. XLII, No. 6 (May, 1963), pp.
51–54. The author says, "The *ease* of learning a foreign language, however, cannot be used as a rationale for offering this subject matter to children in the elementary school. The names of Aztec rulers, Haitian voodoo rituals, or the skill
of making walrus oil might prove to be subjects which children could learn easily.
. . . Are we really to include new areas of study in the already overcrowded elementary school program because young children seem capable in these fields?"
In this article the author cites no intrinsic value for foreign-language study. He
considers it only as an enrichment to social studies. This is, of course, to question
the value of foreign languages not only in the elementary school but at any instructional level. See also my reply to this article, "FLES: A Clarification," *The
National Elementary Principal*, Vol. XLIII, No. 1 (September, 1963), pp. 61–62.

[4] Such a conclusion can, I believe, be inferred from the findings of the Lan-
guage Resources Project directed from 1960 to 1963 by Joshua A. Fishman of
Yeshiva University, New York. See his book, based on his final report to the
United States Office of Education under Contract SAE-9729, entitled *Language
Loyalty in the United States*.

under the following headings: language as a tool, language as communication, language as culture, and language as style.

Language as a Tool

One of the narrowest concepts of language, though one widely held, is that of language as a tool. This instrumental use of language is generally understood to mean that the user can get enough meaning from a printed text to serve him in some specialized field. Even educators who themselves have little or no interest in foreign languages as a liberalizing study, who have relatively little use for them as a means of communication, and who personally may not have been successful in their foreign-language study nevertheless recognize the need for language as a useful tool for gaining access to specialized knowledge. Most graduate schools still require demonstration of ability to read one or two languages, although the required proficiency is often so modest and the demonstration comes so late that the requirement tends to be something of a mockery. As a result many researchers equipped with a Ph.D. degree actually limit their research to sources in English.

This unfortunate fact is documented by three psychologists from Washington University, who found that 65 per cent of 719 holders of the Ph.D. degree in psychology had, in a mean elapsed time of 8.6 years since receiving their degree, not read a single article in the foreign languages they had supposedly learned.[5] As their principal conclusion the authors apparently endorse the following statement contained in "a thoughtful letter" received from one of their respondents:

The point that I would like to emphasize is that it is not simply a matter of continuing the present language requirements, eliminating them, as some would suggest, or revising them, the latter usually in the direction of making them less stringent. There is another possibility, that we revise them in the direction of higher standards, and that this pressure at the graduate school level to make a foreign language requirement for an advanced degree might finally filter down to the high school and grade school

[5] Saul Rosenzweig, Marion E. Bunch, and John A. Stern, "Operation Babel: A Survey of the Effectiveness of the Foreign Language Requirements for the Ph.D. Degree in Psychology," *American Psychologist*, Vol. XVII, No. 5 (May, 1962), p. 239.

levels. This would be the program that I would favor; and to implement it I would urge that psychologists as a professional group carry out studies and exercise influence to demonstrate both the feasibility and the advisability of having one or two foreign languages taught as early as the second grade. Only then will we be able to get away from the present farcical situation of university teachers collaborating in an elaborate process of cheating, setting up requirements that are clearly useless and hoping that candidates will be able to slip through so as to get on to more important things.[6]

Calling attention to Floyd H. Allport's *Theories of Perception and the Concept of Structure,* which summarized research in his special field, Professor of Psychology Sidney S. Culbert turned to the twelve-page bibliography and remarked that all but 3 of the 285 titles were in English and that these 3 were out of date. Asked if this meant that nearly all of the significant research in this field was being done in English, he laughed and said that as a matter of fact about 40 per cent of the journals were published in languages other than English, thus suggesting that in a balanced citation of significant sources non-English titles would have amounted to about five pages. Culbert further remarked that of 562 items in Ulric Neisser's bibliography for *Cognitive Psychology,* only 7 were in German and 2 in French.[7] Yet both of these books are highly regarded and representative of the best contemporary scholarship in this field.

The uncomfortable truth is that most of our scholars and scientists are unable to read more than two or three other languages and that many do not read comfortably even a single foreign language. As a result we are cut off from much valuable research in other parts of the world, which reaches us in translation only and after great delay, if at all. It is now well known that Sputnik, which caught us so completely by surprise, had been described in advance in a Russian periodical and that had our scientists been reading this periodical they would have known on what frequencies reports would be broadcast from Sputnik and would have been able to receive these reports without delay.

At a time when the limits of knowledge are expanding rapidly we are failing to expand our linguistic ability rapidly enough to keep in step. Translations help, but they are expensive, slow, and all too

[6] *Ibid.,* pp. 242–243.
[7] Interview, Sidney S. Culbert.

often unreliable. A better knowledge of more languages by more researchers would put us in a better position to compete successfully in the busy world of research. It is evident that expanded and improved language programs in the elementary school and longer sequences of study in secondary schools are two feasible ways of overcoming our deficiency in this area.

Language as Communication

Thinking man has always sought to transcend the limitations of his own experience and viewpoint by communicating with other thinking men. Once his inquiring mind leads him to compare his ideas with those of others living outside his cultural and linguistic community, he has to learn other languages—for direct spoken communication or for indirect communication through writing. The spoken word, to which ease of travel has in our day given unparalleled importance, has the advantage of immediacy and subtlety of communication. All sorts of intangibles—tone, manner, gesture, facial expression, emphasis, timing, space, and context—give to talk a peculiarly expressive character.[8] Writing, on the other hand, has the advantage of giving us access to the thought of those who have lived before us, in whatever part of the world, and of permitting precise communication with distant contemporaries or with future generations.

In Europe, where people using different languages have always lived relatively closely together, the learning of languages in and out of school has long been a respected tradition. In the United States, separated from Europe by an ocean, the majority of our population has during our early history found more than adequate scope for its ambitions within our own borders, the nearness of Mexico and French Canada notwithstanding. However, conditions have changed with dramatic speed in the last decades. The jet airplane, transoceanic cables, radio, telephone, television, telstar, and space travel all bring us as close to our most distant neighbors on this planet as European countries are to one another. To expect the other fellow in this kind of world always to use our language is a damaging and dangerous admission of inferiority.

[8] See Edward T. Hall, *The Silent Language,* and *The Hidden Dimension;* and Tatiana Slama-Cazacu, *Langage et contexte: Le problème du langage dans la conception de l'expression et de l'interprétation par des organisations contextuelles.*

In the newspapers of December 29, 1952, there appeared the following Associated Press story:

Until the first American trained especially for Indonesian duty was assigned to the Embassy in 1949, all translating was done by natives. To please their employers, they interpreted everything to sound rosy, pro-American. But when American area and language experts began to read the Indonesian newspapers and attend sessions of the National Legislature, the Embassy learned that strong Communist-inspired anti-American feeling was sweeping the country. . . .

State Department officials, at their most optimistic, estimate the Department has only half the area and language experts which it considers a minimum need. . . . One career diplomat recalls that in 1946 the State Department did not have one officer who could read an Arabic newspaper. . . . To find out what Islam was saying in its newspapers, the diplomats had to mail them home to the Library of Congress for translation. . . .[9]

Addressing in 1957 the United States Office of Education Conference to Consider How Foreign Language Programs in the High School May be Redesigned to Serve Better the National Need, Howard E. Sollenberger, dean of the School of Languages of the Foreign Service Institute, Department of State, stated that 75 per cent of new Foreign Service officers "do not have a speaking and reading knowledge of any foreign language that could be considered by us adequate for handling their work and representation requirements overseas."[10] A recent attempt to require language proficiency of new Foreign Service officers has had to be abandoned for lack of qualified candidates in sufficient numbers. Our educational system is simply not yet equal to the challenge.[11]

[9] Quoted by William Riley Parker, *The National Interest and Foreign Languages*, pp. 108–109.

[10] See Marjorie C. Johnston, ed., *Modern Foreign Languages in the High School*, p. 16.

[11] In October 1961, more than five hundred colleges and universities were asked by the United States Department of State to report the progress being made in their foreign-language programs. The purpose of the survey was to test the validity of the department's plan to make language proficiency a requirement for appointment to the Foreign Service. In a letter sent to cooperating universities Herman Pollack, Deputy Assistant Secretary for Personnel of the Department of State, wrote on January 18, 1963, as follows:

"The responses to the survey indicated that, although many institutions are placing increased emphasis on foreign languages, nation-wide resources in the field must be considerably strengthened before college graduates will, as a

And yet the need is pressing: Sollenberger[12] stated in 1957 that there were some 35,000 United States citizens serving as civilian employees of the United States government overseas. He estimated an additional 28,000 Americans who were affiliated with religious organizations, also serving abroad. American business was represented abroad by 22,000, and some 15,000 were with international firms, in technical assistance programs, or serving as teachers or students studying on grants overseas. In one way or another there were in 1957 about 100,000 Americans overseas, not including the Armed Forces.[13]

Commenting on the government situation just before the passage of the National Defense Education Act, Marjorie Johnston has written as follows:

The situation was likened to a treadmill, for in spite of constantly increased efforts there seemed to be no chance of satisfying the need. Six agencies—the Army, Navy, National Security Agency, Department of State, U. S. Information Agency, and the Central Intelligence Agency—have set up full-time language programs for selected personnel in an effort to equip people on the job with the required language proficiency. Not only was it necessary to give advanced specialized instruction in West European languages and to teach additional languages, but it was also necessary to devote a major part of the time to beginning Spanish, to beginning French, and beginning German—languages that should have been learned in our schools and colleges. A few other agencies, such as the Air Force, were contracting with commercial language schools or universities

matter of course, possess significant language proficiency. The Department is convinced therefore that its best interests would be served in the present circumstances by not imposing a firm language requirement at this time. To do so would result in the exclusion of candidates, otherwise highly qualified, because their language skill did not meet an acceptable level of competence.

"In the meantime we propose to emphasize the importance of language skills on the part of candidates who are interested in a Foreign Service career by paying a salary differential to those candidates who otherwise meet all of the qualifications for appointment and who also, at the time of appointment, can pass a speaking and reading test in a modern foreign language that is useful to the Department. This program of positive recognition of language competence will go into effect with those junior officer candidates who take the Foreign Service examination after July 1, 1963."

12 Reported in Johnston, *Modern Foreign Languages in the High School*, p. 13.

13 According to *Business Week* of July 24, 1965 ("Yankees Who Don't Go Home," p. 48), American business abroad was in 1965 represented by 25,000 people, or, if wives and children were included, by 100,000.

to provide intensive training, but most of them, including the International Co-operation Administration, and the Departments of Agriculture, Commerce, Labor, and Interior, the Library of Congress, the Public Health Service, the Bureau of the Census, and others, were unable either to recruit the people needed with language competencies or to provide any instruction on the job.[14]

This international view contrasts sharply with that of the small-town or rural high school, which at best offers two years of one foreign language, frequently Latin. Since most of the graduates of the local high school have in the past remained in town or in the area, the guidance counselor and the school administrators have seen no compelling reason for providing more language instruction in view of the budgetary stringency and the teacher scarcity. So it is that the one or two students who, wishing to see something of the world, might conceivably have wanted to serve their country abroad have been deprived of the opportunity of acquiring the beginning of competence in a foreign language. Of necessity, therefore, most of our future Foreign Service officers and international representatives in business, education, and religion have tended to come from our larger communities, which can provide more ample educational opportunities.

The same cannot be said of our personnel in the Armed Services. Almost every small town and village has contributed to American military forces abroad. Between December 7, 1941, and the end of 1945 an estimated 11,500,000 youths served outside what Parker calls our "comfortable monolingual borders." During the Korean War of 1950–1953 about 3,700,000 served abroad. During the Cold War it was estimated that more than 1,000,000 Americans were stationed abroad in some 900 foreign installations.[15] And as of February 1968, over 500,000 men were on active duty in Vietnam.

But these are cold, if impressive, statistics. What difference does it make in more human terms to be able to communicate? On October 4, 1953, Harold Martin entitled one of his columns, "Signs May Get You a Quick Cup of Coffee, but to Know a People, Learn Their Speech." Martin testified, "I've spent many a harassed hour in foreign lands blocked at every turn because I could not speak the language.

[14] California, State Department of Education, *Looking Ahead in Foreign Languages*, p. 25.

[15] William Riley Parker, *The National Interest and Foreign Languages*, p. 104.

That was merely inconvenience, but it can lead to tragedy too. For I saw a battalion badly bloodied once because nobody could understand what an excited Korean was trying to say—that a strong Red force was lying in ambush, just beyond the hill."[16] Many former GI's—100,000 of them brought back foreign wives[17]—know better than our educators that it is a matter of national concern for more Americans to know more languages.

Roger Hagans, employment specialist of the Creole Petroleum Corporation of New York, reporting to the same conference as did Sollenberger in 1957, declared that all American employees of Creole "must have some degree of proficiency in Spanish or Portuguese."[18] According to the National Foreign Trade Council the value of our foreign trade, including goods and services, rose from less than four billion dollars in 1914 to well over forty-two billion in 1957.[19] By 1966 this figure had risen to forty-eight billion.[20] Hagans pointed out that our trade with Latin America was greater than our trade with any other part of the world in 1957, representing over 27 per cent of our imports and more than 34 per cent of our exports.[21]

In the papers of September 18, 1963, Darden Chambliss, Associated Press Business News Writer, reported on a survey conducted by Associated Press bureaus abroad. He summarized the varied opinions of foreign businessmen about American export business as follows. "They said that too few American salesmen know their way around foreign markets and too few companies adapt to foreign needs. But the American companies that avoid these errors are very successful, showing it's merely a matter of taking the trouble, these foreign buyers say." Comments on the language barrier also varied. One German banker said, "It's nice if the Americans speak our language, but not necessary." On the other hand, "There are many tales of sales literature incomprehensible to a foreign buyer, of technical catalogues requiring tedious translation, of salesmen who offend with

[16] Quoted in *ibid.*, p. 107.

[17] Vanna Phillips, "War Brides 10 Years Later," *Ladies' Home Journal*, Vol. LXXII, No. 7 (July, 1955), pp. 103–108.

[18] Johnston, *Modern Foreign Languages in the High School*, p. 18.

[19] Parker, *National Interest and Foreign Languages*, p. 80.

[20] United Nations, Statistical Office, *Monthly Bulletin of Statistics*, Vol. XX, No. 6 (June, 1966), pp. 98–99.

[21] Johnston, *Modern Foreign Languages in the High School*, p. 17.

their disregard for their customer's tongue." In general, the survey concludes that we could greatly increase our business abroad by learning more about how to satisfy foreign needs. Our businessmen and industrialists are feeling increasingly that they have no choice but to expand their operations overseas because this is the only protection for a capitalistic economy in competition with rival nations and ideologies. Hagans stated flatly that "For the United States concern operating abroad, the problem of language proficiency is directly related to good business practice."[22]

The British, though more experienced than we in foreign trade and though they have long recognized the need of knowing other languages, find it necessary to improve their language proficiency still further, as suggested by a news dispatch in the *New York Times*, entitled "British Businessmen to Get Electronic French Course."[23] Sir Richard Powell, director general of Britain's Institute of Directors, announced plans "to stop the use by British businessmen of 'schoolboy' French" by using up-to-date electronic language laboratories to teach colloquial French, German, Italian, and Spanish. "If we are to make the most of ourselves abroad, we must drop some of our old-fashioned ideas about foreign languages." Sir Richard said, "It is not good enough for a businessman to rub along in schoolboy French. It is neither good business nor especially courteous to assume that English is the master language throughout the world."

From the very beginning, language competence has been considered an essential part of the Peace Corps volunteer's equipment. Intensive foreign-language learning occupies 30 to 40 per cent of the trainee's time in the eight to ten weeks of basic training. Slightly less time during the four weeks of field training, and much more during the four-week overseas training course in the country of assignment. "The strength and value of the whole effort depends upon person-to-person communication between the volunteer and his host country counterparts.[24]

Educated Americans—diplomats, soldiers, businessmen, techni-

22 *Ibid.*, p. 18.

23 *New York Times*, September 22, 1963, p. 31.

24 See George E. Smith, "What Can We Learn from the Peace Corps?" *Audiovisual Instruction*, Vol. VII, No. 9 (November, 1962), p. 638. This article describes the up-to-date techniques used in the Peace Corps language-training program.

cians, educators, missionaries, doctors, lawyers, agriculturalists, tourists—are finding themselves increasingly involved in meetings abroad or in entertaining foreign visitors at home. There is hardly an educated person among us who has not had such an experience and who has not wished at some time that he knew, or knew better, a specific foreign tongue in order to be able to communicate with facility. William Riley Parker best expresses our need for foreign-language training as an aid to greater understanding among peoples:

> Given an atmosphere of good will, an individual traveling abroad can, in a sense, "get by" or "get along" with English or, for that matter, with sign language. (A blind man "gets along" with a seeing-eye dog.) But given an atmosphere of global tension, which is the atmosphere in which we live today, it would seem that no nation, particularly not a nation with frightening power and enviable wealth, can long "get by" without even trying to talk the other fellow's language. One language makes a wall; it takes two to make a gate. That is why Americans, praying for peace and seeking an increase in international understanding, now gather to discuss foreign language study as a means to these ends.[25]

Language as Culture

There is no subject more elusive or more misunderstood than the relation of language to culture. In part the difficulty is caused by a confusion between two basic meanings of the word "culture." Foreign-language teachers have traditionally considered themselves teachers of a foreign culture, especially in their advanced literature courses, and have usually understood "culture" to mean the refinement of a well-educated individual or the intellectual and artistic achievements of a people. It is the newer, anthropological meaning of "culture" as a total way of life, the learned and shared patterns of behavior of a group of people living together, which is only slowly coming to be understood and accepted by language teachers. Consideration of the items on culture and civilization in the Modern Language Association Foreign Language Proficiency Tests for Teachers and Advanced Students and of the great variety that exists in courses on culture in language institutes shows how far we are from any generally accepted concept of culture. Not all of the responsibility for this shortcoming lies with language teachers, however. When they look for comprehensive cultural descriptions of the

[25] Parker, *National Interest and Foreign Languages*, p. 103.

peoples whose languages they teach, they find that the social scientists are still mostly preoccupied with the description of primitive peoples. Only a beginning is being made in describing the patterns of contemporary civilized societies.[26]

Without for a moment discounting the refining influence on the individual provided by the study of foreign language and especially of a foreign literature, it is important to admit that culture in the anthropological meaning is also related to language in a very basic way. In expressing typical feelings, thoughts, attitudes, and values, language is both a vehicle and a mirror of culture. It may be an overt expression of cultural values, as when the French say: "Ce qui n'est pas clair n'est pas français." Or it may communicate a message contrary to the meaning of the words used: "I'm *sure* he's all right." As Edward T. Hall demonstrates, cultural patterns are revealed as clearly by what he calls "the silent language" as they are by words. Hall asserts,

Most Americans are only dimly aware of this silent language even though they use it every day. They are not conscious of the elaborate patterning of behavior which prescribes our handling of time, our spatial relationships, our attitudes toward work, play, and learning. In addition to what we say with our verbal language we are constantly communicating our real feelings in our silent language—the language of behavior. Sometimes this is correctly interpreted by other nationalities, but more often it is not.[27]

[26] See, for example, G. Reginald Bishop Jr., ed., *Culture in Language Learning: Reports of the Working Committees: Northeast Conference on the Teaching of Foreign Languages*, 1960; Robert Lado, *Linguistics Across Cultures: Applied Linguistics for Language Teachers*; Laurence Wylie, Else M. Fleissner, Juan Marichal, Donald Pitkin, and Ernest J. Simmons, "Six Cultures (French, German, Hispanic, Italian, Luso-Brazilian, Russian): Selective and Annotated Bibliographies," in *Reports of Surveys and Studies in the Teaching of Modern Foreign Languages, 1959–1961*, pp. 253–275; Edward Hall, *Silent Language*, and *Hidden Dimension*; Howard Lee Nostrand, "A Second Culture: A New Imperative for American Education," in the College Entrance Examination Board *Curricular Change in the Foreign Languages: 1963 Colloquium on Curricular Change*, and his book *Understanding Complex Structures: A Language Teacher's Handbook*; and Francis Debyser, "The Relation of Language to Culture and the Teaching of Culture to Beginning Language Students," *The CCD Language Quarterly: The Chilton-Didier Foreign Language Newsletter*, Vol. VI, Nos. 1 and 2 (Spring/Summer, 1968).

[27] Edward Hall, *Silent Language*, p. 10.

Each language has a different way of considering human experience, of dividing it, of ordering it. "No two languages are alike; each has to be approached afresh. Some are so dissimilar, English and Navajo, for example, that they force the speaker into two entirely different concepts of reality."[28] An interesting aspect of anthropological study involves the observation of the way in which different languages reflect, in their structure and vocabulary, different outlooks on the world and on life, what the Germans call *Weltanschauung*.[29] Not only do others misinterpret us; we also misinterpret others. Hall remarks,

Americans often do so badly in their job overseas that military officers have a real fear of being assigned to some countries. I once heard a retired admiral talking to an army general about a mutual acquaintance. "Poor old Charley," lamented the admiral, "he got mixed up with those Orientals in the Far East and it ruined his career."[30]

Americans abroad are not always inept; they *can* learn, provided our training programs are sophisticated. Our Peace Corps provides many successful illustrations, as did some of our programs in World War II. Wilmarth H. Starr tells this story of one of his World War II experiences:

It is some 10 years now since, having sought a commission in our military services with a view to contributing my limited knowledge of European languages to the cause, I found myself in the far Pacific, a 90-day wonder as a military strategist and a 17-month wonder as a Chinese scholar. Soon after my arrival in Asia, I witnessed in a striking way the linguistic barriers existing between men of the same nation, for I found myself in the extraordinary position of translator between two Chinese generals, the one from the south speaking to me in broken English, which I in turn rendered in broken Mandarin to the general from the north. The academic question is, Who was the foreigner in that situation?

[28] *Ibid.*, p. 96.
[29] See Ruth Benedict, *Patterns of Culture: An Analysis of Our Social Structure as Related to Primitive Civilizations*; Edward Sapir, *Selected Writings in Language, Culture, and Personality*; John B. Carroll, ed., *Language, Thought, and Reality: Selected Writings of Benjamin Lee Whorf*; Margaret Mead, ed., *Cultural Patterns and Technical Change: A Manual Prepared for the World Federation for Mental Health*; Lado, *Linguistics Across Cultures*; and Robert G. Hayden, "Spanish-Americans of the Southwest: Life Style Patterns and Their Implications," *Welfare in Review* (April, 1966), pp. 14–25.
[30] Edward Hall, *Silent Language*, p. 12.

On another occasion, units of the fleet were immobilized at a critical time for lack of certain information that could only come from Chinese sources. Having been given *carte blanche* to get this information and having learned about Chinese ways, I paid a quite unorthodox call on the distinguished and influential Chinese Mayor of Shanghai. After greeting him with utmost courteousness and a liberal sprinkling of the admiral's compliments, I sat down to several leisurely cups of aromatic tea. Some 45 minutes of casual conversation later, I broached my subject by begging to take leave, mentioning casually that we were sailing in the morning and that the admiral would like the mayor to be the first to know this. The mayor, not to be outdone in courtesy, asked if I would convey his respects to the admiral and would there be, by chance, any information he might send by me to that worthy gentleman. As a matter of fact, there was a small matter that the admiral would very much appreciate knowing about. A few telephone calls were made, some Chinese admirals and generals joined us for another bout with the teacups, and some time later I rejoined the flagship armed with the specific information.

Not my inadequate Chinese, but about seven cups of tea and the exchange of courtesies in an ancient ritual provided the key. An understanding between men rests upon something more than linguistic interchange; its roots extend into the cultural earth in which the men in question have their origins.[31]

George L. Trager and Edward T. Hall have developed a theory of culture,[32] which further illuminates the relation of language to culture. An understanding of this theory will hereafter be indispensable for the modern-foreign-language teacher and will, indeed, contribute greatly to the understanding of educators and all those who seek a broader view of education.

Hall and Trager have found that culture has three levels or aspects, which they call the formal, the informal, and the technical. There is often an overlapping from one aspect to another, the rela-

[31] Wilmarth H. Starr, "Foreign-Language Teaching and Intercultural Understanding," *School and Society*, March 19, 1955. The importance of the cultural aspect, which Starr here emphasizes, has led some social-science educators to discount the language factor altogether. After all, Starr did need some Chinese, too.

[32] First published under the title *Human Nature at Home and Abroad: A Guide to the Understanding of Human Behavior*, and later more fully elaborated by Edward Hall in *The Silent Language*.

tive emphasis differs from culture to culture, and the levels are all subject to change.[33]

Also related are the formal, informal, and technical aspects of learning:

Formal activities are taught by precept and admonition. The adult mentor molds the young according to patterns he himself has never questioned. He will correct the child saying, "Boys don't do that," or "you can't do that," using a tone of voice indicating that what you are doing is unthinkable. . . . An error made by many parents these days is to try to explain formal behavior in the same way one goes about outlining the reasons for technical behavior. This is a signal to the child that there is an alternative, that one form is as good as another! A great mistake.

Informal learning is of an entirely different character from either the technical or the formal. The principal agent is a *model* used for imitation. Whole clusters of related activities are learned at a time, in many cases without the knowledge that they are being learned at all or that there are patterns or rules governing them. . . . Whenever statements like the one that follows are made, one can be sure that the activity is an informal one: "Mother—how does a woman get a man to marry her?" "Well, it's a little hard to describe, but when you get bigger you'll find out. There's plenty of time for learning."

Technical learning, in its pure form, is close to being a one-way street. It is usually transmitted in explicit terms from the teacher to the student, either orally or in writing. Often it is preceded by a logical analysis and proceeds in coherent outline form.[34]

Hall further explains that there are formal, informal, and technical attitudes toward change, pointing out that an attempt by an outsider to change a formal cultural pattern will be met by great, and often emotional, resistance. Even informal patterns are resistant to change except by means of unhurried demonstration. It is in the technical area that change can be effected most easily, for here there is full awareness and analysis, and explanations are more likely to be understood. Gradually our representatives overseas are learning where not to trespass and where proffered assistance will be welcomed, but we are still far from having built into our educational system and especially into our teaching of modern languages

[33] See Edward Hall, *Silent Language*, p. 66 ff., for an interesting passage in which he uses skiing as an example of the three cultural aspects.

[34] *Ibid.*, pp. 69–72.

the knowledge and understanding of these cultural concepts which we need if we are to achieve real proficiency in our teaching.

Language as Style[35]

Modern-foreign-language teachers share with teachers of the classics a consciousness of "initiating oncoming generations into the human traditions of the race," the traditions of artistic and literary expression, "those things which most obviously set us apart from the animal," to use Moses Hadas' words. While the study of literature need not be an exclusive interest, for most language teachers it is an important reason, and for many *the* most important reason, for learning a foreign language. As Mr. Hadas observed in his essay on "Style in Education," "The Greeks subsumed the distinctive qualities of man under the word *logos*, which means 'word,' 'rationale,' 'discourse.' . . . Man is superior to . . . the uneducated because he possesses many *logoi*; the more *logoi* he has the more copiously and subtly and profoundly he can think. The *logoi* were stored up and accessible in a body of literature."[36]

It was the view of Moses Hadas that the word "style" defines civilization and gives it continuity. It is style that Greek educational theory was designed to foster and promote and that is the principal item in the legacy bequeathed to the humanists. It is style that teachers of the humanities must cultivate with special care in a world in which style is on the defensive. How can these teachers do it? According to Hadas, "We teach style, first of all, through the most obvious and immediate and proven of all devices, the *logos*, beginning with its basic meaning 'word,' and then expanding to its fuller meanings of 'rationale' and 'discourse'."[37]

Though even a rudimentary knowledge of a foreign language gives some perspective, as Professor Hadas rightly pointed out, it is obvious that the student of style needs to possess a highly developed and refined knowledge of language. Language skill and refinement of mind and sensibility must in fact go hand in hand. In

---

[35] The use of the word "style" is borrowed from the late Moses Hadas' "Style in Education: Classics and the Classical," in *Curricular Change in the Foreign Languages: 1963 Colloquium on Curricular Change*, from which essay I quote in this section.

[36] *Ibid.*, pp. 1–2.

[37] *Ibid.*, p. 3.

literature, language is the raw material of art. Making use of the full range of expressive possibilities, inducing in the reader emotions all the way from whimsy to terror, or leading him skillfully through the most delicate or compelling patterns of thought, the word artist intertwines sound and sense, and the sensitive reader experiences not only the muscular pleasure of rolling the sounds around on his tongue but all the delights of the imagination. Language teachers rightly feel that it is the study of literature which provides the most liberalizing aspect of language study. For this reason they feel that a college degree requirement that does not include an initiation to a study of a foreign literature in the original tongue falls short of the liberal arts ideal of education.[38]

Language as art—what Hadas called style—is certainly the ultimate to which the foreign-language student may aspire. But ability to apprehend art in a foreign tongue presupposes thorough control of the language, the kind of control that is best acquired by starting early and by pursuing the study for many years. So it is that beginning a foreign language in the elementary school and planning for a long continuity gives the best promise, not only of getting information from a written text or of communicating orally or in writing with foreigners or of sensing the values of an alien culture but also of apprehending the varied effects of the writer-artist.

Conclusion

In our increasingly complex and competitive world foreign languages are indispensable tools for gaining knowledge in a great variety of fields—it is difficult to name a field in which users of different languages are not competing for some form of advantage or excellence—and yet this constitutes the lowest order of justification for including languages in our school programs. Competence in most fields may require nothing more than a reading—or even a translating— knowledge of one or more foreign languages. Ability to speak another language, even haltingly, will, as our Peace Corps experi-

[38] William Riley Parker, Distinguished Service Professor of English, Indiana University, organizer and first director of the Foreign Language Program of the Modern Language Association of America, has clearly stated the case for language study in his article "Why a Foreign Language Requirement?" *PMLA*, Vol. LXXII, No. 2B (April, 1957), pp. 1–12, just as later he has stated "The Case for Latin," (*PMLA*, Vol. LXXIX, No. 4, Part 2 [September, 1964], pp. 3–10).

ence reveals, enable us to cooperate with other nationalities. The effectiveness of our communication is in direct proportion to our linguistic skill—provided we also have some cultural sophistication and human sympathy. Cultural insight, though dependent on knowledge of language, is even more important than mere language skills. Language and culture are in truth so intimately related that our future teacher-training programs will have to take account of both.[39] Finally, as the last step in this process of breaking out of our monolingual and monocultural shell, we should aspire to an appreciation of the most distinguished expressions of creative thought and imagination in another literature.

Foreign languages, therefore, appear to be an essential part of a liberal education. Use of language as a tool for prying basic meaning out of a written text contributes only modestly to a liberating effect. Language as communication comes closer to breaking human barriers. The understanding of language as culture also contributes to the liberalizing process. But only the awareness of language as style can lead the individual to the basic goal of foreign-language study: to the freeing and the cultivation—which is to say, to the education—of the human spirit.

[39] This concept is interestingly presented in a tape recording entitled "A Word in Your Ear," prepared by Walter Goldschmidt and Harry Hoijer. (Published in the *Ways of Mankind Series* by The National Association of Educational Broadcasters, it can be purchased by writing to them at: 119 Gregory Hall, Urbana, Illinois 61803, $3.50.)

3. Why FLES?[1]

THE PREVIOUS CHAPTER took one step toward the justification of foreign-language teaching in the elementary school, a modest first step, that of examining the educational value of foreign languages among our school offerings at any level. Foreign languages have always had a place in our high schools and colleges, however inadequate. Their relative neglect in recent decades is but one indication of our inability to take the long, broad view. To be sure, only a minority of educators and of that part of the public which determines school policy wish to deny a place to languages altogether, but even the majority who accord them a place seem to do so grudgingly, and it is a minimal place at most. The usual limiting of language study to two years serves unwittingly to confirm the often-alleged ineffectiveness of instruction and so fails dismally to supply the skilled users of other languages which we need in our competitive world. The argument in the preceding chapter led to the conclusion that languages should have a prominent place in our schools, that they deserve an emphasis sufficient to assure the acquisition of *adequate* knowledge and skills by many more Americans. It is the purpose of the present

[1] In this chapter I shall make liberal use of data contained in my article "The Optimum Age for Beginning the Study of Modern Languages," *International Review of Education*, Vol. VI, No. 3 (1960), pp. 298–306.

chapter to demonstrate that language learning can be most effective if begun in the early grades of the elementary school, provided instruction in the secondary grades is sequential and efficient.

Nature of Language

Such analysis must, of course, respect (1) the nature of language and (2) the natural process of language learning. Always a few exceptional teachers have understood what language is, but more recently the research of linguists and of cultural anthropologists has provided valuable new insights.[2] Nelson Brooks's definition of the nature of language is pertinent here, for it takes into account the findings of social scientists.

Language is not a book, nor a grammar, nor a dictionary. Language is certainly not writing; indeed it is not even words, for nobody talks in single words. Nor can it be equated with communication. Language lends itself admirably to communication, yet communication can and does take place quite well without language. Above all it cannot possibly be the matching of one linguistic code with another; translation is not language, but only the relating of two languages already well known. Language can be pictured in writing and it may be analyzed and codified in grammar. It may be divided up into words, and these words may be arranged in a lexicon. It serves the literary artist for his art; yet it is what he starts with but not the finished product, so language is not literature. Now if language is none of these things, what is it? We may say that it is learned, systematic, symbolic vocal behavior; a culturally acquired, universal, and exclusive mark of man, grafted upon the human infant's delight in babble.[3]

Summarizing and simplifying, language may be defined as the way a native speaker feels, thinks, and acts when he talks.

[2] See for example Noam Chomsky, "Language and the Mind," *Psychology Today*, Vol. I, No. 9 (February, 1968), pp. 48–51, 66–68. According to Chomsky,

"We can describe the child's acquisition of language as a kind of theory construction. The child discovers the theory of his language with only small amounts of data from that language. . . . It is unimaginable that a highly specific, abstract, and tightly organized language comes by accident into the mind of every four-year-old child. . . . The child cannot know at birth which language he is going to learn. But he must 'know' that its grammar must be of a predetermined form that excludes many imaginable languages" (p. 66).

[3] See Marjorie C. Johnston, ed., *Modern Foreign Languages in the High School*, pp. 136–137.

Process of Language Learning

How language came to be learned by man is one of the unsolved mysteries, a mystery that is re-enacted every time a baby is born. Susanne K. Langer remarks that "Between the clearest animal call of love or warning or anger, and a man's least [i.e., most] trivial *word*, there lies a whole day of Creation—or in modern phrase, a whole chapter of evolution."[4] In the individual this chapter of evolution takes place between birth and about age five and the most miraculous part occurs earliest. It is no wonder that the subject of infant speech has attracted so many students. Despite the studies of Bellugi, Brown, Jacobson, Langer, Lenneberg, Leopold, Lewis, McCarthy, Piaget, Preyer, the Sterns, Watts, and many others, the exact nature of the miracle escapes us and the learning of speech by man remains a mystery.[5]

EARLY LEARNING. From the moment of birth the human infant makes vocal noises and unconsciously begins to enjoy a truly remarkable capacity for producing—at least potentially—all the sounds in all the three to six thousand languages spoken on this planet. After a study of sample recordings of the vocalization of a single infant in the first year of life Charles Osgood states that "The first observation of note was that within the data for the first two months of life may be found all of the speech sounds that the human vocal system can produce."[6] As a developing social creature the infant would, of course, like to share his pleasure with those around him. The unhappy truth is that only a small part of his sound production meets with a response from the linguistically limited grownups who attend him, and so only those sounds belonging to the particular language of his community are reinforced and the others gradually slip into disuse. As time goes on, he not only loses his taste for inventing and practicing sounds but also his aptitude for imitating sounds accurately.

[4] Susanne K. Langer, *Philosophy in a New Key: A Study in the Symbolism of Reason, Rite, and Art*, p. 94.

[5] For a discussion of possible origins of language and of the process of language learning see Chapter 16, "Language Behavior," in Charles E. Osgood, *Method and Theory in Experimental Psychology*; Ursula Bellugi and Roger W. Brown, eds., *The Acquisition of Language*; and E. H. Lenneberg, *Biological Foundations of Language*.

[6] Osgood, *Method and Theory in Experimental Psychology*, p. 684.

An infant also observes the behavior of his family and friends as they make noises through their mouths. Little by little this behavior suggests the meaning of these noises. In time the noises convey significance even without the accompanying behavior; that is, they acquire their full symbolic meaning. Gradually he discovers that he can use his voice to affect the behavior of those around him. How successful he is in this, as well as in adjusting his behavior to that of others, depends in part on his skill in using this instrument called language.

This analysis suggests two facets in the language-learning process, the inventive and the imitative. "The mother helps, but the initiative comes from the growing child," says Dr. Wilder Penfield, former director of the Montreal Neurological Institute.[7] Of the two, authorities have come to consider the inventive aspect as the more important. Werner Leopold goes so far as to assert that "pronunciation is the only part of language that is chiefly imitated."[8] He is even more explicit in his *Speech Development of a Bilingual Child* when he writes concerning his daughter, who was raised bilingually,

> The diary at this point reveals my astonishment at the course which the development took. From the literature on child-language I had expected a stage of mechanical sound-imitation, with later induction of meaning for words thus acquired. . . . In Hildegard's case, the phase of mechanical imitation was completely lacking; meanings were always developed before sound-forms. The impulse for any kind of imitation was strikingly weak in this child.[9]

Nelson Brooks, using terms invented by the Swiss linguist Ferdinand de Saussure,[10] reflects a similar point of view: "In the case of the infant, there is a fascinating contest between his inborn potential for the use of *parole*[11] and the community's highly systematized practice of *langue*.[12] Of course, the latter always wins, and imposes

[7] Wilder G. Penfield, *Speech and Brain-Mechanisms*, p. 240.

[8] The Modern Language Association of America, "Childhood and Second Language Learning," *FL* [Foreign Language] *Bulletin*, No. 49 (August, 1956), p. 3.

[9] Werner F. Leopold, *Speech Development of a Bilingual Child: A Linguist's Record*, Vol. I, p. 22.

[10] Ferdinand de Saussure, *Cours de linguistique générale*, translated by Wade Baskin under the title *Course in General Linguistics*.

[11] The individual's language.

[12] The language of the community.

its will on the loser almost completely."[13] And Dorothy McCarthy summarizes thinking on the subject when she writes: "Most present-day psychologists seem to agree with the opinion of Taine (1876) that new sounds are not learned by imitation of the speech of others, but rather that they emerge in the child's spontaneous vocal play more or less as the result of modulation, and that the child imitates only those sounds which have already occurred in its spontaneous babblings."[14]

Language learning in the early stages consists, according to Penfield, of the acquisition of "speech units," by which he means the conditioned learning of the sound system and forms of a language by the assimilation of a set of utterances or structures. This is what Aage Salling, following Otto Jespersen,[15] calls *det lille Sprog* (the little language) in a book of the same title. Salling's theory states that, although the pupil may have a small vocabulary, he will be able to express personal feelings by his use of it.[16]

Once the child has learned the basic speech units he is ready for the stage of vocabulary expansion. "At three years the child begins to use prepositions and plurals with some facility. Sheer rate of learning new words is at a peak. The three-year-old may be acquiring language at the rate of about 400 new words in six months; and from 2½ to 3½ years his total vocabulary nearly doubles."[17]

FRANÇOIS GOUIN'S OBSERVATIONS. François Gouin, best known for the "Gouin Series," which still continues to exert a beneficial influence on beginning language textbooks, has given a fascinating account of the way a three-year-old learns language.[18] Gouin describes so vividly his three-year-old nephew caught in the act of learning

[13] Nelson Brooks, *Language and Language Learning: Theory and Practice,* pp. 21–22.

[14] Dorothy McCarthy, "Language Development in Children," in Leonard Carmichael, *Manual of Child Psychology,* pp. 494–495.

[15] Otto Jespersen, *Language: Its Nature, Development and Origin,* pp. 105 ff.

[16] Quoted from a summary in English printed at the end of *Det Lille Sprog,* p. 133, and republished in *The French Review,* under the title "The Principle of Simplification," Vol. XXVIII, No. 2 (December, 1954), pp. 153–159.

[17] Arnold Lucius Gesell and Frances L. Ilg, "Development Trends in Language Behavior," *FL* [Foreign Language] *Bulletin,* No. 49 (August, 1956), p. 7.

[18] François Gouin, *L'art d'enseigner et d'étudier les langues.* I quote from the ninth English edition, *The Art of Teaching and Studying Languages,* translated from the French by Howard Swan and Victor Betis.

a whole segment of language that it is worth reproducing this description at length in his own words, since his book has long been out of print.

Gouin had been spending several months of study in Germany and had been wrestling futilely with the problem of learning German well enough to follow university lectures. He had returned to France for the spring vacation and was visiting relatives. He remarks that "in taking leave . . . ten months before, I had kissed good-bye to one of my little nephews, a child of two and a half years, who was beginning to run about, but could not yet talk. When I entered the house on my return, he began chatting with me about all sorts of things quite like a little man."

The uncle thought to himself,

"The child has not yet seen everything, has not yet perceived everything. I should like to surprise him in the presence of some phenomenon entirely fresh to him, and see what he would do—on the one hand to express this phenomenon to himself in the aggregate and in all its details, and then to assimilate the expressions gathered, attempted, or invented by him on the occasion of this phenomenon.

"One day the mother said to the child, 'Would you like to come along with me, I am going to the mill; you have never seen a mill; it will amuse you.' I was present; I heard the proposition; and the words, 'you have never seen a mill' recalled my watchword to me.

"The little lad went along with his mother. He went over the mill from top to bottom. He wanted to see everything, to hear the name of everything, to understand about everything. Everything had to be explained to him. He went up everywhere, went into every corner, stopped before the tick-tack, listening long in mute astonishment. He curiously examined the bolters, the millstones, the hoppers. He made the men open the flour-store; he pulled back the curtain of the bran-room, admired the turning of the pans and belts, gazed with a sort of dread at the rotation of the shafting and the gearing of the cog-wheels, watched the action of the levers, the pulleys, the cranes lifting through space the sacks stuffed full of wheat. All the time his eyes eagerly followed the millers, whitened with flour, moving about here and there, loading and unloading sacks, emptying some, filling others, stopping the motion of the wheels, silencing one clattering wheel and then starting another.

"Finally the child was led to the great water-wheels outside. He lingered long in ecstasy before these indefatigable workers, and before the mighty, splashing column of water, which, issuing from the mill-pond, already full to overflowing, rushed white with foam along the mill-race, fell in roaring torrents into the floats of the water-wheel, setting and keeping in motion with thunderous roar the giant wheels, with all this immense and marvelous mechanism turning at full speed beneath their impulsion, driving, devouring the work with a bewildering rapidity.

"He came away deafened, stunned, astounded, and went back home absorbed in thought. He pondered continually over what he had seen, striving to digest this vast and prolonged perception. I kept my eyes upon him, wondering what could be passing within him, what use he was going to make of this newly acquired knowledge, and, above all, how he was going to express it.

"In the child the intellectual digestion, like the physical digestion, operates rapidly. This is doubtless owing to the fact that it never overloads its imagination any more than its digestive organs.

"At the end of an hour he had shaken off his burden. Speech returned. He manifested an immense desire to recount to everybody what he had seen. So he told his story, and told it again and again, ten times over, always with variants, forgetting some of the details, returning on his track to repair his forgetfulness and passing from fact to fact, from phrase to phrase, by the familiar transition, 'and then . . . and then . . .' He was still digesting, but now it was on his own account; I mean, he did not stay to think any further over his perceptions; he was conceiving it, putting it in order, moulding it into a conception of his own.

"After the discourse came the action; after Saying came Doing. He tormented his mother until she had made him half a dozen little sacks; he tormented his uncle until he had built him a mill. He led the way to a tiny streamlet of water nearby; and here, whether I would or no, I had to dig a mill-race, make a waterfall, drive in two supports, smooth two flat pieces of wood, find a branch of willow, cut two clefts into it, stick the pallets into these clefts; in short, manufacture a similacrum of a large wheel, and then, lastly, place this wheel beneath this waterfall and arrange it so that it would turn and the mill would work.

"The uncle lent himself with great willingness to all these fantasies, acquitted himself in the enterprise as well as he could. During all this time I watched each movement of the importunate little fellow attentively. I noted each of his words, each of his reflections, striving to read the interior thought through the work or the external pre-occupation.

"When the mill was definitely mounted and set agoing, the little miller filled his sacks with sand, loaded them on his shoulder with a simulated effort accompanied with a grimace; then, bent and grunting beneath the weight, carried his grain to the mill, shot it out and ground it, so reproducing the scene of the real mill—not as he had seen it, but as he had afterwards 'conceived' it to himself, as he had 'generalised' it.

"Whilst doing all this, he expressed all his acts aloud, dwelling most particularly on one word—and the word was the 'verb,' always the verb. The other terms came and tumbled about as they might. Ten times the same sack was emptied, refilled, carried to the mill, and its contents ground in his imagination.

"It was during the course of this operation, carried out again and again, without ceasing, 'repeated aloud,' that a flash of light suddenly shot across my mind, and I exclaimed softly to myself, 'I have found it! Now I understand!' And following with a fresh interest this precious operation by means of which I had caught a glimpse of the secret so long sought after, I caught sight of a fresh art, that of learning a language. Testing at leisure the truth of my first intuition, and finding it to conform more and more to the reality, I wandered about repeating to myself the words of the poet, 'Je vois, j'entends, je sais'—'I see, I hear, I know!' "[19]

LANGUAGE SKILLS. Authorities agree that by the age of five and a half, on the average, a child has completely assimilated the basic language skills; he is capable, within the limits of his exprience, of understanding anything that is said by those around him and of saying anything he wishes within the same limits and with a pronunciation and intonation that conform perfectly to those of his community. In the words of Professor Ruth G. Strickland, "The child of five years is speaking about as well as the adults in his environment."[20]

[19] *Ibid.*, pp. 34–38.
[20] Ruth Gertrude Strickland, *The Language Arts in the Elementary School*, p. 101.

The size of a child's vocabulary also astonishes grownups, whose rate of learning has by comparison almost come to a halt. Mary Katherine Smith, using the Seashore-Eckerson English Recognition Vocabulary Test,[21] found that "For grade one, the average number of basic words known was 16,900, with a range from 5,500 to 32,800. . . . For grade one the average number of words in the total vocabulary (basic plus derivative words) was 23,700, with a range from 6,000 to 48,800."[22] In a study of children's active vocabulary Henry D. Rinsland used written sources supplemented by children's conversation to count 5,099 different words used by first graders out of 353,874 running words.[23] It would be ludicrous, were it not so tragic, to ponder the fact that American children with recognition vocabularies of many thousands of words are being systematically stultified in their early reading instruction by the use of primers based on vocabularies of only a few hundred words.[24]

Optimum Age for Foreign-Language Study

It is for the very young learner but a short, almost imperceptible, step from learning his own language to learning one or more other languages. According to Wilder Penfield, "A child who is exposed to two or three languages during the ideal period for language learning pronounces each with the accent of his teacher. If he hears one language at home, another at school, and a third perhaps from a governess in a nursery, he is not aware that he is learning three languages at all. He is aware of the fact that to get what he wants from the governess he must speak one way and with his teacher he must speak in another way. He has not reasoned it out at all."[25]

One of the best known examples of children's multilingual abilities is that cited by the British psychologist J. W. Tomb:

[21] For an interesting description of the procedure and result of measuring the size of children's vocabulary see Robert H. Seashore, "How Many Words Do Children Know?" *The Packet*, Vol. II, No. 2 (November, 1947), pp. 3–17.

[22] Mary Katherine Smith, "Measurement of the Size of General English Vocabulary through the Elementary Grades and High School," *Genetic Psychology Monographs*, Vol. XXIV, Second Half (November, 1941), pp. 343–344.

[23] Henry D. Rinsland, *A Basic Vocabulary of Elementary School Children*, p. 12.

[24] See Jeanne Chall, *Learning to Read: The Great Debate*.

[25] Penfield, *Speech and Brain-Mechanisms*, p. 253.

It is a common experience in the district in Bengal in which the writer resided to hear English children three or four years old who have been born in the country conversing freely at different times with their parents in English, with their *ayahs* (nurses) in Bengali, with the garden-coolies in Santali, and with the house-servants in Hindustani, while their parents have learnt with the aid of a *munshi* (teacher) and much laborious effort just sufficient Hindustani to comprehend what the house-servants are saying (provided they do not speak too quickly) and to issue simple orders to them connected with domestic affairs. It is even not unusual to see English parents in India unable to understand what their servants are saying to them in Hindustani and being driven in consequence to bring along an English child of four or five years old, if available, to act as interpreter.[26]

Such observations could of course be multiplied indefinitely. Almost any American family with young children which has lived abroad for a considerable length of time has observed this, to grown-ups, fantastic language-learning ability of children. Missionaries are often in a particularly good position to testify. One American missionary family in Vietnam tells this story: When they went out to Vietnam, there were three of them, father, mother, and four-year-old daughter. Shortly after their arrival a son was born. The parents' work took them on extended trips to the interior of the country, at which times they left their children in the care of a Vietnamese housekeeper and nursemaid. When the time came for the young son to talk, he did in fact talk, but in Vietnamese. Suddenly the parents realized that they could not even communicate with their son except by using their daughter as an interpreter.

Another story is told by the British language educator, E. V. Gatenby, who cites the case of a bilingual Turkish novelist named Halide Edip who comments in her memoirs that she had reached the age of twelve before she became aware that she spoke two languages, English and Turkish.[27] Bruce Hutchison quotes Louis St.

[26] J. W. Tomb, "On the Intuitive Capacity of Children to Understand Spoken Languages," *British Journal of Psychology*, Vol. XVI, Part 1 (July, 1925), p. 53. This example is also cited in the UNESCO tape recording entitled "The Other Man's Language," prepared after the UNESCO Conference in Ceylon, August 1953. Demonstrated on the same tape is the easy bilingualism of an English girl of eleven who has spent much time in France.

[27] E. V. Gatenby, "Popular Fallacies in the Teaching of Foreign Languages," *English Language Teaching*, Vol. VII, No. 1 (Autumn, 1952).

Laurent, the former Prime Minister of Canada as follows, "I thought," he used to say in later years, "that everybody spoke to his father in French and his mother in English."[28] One of my colleagues, on a mission in Rio de Janeiro, told of meeting a small girl of five or six whose father was German, whose mother was Polish, who had a Russian grandparent, and who had traveled in Germany, France, England, Morocco, and Argentina, before settling in Brazil. At the time my friend met her she was prepared to expect that every new stranger she met would speak differently, but seemed not in the slightest upset by this expectation.

Research and observation combine to demonstrate that in learning to understand and speak foreign languages the child has a big advantage over the adolescent and the adult.[29] Ronjat describes with what ease his bilingual son Louis moved back and forth between France and Germany.[30] Penfield asserts that "There is an age when the child has a remarkable capacity to utilize those areas [of the brain] for the learning of the language, a time when several languages can be learned simultaneously as easily as one language. Later, with the appearance of capacity for reason and abstract thinking, this early ability is largely lost."[31]

Susanne K. Langer characterizes this favorable language-learning age by saying that "There is an *optimum period of learning*, and this is a stage of mental development in which several impulses and interests happen to coincide: the lalling, the imitative impulse, a natural interest in distinctive sounds, *and a great sensitivity to 'ex-*

[28] Bruce Hutchison, *Mr. Prime Minister, 1876–1964*, p. 288.

[29] The educational advantage emerges clearly from John B. Carroll's "Foreign Language Proficiency Levels Attained by Language Majors Near Graduation from College" (*Foreign Language Annals*, Vol. I, No. 2 [December, 1967], pp. 131–151). Carroll states that while this data cannot be used to give unqualified support to the FLES movement, "The conclusion that does seem to emerge from the data is that for those students who were enabled to start French or Spanish in the elementary school and who liked the language study well enough to impel them to continue with it to the point of graduating from college with a language major, their start in elementary school gave them a distinct advantage, on the average, over those who started later" (p. 137).

[30] Jules Ronjat, *Le développement du langage observé chez un enfant bilingue*.

[31] Wilder G. Penfield, "A Consideration of the Neurophysiological Mechanisms of Speech and Some Educational Consequences," *Proceedings of the American Academy of Arts and Sciences*, Vol. LXXXII, No. 5 (May, 1953), pp. 201–214.

pressiveness' of any sort. Where any of these characteristics is absent or is not synchronized with the others, the 'linguistic intuition' miscarries."[32] She points out the educational consequences of not taking advantage of the mental development corresponding to the individual's particular age. "The tendency to constant vocalization seems to be a passing phase of our instinctive life. If language is not developed during this period, the individual is handicapped . . . by a lack of spontaneous phonetic material to facilitate his speaking experiments. The production of sounds is conscious then, and is used economically instead of prodigally."[33] Conditioned learning seems to be at a peak at birth and to decline progressively; conceptual learning, at its low point at birth, seems to increase with age.

At what point does conceptual learning outweigh conditioned learning? Tentatively, it seems that age ten approximates the dividing line,[34] that before this age speech habits in the first language are not so fixed as to interfere seriously with the learning of new speech habits. It has been noted, for example, that foreigners who come to the United States before the age of ten are much more likely than those who arrive later to speak English without an accent. Those who come later usually speak with an accent, which is the more marked the older they are on arrival.

All the evidence so far examined confirms the conclusions expressed in the Modern Language Association *FL* [Foreign Language] *Bulletin*, No. 49. At a meeting held in May, 1956, the conferees were asked: Is it possible to determine an optimum age, from

[32] Langer, *Philosophy in a New Key*, p. 110.

[33] *Ibid.*, p. 19.

[34] This hypothesis is graphically represented by the figure below, taken from my article, "Optimum Age," p. 303.

Figure showing hypothetically the relation of learning to age.

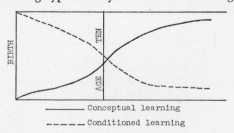

————— Conceptual learning

————— Conditioned learning

the standpoint of the child's physiology and psychology, for beginning the learning of a second language? In their report they replied:

Several conferees (Penfield, Ilg, Leopold) were inclined to think that *ideally* the best starting age is at birth. However, since the group was considering language learning in relation to school and since the first language is normally "set" by the age of four or five, it was decided to select four as the earliest age to be recommended. As is stated below, the years from four to eight are regarded as very favorable. The imitative capacity of the child in this early period is considered by Dr. Ilg as the best for language learning. She added that at eight the child is group-minded, expansive, and receptive. At this age, when expansion and imitation are at their height, the child can under favorable conditions be expected to learn a second language with a rush. At eight also the child begins to hold to patterns and at nine he fixes them.[35]

The conference therefore drafted the following consensus:

The optimum age for *beginning* the continuous learning of a second language seems to fall within the span of ages four through eight, with superior performance to be anticipated at ages eight, nine, ten. In this early period the brain seems to have the greatest plasticity and specialized capacity needed for acquiring speech.

The specialized capacity includes the ability to mimic accurately the stream of speech (sounds, rhythm, intonation, stress, and so forth) and to learn and manipulate language patterns easily. Support for the conviction that the brain has greater plasticity for speech learning during the first decade of life comes from the fact that, in cases of gross destruction of the cerebral speech areas, return of normal speech occurs much more rapidly and more completely than at a later age.[36]

Rewards of Bilingualism

Not only physiological and psychological but also social, political, and economic considerations provide strong reasons for learning languages early.[37] Ignorance of languages is recognized as a barrier

[35] Modern Language Association, "Childhood and Second Language Learning," p. 5.

[36] *Ibid.*, p. 6.

[37] For example, the situation in the Philippines may serve to enlighten us on this subject. See particularly the "Iloilo Experiment" as described by Clifford H. Prator, Jr., in his *Language Teaching in the Philippines*, pp. 23–33; see also United Nations, Educational, Scientific, and Cultural Organization, *The Use of*

to communication among nations. What is less vividly realized is that monolingualism is also a serious barrier to understanding among ethnic groups within a nation. There are countries in which conditions would be greatly improved if from an early age all children acquired a useful control of a second language: English or French in Canada, Sinhalese or Tamil in Ceylon, French or Flemish in Belgium, for example. And in our own country the early mastery of a second language by English-speaking children (French in New England and Louisiana; German in Pennsylvania, Texas, and various parts of the Midwest; Chinese and Japanese on the Pacific coast; and Spanish in New York, Florida, and the Southwest, for example) could be expected to improve the social relations between linguistic groups and would help us better to assimilate our minority groups politically and economically. Healthy, constructive attitudes can best be inculcated in the very young. As H. H. Stern points out,

> The postwar approach to international tensions has laid much stress on the causes of nationalism, aggressiveness, and prejudice in the minds of children. An international outlook came to be regarded not as something that can be grafted on a prejudiced adult mind. It must grow and must be fostered from infancy. This was seen partly as a question of furthering mental health, . . . but partly also as a matter of contacts, exchanges, travel and study in other countries—and also the learning of languages. Everywhere in these attempts the language barrier seemed to be the one major obstacle that prevented a thorough-going internationalism. Looked at in this light, an early acquaintance with other countries and their languages became an essential of the most basic education anywhere.[38]

The Union of South Africa, "the most bilingual country in the world today," presents a good example of tolerance for minority languages.[39] In contrast to Canada, where, according to Whitaker's Almanac, only 12 per cent of the population speaks both French and English, over 80 per cent of the three million white population

---

Vernacular Languages in Education, pp. 123–133; and Philippine Center for Language Study, "Philippine Language-Teaching Experiments," pp. 78–157.

[38] H. H. Stern, *Foreign Languages in Primary Education: The Teaching of Foreign or Second Languages to Younger Children*, p. 3.

[39] Ernst Gedeon Malherbe, Inaugural Address, in United Kingdom, National Commission for UNESCO, *Bilingualism in Education*, Report on an International Seminar on Bilingualism in Education, Aberystwyth, Wales, August 20–September 2, 1960, p. 8.

speak both Afrikaans and English, according to an estimate by E. G. Malherbe.[40] The explanation of this relatively happy state of affairs is to be found in the officially sponsored bilingual educational system, which in turn rests upon a spirit of tolerance and respect between the two language groups. In addition, "all indigenous African pupils are taught their vernacular language as well as at least one of the official European languages.[41] Despite the essentially favorable picture that Malherbe draws in his inaugural address and in an earlier book,[42] the ideal will not be achieved until parallel but separate classes in Afrikaans and English have all been converted to the dual-medium system of instruction.

There have been some psychologists who have regarded bilingualism as a hazard to normal maturation. Such phenomena as stuttering, for example, have been attributed to it. But H. H. Stern points out that "when it is claimed that there is a causal connection between bilingualism and emotional instability, it has to be remembered that bilingual groups are often minority groups and in those situations it may be the culture conflict, the lack of status of the minority or prejudice against the minority which cause emotional difficulties; the language itself may not be the primary factor."[43]

The advantages and disadvantages of bilingualism have been reviewed often.[44] Seth Arsenian wrote in 1937, "It has been observed ever since the time of Petrarch and Dante that the free development of national vernaculars has constituted a stimulating and propelling force that has led to a regeneration of national cultures."[45] As a hor-

[40] *Ibid.*, p. 9.   [41] *Ibid.*, p. 10.

[42] Ernst Gedeon Malherbe, *The Bilingual School: A Study of Bilingualism in South Africa.*

[43] Stern, *Foreign Languages in Primary Education*, p. 16.

[44] See, for example, International Bureau of Education, Geneva, *Conférence internationale sur le bilinguisme: Le bilinguisme et l'éducation;* Uriel Weinreich, *Languages in Contact: Findings and Problems*, p. 73; United Kingdom, Ministry of Education, Central Advisory Council for Education (Wales), *The Place of Welsh and English in the Schools of Wales;* Einar Haugen, *Bilingualism in America: A Bibliography and Research Guide;* University College of Wales, Faculty of Education, *Bilingualism: A Bibliography with Special Reference to Wales;* and United Kingdom, National Commission for UNESCO, *Bilingualism in Education.*

[45] Seth Arsenian, *Bilingualism and Mental Development: A Study of the Intelligence and the Social Background of Bilingual Children in New York City*, p. 14.

rible example" of the *degeneration* of culture, both ancestral and adoptive, Mildred Boyer tells how "Texas Squanders Non-English Resources"[46] and illustrates her point vividly by reproducing photographically, together with his teacher's interpolations, a letter written by a junior-high-school student who was caught speaking Spanish in school.[47]

In a resolutely impartial report a British committee studying the bilingual situation in Wales concluded: "It appears wisest at the present juncture to accept that body of opinion that bilingualism in itself is neither an advantage nor a disadvantage to the mental development of a normal child."[48] H. H. Stern notes certain weaknesses in some of the earlier studies of bilingualism: "(a) that no distinction was made between various types and degrees of bilingualism; (b) that social and economic factors were not always taken into account; and (c) that the statistical procedures used to validate conclusions were often inadequate."[49] A recent study in Montreal, which does take these factors into account, shows that, contrary to the general belief that bilingualism and intelligence have a negative correlation, bilingual children are markedly *superior* to monolinguals in both verbal and nonverbal intelligence.[50]

After weighing the conflicting testimony in this field, Nelson Brooks reaches the following reasonable conclusion: "Even if it were proved (as it has not been) that . . . children are below standard in English vocabulary because of bilingualism, the lack of a few lexical items in the mother tongue at a given age may be a modest price to pay when, in exchange, one is in possession of all the structure and a sizable vocabulary of a second language."[51]

Bilingualism and multilingualism have long fascinated individual educators and have been the subject of much educational experimentation. The Spaniard, José Castillejo, has reported that

---

[46] Mildred Boyer, "Texas Squanders Non-English Resources," *Texas Foreign Language Association Bulletin*, Vol. V, No. 3 (October, 1963), pp. 1–7.

[47] *Ibid.*, pp. 1, 3.

[48] United Kingdom, *Place of Welsh and English in the Schools*, pp. 42–43.

[49] Stern, *Foreign Languages in Primary Education*, p. 15.

[50] Elizabeth Peal and Wallace E. Lambert, "The Relation of Bilingualism to Intelligence," *Psychological Monographs, General and Applied*, Vol. LXXVI, No. 27 (1962), pp. 1–23.

[51] Brooks, *Language and Language Learning*, p. 42.

His school [in Madrid] received boys and girls between the ages of three and five and instructed them in Spanish, French, and German. All of the children received instruction in the mother tongue and in at least two foreign languages. A few were taught four languages. The children came from superior homes, the size of the classes was limited to a maximum of fifteen, and the general curriculum was restricted. No teacher was permitted to use any language but his own in the classroom, the playground or the dining rooms. Consequently the pupils identified the language with the person who taught it and it was found that they did not mix the various languages.[52]

Castillejo concludes that "the accumulation of several languages neither disturbs nor overloads the mind of the child, because to him they are not multiple. He does not distinguish them . . . he does not even notice the differences between them. The child of five years could not tell his mother whether the songs were in French or English. His only explanation was 'this is the fair-haired teacher's, and this is the brown-haired teacher's'."[53]

H. H. Stern describes, among several others, the bilingual program of the Ecole Active Bilingue—Ecole Internationale de Paris.[54] This school, founded in 1954, partly subsidized by the French Ministry of Education and recognized by UNESCO, provides a thorough education in French and English to children between the ages of three and eleven. Although the official French curriculum is taught throughout the primary classes, English, too, is taught by native speakers of English for periods varying from forty-five minutes to two hours a day. More exactly, children are not taught English but rather are immersed in an English language bath. "Thus one mother one day complained that her daughter had said she had no English lessons, but three weeks later the same mother reported that, to her great surprise, she had overheard her little girl spontaneously chatting in English with her dolls."[55]

The John F. Kennedy School, German-American Community School, founded in 1960 in West Berlin, comes closest to achieving a

---

[52] José Castillejo y Duarte, "Modern Languages in an International School," *New Era in Home and School,* January, 1933.

[53] Quoted from the United Kingdom, *Place of Welsh and English in the Schools,* p. 43.

[54] Stern, *Foreign Languages in Primary Education,* pp. 58–59, 72–74.

[55] *Ibid.,* p. 59.

balanced bilingualism. This special bilingual elementary school is under the supervision of the Berlin Board of Education. Although part of the German public school system, this school has a joint advisory committee of seven Americans and six Germans appointed by the mayor of Berlin. Combining features of both the American and German educational systems, the school in 1963 provided instruction in English and German to about 360 pupils, of whom half were German and half American and other nationalities. The teaching staff is international but primarily German and secondarily American. All teachers are bilingual, and they teach bilingually, moving back and forth easily from one language to the other and encouraging the children to respond in either language. Under these conditions it is not surprising to find the atmosphere lively but informal, as it was when I visited the school in September of 1964.

In the fall of 1963 the Dade County (Florida) Public Schools launched a bilingual program in the Coral Way School in Miami. This is believed to be the first American public elementary school since World War I to have a fully developed bilingual program. I shall have occasion in a later chapter to describe this program as well as some of the many bilingual programs that are beginning to multiply especially in the Spanish South and Southwest. What makes bilingual schooling relevant to FLES—of which it is but one important aspect—is that it contributes a totally new dimension to language learning. In bilingual programs the second language is not merely a subject of instruction but also a medium of learning. Such programs provide a setting in which children learn informally, on the playground as much as in the classroom, from one another.

These experiments are of special interest and give promise of language learning in school at its best. At the moment it is important to decide whether, in monolingual areas as well, foreign-language instruction, benefiting perhaps from bilingual programs, can be carried on more efficiently in the elementary school than in high school or college. The preponderance of evidence points to the fact that very young children do learn more easily and more effectively to understand and to speak other languages than do adolescents or adults. As Wilder Penfield points out, the child's brain is so constituted as to learn foreign speech easily. Moreover, young children who learn under favorable conditions suffer none of the inhibitions experienced by older language learners.

This is not to say that older people do not learn other aspects of language more efficiently than do children. With the development of the analytical faculties and with the disciplining of the mind it goes without saying that adolescents and adults are able to learn *about* a language more efficiently than are children. Thus they can perhaps more easily acquire a useful and comprehensive knowledge of the structure than they can an intimate "feel" of the language. The following incident is suggestive: An American lady was riding in a Paris cab with her nine-year-old daughter and two French children. The children were chattering away in French, and the sound "shoo" kept recurring frequently. No longer able to restrain her curiosity, the mother said, "Nancy, what are you talking about a shoe for?"—"Oh, Mother," replied Nancy, "we're not talking about a shoe; we're talking about *choux*, cabbages; can't you hear the difference?" Many language teachers feel that it is not their obligation to provide a *Sprachgefühl* but rather to create an understanding of language structure, culture, and literature. As H. H. Stern remarks, "These objectives are not invalidated. But they constitute an advanced stage of linguistic activity which is all the more rewarding the more it is based on an unselfconscious bilingual experience."[56]

The earlier the start the better. The theoretical evidence, confirmed by educators who have had an opportunity to observe, supports the view that first graders acquire skill in understanding and speaking a second language better than third graders, that children in the kindergarten acquire the feel for a second language even more intimately than first graders, and that preschool children are perhaps best endowed of all to take full advantage of the language-learning powers of the human brain.[57]

[56] *Ibid.*, p. 14.

[57] V. S. Ginsberg ("An Experiment in Teaching Pre-School Children a Foreign Language," *Soviet Education*, Vol. II, No. 11 [September, 1960]), reporting on an experiment in Leningrad, concludes that "Sounds are mastered more easily in the second grade than in the fourth, but less easily than in kindergarten. Children in the second and fourth grades can study for much longer periods than preschool children but it takes them longer to memorize the same material. The degree to which the material was retained when the lessons were based on visual presentation and aimed at developing oral speech habits was fully satisfactory. After the summer vacation, the pre-school children recalled what they had been taught much more rapidly and fully than school children" (*ibid.*, pp. 18–25).

Conclusion

If then our objective is to give to great numbers of our future American citizens the opportunity to become skillful in other languages, the best way to do it is to provide the opportunity to begin such learning in the very earliest grades of the elementary school, or even through preschool experiences, and to continue in a carefully executed sequential program in the secondary school.

This chapter completes the argument begun in the preceding chapter. For those citizens who reject altogether the educational advantage of including one or more foreign languages in our school program, the advantage of an early beginning will have no appeal. But for those who recognize that knowledge of other languages contributes to the education of the individual, to our cultural maturity, and to our national security, the advantage of an early start—assuming always that instruction can proceed under favorable circumstances—seems indisputably to recommend itself. Educational objectives and the psychology of learning appear to join advantageously to give both theoretical and practical reasons for the inclusion of foreign-language learning in American elementary-school education. From the evidence available language learning in the early grades—the earlier the better—when conditions are favorable, is, therefore, justified on the basis of educational efficiency.

4. History of Foreign-Language Teaching in the Elementary School: 1840–1920

IN THE INTRODUCTION two commonly held misconceptions were discussed: the first, that in the United States the teaching of foreign languages in the elementary school is only two decades old and therefore without a history, and the second, that in Europe and other parts of the world it is an integral part of the primary-school program.

What *is* true is that, contrary to the situation in the United States, where languages have had a too restricted place, in other parts of the world they have traditionally had an honored place, not in the primary grades but in academic secondary schools, which most commonly begin with the fifth or sixth school year. In European schools of this type several languages are studied, sometimes Greek as well as Latin, and usually two or three modern languages. European educators are, therefore, surprised to learn what happens in our high schools to a student interested in languages. Our guidance counselors, who strongly influence the selection of subjects to be studied, tend to discourage a student, no matter how serious or how gifted, who wants to study two or more languages, and they usually advise only two years' study of one language. In contrast, European students normally start their language study at the beginning of the secondary-school course, when they are between ten and twelve years old, and, once begun, the study of a second language is continued for from four to nine years.

Practices in Other Countries

A summary of the practice in a number of countries will illustrate this point.[1]

ARGENTINA. In 1960 the teaching of English was authorized in five pilot primary schools in Buenos Aires. Fourteen additional schools were authorized in 1961. By 1962 oral English instruction, begun in grade two, was continued through the remaining four grades of these schools. Studying modern languages in the five-year secondary school has long been traditional.

AUSTRALIA. A majority of pupils start French at about age twelve in the first year of the four- or six-year secondary school and continue it throughout the remaining grades.

AUSTRIA. A three-year kindergarten and a four-year primary school (*Volkschule*) precede the secondary schools. Foreign-language instruction begins in the secondary school, at age eleven, and continues for from four to eight years. Students attending the *Hauptschule* (general high school), the terminal school for the majority of Austrian children, have four years of instruction, in grades five through eight, in one modern language. Students attending one of the various types of rigorous university-preparatory *Mittelschulen* (academic high schools) study at least two foreign languages. *Gymnasium* (classical high school) students study one modern language for eight years (during the last four years, in the upper division, as an elective). They also have to take six years of Latin, from what corresponds to our seventh grade on, and four years of classical Greek. In the *Realgymnasium* (modern classical high school) they take eight years of one modern language and four of another. The principal modern language is English, taken by more than 80 per cent of the students attending *Mittelschulen*, and the second is French.[2]

DENMARK. The primary school comprises seven grades. Since 1959 English instruction begins in the sixth grade, when pupils are about

[1] The main source of the data contained in the following pages is United Nations, Educational, Scientific, and Cultural Organization, "Second Language Teaching in Primary and Secondary Schools," *Education Abstracts*, Vol. XIII, No. 3 (1961).

[2] For this information I am indebted to Wilhelm Schlag, Cultural Affairs Officer, Austrian Consulate General in New York.

twelve, and continues for seven years, but in an increasing number of schools language training begins in the fourth or the fifth grades. German is generally begun in grade seven, Swedish in grade eight, Latin and French in grade ten.

ENGLAND. Except for a very few state primary schools, which are experimenting with early modern-language instruction, and except for private preparatory schools, where language instruction begins at the age of eight or nine, there is no language instruction before secondary school. It begins usually at about age eleven and continues for five years.

FRANCE. Foreign-language instruction begins in the first year of the secondary school, between ages ten and twelve, and continues for seven years. A few cities are experimenting with English in primary schools, among them Paris and Arles. The latter city is twinned with York, Pennsylvania, where in 1952 French was introduced experimentally into one elementary school and in 1957 extended to all elementary schools in the fifth and sixth grades.[3]

FEDERAL REPUBLIC OF GERMANY. About 21 per cent of the pupils in primary schools study a modern language, usually English, in the fifth or final grade. In the intermediate schools (*Mittelschulen*) English is compulsory from the fifth through the tenth year, while French or sometimes Spanish is an additional option. Pupils in the mathematics-science type of *Gymnasium* usually start with English in grade five and add either French or Latin in the seventh grade. In the modern-language type of *Gymnasium* pupils add a third language (Latin, French, or Russian) in the ninth grade and continue all three through the thirteenth or final secondary grade. In the classical type Gymnasium Latin is compulsory from grade five, English or French from grade seven, and in grade nine Greek is added.

HUNGARY. The study of Russian is compulsory from the fifth grade of the eight-grade primary school. Pupils who do well are permitted to choose a second language, English, French, or German. Study of two languages, Russian and English, has recently been made compulsory, as an experiment, in the four secondary grades of the twelve-year school.

INDIA. Here, where the situation is complicated by the fact that children have to study the language of their region as well as Hindi,

[3] Marguerite Eriksson, Ilse Forest, and Ruth Mulhauser, *Foreign Languages in the Elementary School*, pp. 116–117.

their national language, English is begun in the secondary school, usually in the sixth school year or a little later.

IRAQ. The primary school has six grades and the secondary school five. English is begun at age eleven in the fifth primary class and is continued for seven years, throughout the secondary school.

MEXICO. Foreign-language instruction does not begin before the secondary school, when pupils are fourteen, except in a few private schools.

NORWAY. As in Denmark, the primary school continues through the seventh grade. Instruction in English begins in the sixth grade and continues for six or seven years. Four years of instruction in German and three in French are usually added.

SWITZERLAND. The varying local arrangements complicate the situation in Switzerland. In some cantons the primary school includes grades one to nine, in which case modern-language instruction begins in grade six. In other cantons the secondary school begins with the fifth grade, where one language is compulsory and a second optional.

UNION OF SOVIET SOCIALIST REPUBLICS. In the Soviet ten-year school, foreign-language instruction begins in grade five at age twelve. Exceptions are the special language schools, of which the best known are one each for English, French, and German in Moscow, in which instruction begins in grade one and the second language is used as the medium of instruction for some subjects in the upper grades. An announcement in the *Soviet Weekly* tells of a successful four-year experiment in teaching English to five-year-old children in the kindergarten in Stalinabad, capital of Tajik. At the same time, perhaps as a result of this success, the Soviet Government announced that "If the parents desire it, children will be able to start their foreign-language studies in kindergarten or in the lower forms at general schools. . . . By 1965 there will be at least another 700 general schools which teach a number of subjects in a foreign language."[4] It is interesting to contrast this situation with ours, for in several states we have laws that restrict to one hour a day the use of a foreign language in the classroom of our public schools.

To summarize, in other countries foreign-language instruction normally begins in the fifth or sixth year of school, when children are between ten and twelve years old. Usually this is the beginning

[4] *Soviet Weekly*, No. 1011, June 15, 1961.

of the secondary school, but in Denmark, Germany, Hungary, Iraq, Norway, and in parts of Switzerland one or both of these grades are included in the primary, or elementary, school. Argentina, England, Denmark, France, Germany, Hungary, and the Soviet Union show a trend toward beginning language instruction earlier than in the past. If these experiments are successful and if the problem of finding qualified teachers can be solved, the practice can be expected to spread. Except for this experimentation, present practices are still essentially those which have been traditional throughout the modern epoch of European education. Thus, in Europe and in Europeanized systems of education, where secondary education begins earlier than in the United States and is more seriously academic, foreign-language instruction begins from two to four years earlier than in the United States and continues from two to seven years longer. To call it FLES is slightly misleading, however, for it has not generally been identified with elementary education and the methods employed have been more characteristic of secondary than of elementary instruction.

Practices in the United States have fluctuated much more than in Europe. Contrary to the assertions of certain writers, who trace the teaching of modern languages in the elementary school back to 1952 only, the story of foreign-language instruction in the elementary grades takes us back about a century and a quarter, to the very beginning of our free public schools. In this and the following chapter I shall not only sketch the history and present status of FLES but also shall distinguish between the older and newer concepts regarding it.

Early FLES Programs

From our very origins we have been a polyglot nation.[5] As early as 1564 French Huguenots came to Florida. In 1565 the Spanish founded Saint Augustine. The Dutch settled Manhattan about 1625 and the Swedes Delaware a few years later. Moving down from Canada the French established trading posts in the Northwest in the latter part of the seventeenth century and remained in control of the

[5] For the information contained in the following pages I am indebted principally to Charles H. Handschin, *The Teaching of Modern Languages in the United States;* and to E. W. Bagster-Collins, "History of Modern Language Teaching in the United States," in *Studies in Modern Language Teaching.*

Mississippi and Ohio valleys until the close of the French and Indian Wars in 1763. French influence was also important in the South, especially in Louisiana, whose settlement began in the early decades of the seventeenth century, and in Charleston, South Carolina, which, after the Revocation of the Edict of Nantes in 1685, became a center of French influence. The first important arrival of Germans took place in 1683 in the area of Philadelphia. During the following century Germans representing various religious sects spread gradually in all directions. As the frontier moved westward in the early nineteenth century, it also embraced a Spanish-speaking population in California, Colorado, Arizona, New Mexico, and Texas.[6] But it was the renewal of immigration from all the countries of Europe, beginning in the eighteen-thirties and swelling into successive waves throughout that century and into the present century, that brought the greatest number and variety of speakers of other languages. Their number today is conservatively estimated to be about nineteen million.[7] Their presence exerted a considerable influence on our public education before World War I.

GERMAN IN ELEMENTARY SCHOOLS. German, like other foreign languages, was initially taught in church schools, the earliest of which was founded in 1702 in Germantown, Pennsylvania. The first enterprise in any community was the founding of a church, and soon thereafter instruction by the minister in the catechism began, often followed by the establishment of denominational schools. The quality of these schools naturally depended on the teachers. There were exceptional ones of high caliber, but as a class the clergymen of the early Republic were not highly educated, nor did the low salaries attract able men. Charles Handschin quotes the following estimate of the German denominational schools as of 1868, submitted to the United States Commissioner of Education by Dr. A. Douai, a German educator and leader in the German movement in the United States:

---

[6] For the story of the Spanish-speaking people in the United States, see Carey McWilliams, *North from Mexico: The Spanish-Speaking People of the United States;* and Jane MacNab Christian and Chester C. Christian, Jr., "Spanish Language and Culture in the Southwest," in Joshua A. Fishman, *Language Loyalty in the United States: The Maintenance and Perpetuation of the Non-English Mother Tongues by American Ethnic and Religious Groups.*

[7] Fishman, *Language Loyalty in the United States,* p. 45.

During the last two or three decades, it is true, a sufficient number of able German teachers came over from the mother country, so that the character of these denominational schools might have been extensively improved. But there being little intelligence among the congregations and their clergy, they could not understand the requirements of a good school, and that able teachers cannot be expected to thrive on so low salaries as from $200 to $400 a year, and to perform, into the bargain, the menial work of sextons and attendants to their ministers. Thus it is that hardly half a dozen of the several hundred schools of this kind have ever been worthy of the name of schools . . . and that from 2,000,000 to 3,000,000 descendants of Germans now in the country have fully, or almost fully, lost the understanding and use of their native language.[8]

E. W. Bagster-Collins observes that there was an important educational difference between the early German colonists who came to seek freedom from religious and social oppression and the immigrants of the nineteenth century. The latter sought greater economic opportunities and were often skilled workers with considerable schooling. They wanted a good education for their children, and finding our common schools inferior to those with which they were familiar in Germany, they founded private and parochial schools, which for some decades competed successfully with the public schools despite the fact that parents had to pay tuition as well as taxes. "Even as late as 1865 there were in Milwaukee over 5,000 children attending private schools as against 7,000 in the public schools."[9]

It was inevitable that German immigrants should want to maintain their language and way of life, especially in communities where they were the majority or a large minority of the population. At the same time it was a matter of concern to Americans in a still young republic that speakers of other languages be assimilated to American speech and way of life. In order to draw German children into the American public school and to prevent their threatened isolation from the common stream of American civilization, Ohio passed on the nineteenth of May, 1840, a law that made it "the duty of the Board of Trustees and Visitors of common schools to provide a number of German schools under some duly qualified teachers for

8 Handschin, *Teaching of Modern Languages*, p. 31.
9 Bagster-Collins, "History of Modern Language Teaching," p. 15.

the instruction of such youth as desired to learn the German language or the German and English languages together."[10]

In 1840, as a result of this law, Cincinnati introduced German instruction in the grades as an optional subject and is thus credited with having initiated foreign-language instruction in the public elementary schools of the United States. The Cincinnati plan of organization served as a model for many of the programs that began in the following decades. New York introduced both German and French in the grades in 1854. St. Louis followed with German only, in 1864. By 1889 Baltimore, Buffalo, Chicago, Cleveland, Columbus, Dayton, Denver, Indianapolis, Milwaukee, San Francisco, and St. Paul were also offering German in the elementary grades. Boston joined this group in 1895.

GERMAN ENROLLMENTS, 1840–1919. Thanks to the research of Charles Handschin, E. W. Bagster-Collins, and Professor Frances Ellis,[11] some fragmentary statistics on the number of children involved in these programs are available. They are arranged in tabular form in Table 1. It has been estimated that in 1872–1873 one-third of all elementary pupils in Cleveland were in German classes; and in 1875 there were 5,146 children taking German, of whom 3,438 were of German and 1,708 of English-speaking parentage. In Dayton more than one-quarter of the elementary-school children were studying German in 1875–1876. In Cincinnati in 1914, there were some 14,649 children enrolled in German classes of a total elementary-school population of 43,241. Two years later the effects of the war were already apparent, for the number had fallen to 13,800, and in 1917–1918 the numbers had dropped to about 7,000. Of the children taking German in Buffalo in 1917, 22 per cent were of German parentage, 50 per cent of American parentage, and the remaining 28 per cent were children having parents of various other nationalities. In Indianapolis the enrollment in German in the district schools in 1901 was 6,699, about one-quarter of the total school population, of whom 2,363 were of German parentage and 4,336 of non-German origin.

[10] Quoted in *ibid.*, p. 14, from the *Twelfth Annual Report of the Condition of the Common Schools in Cincinnati, 1841.*

[11] Frances H. Ellis, "Historical Account of German Instruction in the Public Schools of Indianapolis, 1869–1919," *The Indiana Magazine of History*, Vol. L, No. 2 (June, 1954).

TABLE 1. *Sample Annual FLES Enrollments*[a]

Place	Program begun in	Conjectured life of program (years)	Enrollment	Year
Cincinnati	1840	79	14,649	1914
			13,800	1916
			7,000	1918
New York	1854	65	21,005	1873
			4,675	1877
			11,026	1885
			26,632	1895
St. Louis	1864 (–1888)	24	450	1864
			2,000	1868
Chicago	1865	54		
Indianapolis	1869	50	3,096	1895
			6,699	1901
			6,963	1902
			6,501	1909
			8,161	1916
Cleveland	1870	49	5,146	1875
San Francisco	1871	20	3,068	1871
			2,806	1878
			1,627	1888
Baltimore	1874	45		
Boston	1895	5	656	1896
			1,013	1897
			1,281	1915
Buffalo			10,590	1912
Columbus			2,122	1882
Dayton				
Denver			7,000	1867
Milwaukee			35,849	1917
Total enrollment			203,815	
Average annual enrollment per program			8,152	
Average annual enrollment for 14 programs			114,128	
Average life of 9 programs		43		
Estimated total FLES enrollments (1840–1919)			4,907,504	
Estimated minimum persons affected (1840–1919)			1,000,000	

[a]Composite figures taken from E. W. Bagster-Collins, "History of Modern Language Teaching in the United States"; Frances H. Ellis, "Historical Account of German Instruction in the Public Schools of Indianapolis, 1869–1919"; and Charles H. Handschin, *The Teaching of Modern Languages in the United States.*

FRENCH IN ELEMENTARY SCHOOLS. With the Louisiana Purchase in 1803, some twenty thousand French speakers became American citizens,[12] and French continued for many years to be the medium of instruction in the schools of the area. The Civil War and the years of Reconstruction terminated this situation, but provision for instruction of French in the public schools was made in the Louisiana state constitution of 1879 and reaffirmed by the Statutes of 1906, Section 212.[13]

Contrary to the situation in areas of concentrated German population the predominant French speakers in Louisiana did not produce any extensive French program in the public elementary schools. Instead, the upper and middle classes sent their children to private, parochial, or convent schools in which French was taught.

In other parts of the country French appeared only sporadically in elementary-school programs.[14] As mentioned, French, as well as German, instruction was begun in New York schools in 1854 in grades seven and eight. According to a report for 1873 there were 1,609 pupils enrolled in French as compared with 19,396 in German. In 1877, as a result of a more restrictive policy of the board of education, the enrollment was only 452 in French and 4,223 in German. In 1879 these languages were restricted to grades seven and eight. The board must later have liberalized its policy, for in 1885 the enrollment figure for French was 1,979 and for German 9,047. In 1890 both French and German were allowed in grades four through eight. In 1895 the French enrollment in New York was 3,134 and the German 23,498. In 1903 French, German, and Latin were made optional in the eighth grade only. This arrangement continued until World War I.[15]

San Francisco began in 1867 to create a few "cosmopolitan schools," which were in operation by 1871. Pupils in the primary grades of these schools took either French or German for an hour and a half daily. In the "grammar" (intermediate) grades both languages were taken and filled nearly half of the working day. In 1871

[12] Thomas Perkins Abernethy, *The South in the New Nation, 1789–1819*, p. 253.

[13] Handschin, *Teaching of Modern Languages*, pp. 28–29.

[14] George B. Watts, "The Teaching of French in the United States: A History," *The French Review*, Vol. XXXVII, No. 1 (October, 1963), pp. 49–56.

[15] Bagster-Collins, "History of Modern Language Teaching," pp. 19–20.

the enrollment in French in the primary department was 763 and in German 2,305. Both languages were studied by 900 children in the grammar department. The policy here as in so many places was vacillating, however, and by 1878 the languages were dropped from the first grade. The French enrollment that year was 683, while 2,123 pupils were enrolled in German, of whom, it is interesting to note, all but 302 were of German parentage. By 1888 the number of French pupils had fallen to 176 and the German to 1,451 in three cosmopolitan schools. In a reorganization of the curriculum in the early nineties both languages were dropped from the elementary schools. The superintendent's report of 1892 speaks of this foreign-language study as among the "educational hobbies" of the past.[16]

In 1895, at about the time the San Francisco superintendent became disenchanted, the Boston superintendent became enchanted with FLES. Moved by the report of the Committee of Ten,[17] which recommended beginning foreign-language instruction in the elementary school, he proposed to add French, German, and Latin to enrich the elementary course of study. French instruction began in 1895 in three schools, was extended the following year to nine schools, with an enrollment of 656 pupils distributed among various grades, reached 1,013 pupils in eleven schools in 1897, and then was suddenly dropped, only to be reinstated again later. Apparently no adequate provision was made to establish any real policy or to appoint qualified teachers. In 1915 committees of teachers prepared syllabi for French and German and in 1916 for Italian and Spanish. In 1915 there were in the seventh and eighth grades thirty-two modern-language classes with a total of 1,281 pupils.[18] Here as elsewhere World War I ended FLES.

SPANISH, POLISH, AND ITALIAN. Bagster-Collins also makes brief mention of Spanish, Polish, and Italian in the elementary schools.

Spanish was almost completely limited to the territory that became New Mexico in 1912. In 1890 a majority of the population could not speak English, and Spanish continued for many years to be the medium of instruction in the schools. A state law in 1915

[16] *Ibid.*, p. 24.

[17] Appointed by the National Education Association in 1892. The report of this subcommittee is contained in the *Report of the Committee on Secondary School Studies*, pp. 96–103.

[18] Bagster-Collins, "History of Modern Language Teaching," p. 24.

provided that Spanish might be taught in any public school if the majority of the board of education so desired.

In 1913 Polish and Italian, as well as German, were taught in Milwaukee schools. The law provided that in districts where 75 per cent of the parents so desired, these languages might be introduced. In this year enrollment in Polish, distributed among several schools, was 2,387, and in one or two schools some 770 children were studying Italian. By 1917 these figures had risen to 3,553 and 900 respectively, as compared with 31,306 in German. The hysteria of World War I not only relegated German language study to limbo but momentarily terminated all FLES programs.

The Scope of FLES, 1840–1920. Data on FLES in the period from 1840 to 1920 has been collected in only fourteen of our larger cities. There must have been other programs about which nothing is known, some perhaps of only short duration. Still others were continuous for half a century or longer. For example, the Indianapolis program, which is barely mentioned by Bagster-Collins, was, as Professor Frances Ellis of Indiana University points out, continuous from 1869 to 1919.

Only the most approximate estimate of the numerical significance of these pre-World War I programs is possible. By adding the 25 annual enrollment figures that are cited by Bagster-Collins and Ellis,[19] an approximate total enrollment of 203,815 is reached. Dividing by 25 gives an average annual enrollment per program of 8,152. If this figure is multiplied by 14, the number of known programs, an estimate—again very approximately—of 114,128 as the annual overall enrollment is established. Multiplying by 43, the average number of years of these programs, gives an estimate of the total enrollments in FLES programs between 1840 and 1920. This figure shows 4,907,504 enrollments. How many children were involved is not known, for there is no way of estimating how many years a given pupil remained in a specific program. Guessing arbitrarily 4.9 years—surely an overestimate—gives one million as the minimum estimated number of pupils in this first period of FLES.

This figure takes on significance if it is compared to the enrollment figures compiled by the Modern Language Association in the last few years. The total number of children found to have been en-

[19] See Table 1.

rolled in elementary-school foreign-language programs in these surveys was respectively 145,643 in 1953, 209,549 in 1954, 271,617 in 1955,[20] and 1,030,097 in 1960.[21] The figure of 113,002 may not seem very impressive as compared with these later figures until the total public elementary-school population (nursery and kindergarten through grade eight) in 1900, which was 14,983,859,[22] is compared with the elementary-school population in 1960, which was 32,413,000.[23] These statistics show that, if the estimates are not too inaccurate, pre-World War I FLES was relatively more impressive than the enrollments of 1953 and comparable to the enrollments of 1954 and 1955. Only after the passage of the National Defense Education Act of 1958 did FLES enrollments reach a point of being four to five times as large, relatively, as in the earlier period.

Organization of German FLES Programs

The research of Handschin, Bagster-Collins, and Ellis provides valuable information about the organization and quality of some of the early German FLES programs, which Bagster-Collins describes as follows:

Special schools were set apart where they [the schools] were demanded and called either German or German-English schools. In Cincinnati the German schools were attended during the early period only by children of German parentage. In other places, St. Louis for example, it was regarded as bad educational policy to segregate populations in this manner. German-English schools were therefore created which were attended by all children, regardless of parentage or native speech, and in which the emphasis was upon the English language. The German-English school was apparently the type most generally developed.[24]

In the German schools the classroom teachers gave instruction in both languages. In the German-English schools either special teachers taught German or a "parallel class system" was developed. The

[20] Kenneth W. Mildenberger, *Status of Foreign Language Study in American Elementary Schools, Fall Term, 1953*, p. 11, *1954*, p. 1, *1955*, p. 1.

[21] The Modern Language Association of America, *Reports of Surveys and Studies in the Teaching of Modern Foreign Languages, 1959–1961*, p. 2.

[22] U.S., Department of Commerce, Bureau of the Census, *Historical Statistics of the United States, 1960*, p. 207.

[23] *Ibid.*, *1963*, p. 128.

[24] Bagster-Collins, "History of Modern Language Teaching," p. 16.

following plan was in operation in Cincinnati in 1914: "In the lower grades of the larger schools two teachers were assigned to two classes, one teaching German and the other English to both classes, alternately, the German teacher in addition taking charge of such branches as drawing, music, and primary occupation work. The upper grades were generally taught by a German supervising assistant."[25]

The amount of time devoted to German instruction varied considerably. In general it ran from twenty minutes a day to an hour and a half or more. In Cleveland in 1869–1870 equal time was given to instruction in both German and English, and in 1914 German was taught in Cincinnati from thirty minutes to ninety minutes daily, according to local conditions. The maximum time devoted to German, however, never exceeded nine hours per week.

THE MILWAUKEE COURSE OF STUDY. Bagster-Collins describes the German course of study in Milwaukee in 1911 as an example of how German was taught.

There were two courses, one chiefly for children whose parents spoke German, the other for children of non-German speaking parents. The general plan pursued was the same for both courses, the chief difference being in the amount of ground covered. Doubtless also greater use was made of English in those classes containing children from English-speaking homes. The center of instruction was the reader, comprising a single "Fibel" [primer] and later four graded readers. The selections were taught by the question and answer method and afterwards reproduced orally and in writing. Oral work and the vocabulary were also developed, in the earlier stages at least, by means of objects and pictures. Some of the selections were assigned for cursory reading. Special attention was given to exercises and dictation and memory work. Beginning with the third grade, supplementary material, either read by the teacher or by the pupils, was included in the work. It consisted of the following texts in the order given: "Märchen" by Amalie Godin, "Märchen" by Forster, "Allerlei" by Agnes Fahsel, "Märchen" by Grimm and Hauff. Grammar lessons of simple nature evidently first began in the fifth grade and were drilled partly by means of translation from English into German.[26]

[25] Quoted in *ibid.*, p. 17, from Cincinnati Public Schools, *85th Annual Report*, 1914, p. 68.
[26] *Ibid.*, p. 22.

THE BALTIMORE COURSE OF STUDY. About 1899 the Baltimore course of study was similar to the Milwaukee course but more closely correlated with other subjects. "Mental arithmetic was taught in German in the first three grades. Beginning with the fourth grade, sections taken from the regular geography, physiology, and history textbooks were used for translation purposes, particularly for translation from English into German. It was also suggested that universal history should be taught from the fourth grade on, in the form of brief oral biographies to be given by the teachers. In the fifth grade, for example, sketches of such outstanding men associated with Greek history as Miltiades, Aristides, Themistocles . . . were to be narrated to and exacted from the children by the teachers."[27]

EXAMINATIONS. One of the best ways to judge the objectives of a course of study is to see what kinds of examinations are used. Bagster-Collins reproduces the final examination for the eighth grade in the Cleveland elementary schools given in June of 1875 to pupils of German parentage. The examination consists of five parts, of which the first is a free composition on the subject of Frederick the Great. The second, on grammar, asks the student to write a simple sentence, a complex sentence, a compound sentence, a coordinating conjunction of comparison, one of contrast, a clause used as an object, one used as an attributive, a dependent adverbial clause of place, one of time, one of manner, and one of cause. The exam also contained two translation passages, one to be translated from English into German, consisting of nine verses taken from *Julius Caesar*, and the other to be translated from German into English, consisting of seven lines from *Wilhelm Tell*. The fifth and last question on the exam was to write from memory the last two stanzas of the poem entitled "Lützow's wilde Jagd."[28]

Teacher Training for German FLES Programs

As in our day, the supply of adequately qualified teachers was far from sufficient. Native Germans and Austrians, who were hired as

---

[27] *Ibid.*, p. 22, quoted from the *Report of the Board of Commissioners of Public Schools of Baltimore*, 1899, p. 165.

[28] *Ibid.*, p. 23.

special teachers, were sometimes deficient in their knowledge of English and not always at home in the American school system. Their number was supplemented by native American teachers of German who were graduates of high schools or German church schools. What little training the teachers were given was usually furnished by city supervisors of German. A few cities provided special training in their normal schools. Thus Cincinnati started a German teacher-training program in 1871, Cleveland followed in about 1875, and St. Louis had one in operation at least as early as 1882. The establishment of the Lehrer-Seminar at Milwaukee in 1878, supported by the National German American Teachers' Association, was the most successful, but its graduates, though well-prepared, were far too few to meet the needs of the situation.[29]

Frances Ellis quotes from a report by a supervisor of German in Indianapolis who described the up-to-date teaching procedure used by a whole group of teachers he had recruited and whom he oriented and supervised very carefully. "In all classes German is the principal medium of communication. The entire course is based on the spoken language. The vocabulary, word forms, and constructions learned orally are reviewed in the form of exercises in reading, writing, and translation. The systematic study of German grammar is begun in the sixth grade."[30]

EVALUATION OF FLES IN BUFFALO. Lacking careful guidance, teachers often performed in mediocre fashion. Bagster-Collins describes the result of a survey in 1914–1915 of the work done in German in the elementary schools of Buffalo.

Most of the instruction observed was purely perfunctory, consisting of so many pages of a book. There was no plan in selecting or teaching vocabulary; the conversational exercises had no direction; the pronunciation was poor; the teachers were working blindly. . . . After six years of instruction, the pupils were required to take a uniform examination, roughly equivalent to one's years work in the foreign language in high school. In 1912–13, 740 or seven per cent of the total number who were registered in German took this simple test. Just under 400 or three per cent took an examination for advanced credit. Measured by these results, nearly ten thousands pupils were taught by sixty-seven teachers in forty-three schools

29 *Ibid.*, p. 21.
30 Ellis, "Historical Account of German Instruction," p. 360.

in order that approximately four hundred may get what they would have been able to obtain under two or three teachers in one year of the high school course.[31]

The testimony is eloquent, but one caution must be observed: What is undoubtedly being measured in these examinations is not so much the skill in understanding and speaking as the knowledge of grammar. It is precisely the language skills at which young learners become most adept when the instruction is adequate, as obviously it was not here.

IMPORTANCE OF FLES SUPERVISOR. Ellis points out that the German supervisor was the key to the situation. Robert Nix, who was supervisor in Indianapolis from 1894 to 1910, not only guided his teachers closely—"during the year 1902, for instance, thirty-five meetings for teachers of German were held"—but he also had the authority to examine and select teachers. One examination was used as a prerequisite for the license to teach German, another was used for those already licensed. "Of the thirty-one applicants who took the examination in 1902, only twelve, four men and eight women, obtained the required average of seventy-five per cent. The three highest, all men, were native Germans, trained in either a teachers' seminary or at various German universities; four others had immigrated to the United States at an early age and like the remaining five candidates had had their training at American universities and normal schools, or were merely graduates of an Indianapolis high school."[32]

In 1910 Peter Scherer was appointed to succeed Robert Nix, with the title of Director of German. His report to the superintendent, dated May 20, 1915, reveals much about the requirements for the teacher's license.[33]

Under the direction of supervisors of the caliber of Nix and Scherer, a FLES program could prosper, as it did for a time in Indianapolis. Adequate selection and supervision of teachers presupposes the existence of competent supervisors, whose satisfactory performance

[31] Bagster-Collins, "History of Modern Language Teaching," p. 31, quoted from *Examination of the Public School System of the City of Buffalo*, 1916, pp. 105 ff.

[32] Ellis, "Historical Account of German Instruction," p. 360.

[33] See Appendix H, Part 1.

in turn is not possible without the support of school administrators, school board, and taxpayers.

History of German FLES in Indianapolis

A brief sketch of the origin, development, and sudden death of one typical program, which has been thoroughly investigated by Frances Ellis of Indiana University, summarizes this first chapter of the FLES story in the United States. Miss Ellis tells this story "from its first stirrings in the [eighteen] fifties and its legal entrance in 1869 to its abrupt decline in 1918 and its equally legal exit one year later. Vital years those of more than half a century, in which men both on the Indianapolis School Board and off strove ceaselessly, even in the face of defeat, to bring about the fruition of German instruction in the Indianapolis Public Schools. German newspapers, too, especially *Der Tägliche Telegraph*, played no small part in determining its progress."[34]

Free public schools were established in Indianapolis in 1853. In 1856 the Indianapolis City Council considered a resolution "That a portion of the school fund be appropriated to educate the German children of the city in their own language, or for the employment of a German teacher for their instruction."[35] German was available in private schools, but there were many Germans who could not afford to send their children to private schools and who nevertheless wanted them to have the benefit of German instruction. The resolution was tabled, as were other similar resolutions later.

Instead, to help meet the increasing demand for instruction in German, a new private school, Die Deutsche-Englische Schule, was founded in 1857. "Free from sectarianism it seems to have been an outstanding private school and to have exerted an influence for thoroughness and high standards throughout the twenty-five years of its existence (1857–1882). As a matter of fact it was not until the public schools themselves were worthy competitors that its own attendance dwindled and it was forced to close."[36]

In 1863 the Board of School Trustees was petitioned to employ

---

[34] The following account is based entirely on Miss Ellis' study, already cited, now unfortunately out of print (Ellis, "Historical Account of German Instruction").

[35] *Ibid.*

[36] *Ibid.*, p. 121.

German teachers to teach German in the public schools, but the petition was denied. Not until 1865 is there evidence that a part-time teacher of German was employed. However, the law prescribed, ironically, that all instruction must be done in English. In addition, the first teacher resigned within a few months, as did a second appointee. As Professor Ellis comments, "with German taught in English and with three teachers within one year the advent of German instruction does not seem to have been too auspicious."[37] Nevertheless, these efforts of 1865 mark the beginning of German instruction in the grades in Indianapolis.

POLITICS AND FLES. In 1867 *Der Tägliche Telegraph* led a spirited campaign to urge the Indiana state legislature to amend the state school law. In an editorial printed in English on "Indiana and the Immigration Question," *Der Tägliche Telegraph* pointed out that "Indiana had not had its share of immigrants, that they went to Illinois and Missouri; second, that Indiana had a bad name, as it was generally believed that the Germans in Indiana were not being treated in a liberal, generous, and cosmopolitan spirit; third, that the legislature should consider measures to counteract the above two points, both by authorizing that the laws, the proceedings of the legislature, and the educational and agricultural reports be published in the German language, and by permitting instruction in the German language to be introduced into the public schools."[38] Further editorials stressed that "by all these measures our state authorities will be able to attract to Indianapolis in the course of a few years over 100,000 industrious and thrifty German immigrants who will take up our wild lands, till our rich soil, help us in developing our manufactures and working our mines and increase our general wealth and prosperity."[39] The newspapers also taunted the legislators with the assertion "that the German-English Freischule was accomplishing much more than the public schools." The legislature became sensitive to the pressures and finally William E. McLean, chairman of the Committee on Schools and Education introduced a bill providing for the teaching of German in the public elementary schools of the state. Another member of the committee, Emil Bis-

[37] *Ibid.*, p. 123.
[38] *Ibid.*, p. 124.
[39] *Ibid.*, p. 125.

chof, drew upon himself the ire of the German population and of the newspapers by opposing the bill. He and the others who opposed the bill contended that the present law was adequate in that it permitted local authorities to authorize instruction in German. At the same time, however, "they wanted only the English language taught to the youth of the country."[40] However, the citizens came to the support of the papers. The *Telegraph* of March 9, 1867, announced that "Letters are pouring in upon us from all sides, expressive of the profound indignation felt by the Germans of Indiana at the outrageous conduct of Emil Bischof with regard to the immigration question, especially to the amendment to the school law."[41]

Having failed in its campaign in 1867, the German newspapers and population renewed their efforts in the legislative session of 1869. A new amendment was introduced and referred to the Committee on Education and was discussed in the House on February 8, 1869. On February 9, 1869, the House passed the bill seventy-seven to seven. Owing to political complications, however, the Senate was not of a mind to consider the bill, until the *Telegraph* rallied support. It called on all Germans interested in the amendment to come to the Senate chamber.

The next morning, promptly at nine o'clock, Germans from all parts of town, from all social circles, from all churches and all political parties arrived to take part in a demonstration in the senate chamber. . . . According to the newspaper accounts, the habitués of the State House were dumbfounded at the flood of Germans. . . . Hastily the Senate convened and, after a vote of suspension of rules the school bill was third on the agenda. The two other bills were read and discussed; there were messages; also pages running back and forth; but the German delegation had said it would not leave the place until the bill had been voted upon. Finally it was in order. It was read and the battle started. There was much debate. Amendments were introduced relative to teachers, to having a majority of parents of the pupils petition instead of but twenty-five, to have French and Spanish included, etc. The arguments for the bill seemed to be more forceful, however, than those against it, and so it came to a vote and as the *Telegraph* expressed it "many a Saul became a Paul." Thirty-seven votes were cast in favor of the bill and only three against it. The members of the German delegation waved their hats and congratulated each other

[40] *Ibid.*, p. 126.
[41] *Ibid.*, p. 128.

None among them, they agreed, had ever spent a morning to a better purpose.[42]

The following amendment was finally signed by the governor on May 6, 1869:

Section 1. *Be it enacted by the General Assembly of the State of Indiana,* that section one hundred and forty seven . . . be amended to read as follows: . . . and that whenever the parents or guardians of twenty-five or more children in attendance at any school of a township, town, or city shall so demand, it shall be the duty of the School Trustee or Trustees of said township, town, or city, to provide efficient teachers and introduce the German language as a branch of study into such schools; and the tuition in such schools shall be without charge: *Provided,* such demand is made before the teacher for said district is employed.[43]

SUPERINTENDENT SHORTRIDGE. Curiously enough, a full year later not a single petition had been received, and again the *Telegraph* was moved to spur the Germans of Indianapolis into action. This apparent lethargy is to be accounted for by the fact that German had already been taught in the grades for four years though without specific legislative endorsement. Citing Superintendent Shortridge's report of 1868–1869, Ellis explains that "a total of 866 pupils had received instruction. . . . The average number who continued the study through the entire year was . . . 642. Four teachers had been employed full time for this purpose; they labored hard, and as a class were second to no others in the schools." What difference the new legislation made is conveyed in carefully restrained language by Superintendent Shortridge: "It affords me pleasure to report the comparatively prosperous condition of this department of our school system. We have already done much, and I am satisfied that, with the experience of the past year, we shall do much more next, toward putting it on an efficient and permanent basis, as a part of the public school system of the city."[44] In April, 1871, Superintendent Shortridge reported "that for the past month 535 pupils had been studying German, 116 of which were English speaking and 419, German."[45]

[42] *Ibid.,* pp. 135–136.
[43] *Ibid.,* pp. 136–137.
[44] *Ibid.,* p. 137.
[45] *Ibid.,* p. 253.

A second petition was received in July of 1871, and the board realized that with improved methods and growing population there would soon be an expansion in German instruction. For this reason it drew up a set of regulations, which remained in force almost unchanged until 1900, when there was a drastic revision.[46]

Superintendent Shortridge's report of June 19, 1874, shows "a total of 718 pupils studying German in the district schools and 138 in the high schools. The total enrollment in all the public schools at that time was 7,801.[47]

The German citizens of Indianapolis were not satisfied with the quality of instruction, and in February of 1875 they petitioned that the time devoted to German instruction be increased. There was a general feeling that "the results to date were not at all good and would not be until the entire system underwent a thorough change." It was suggested that "two school houses, one north and one south, be designated for the explicit purpose of devoting half the time to English and half to German."[48]

This suggestion was not adopted, but instruction was consolidated. Whereas German-speaking pupils had begun their German in grade 2A (grade two, second semester) and had continued it through 8A (grade eight, second semester) and English-speaking pupils had not begun their German until 6A (grade six, second semester), "all pupils, American as well as children of foreign parentage, now had to begin in the C Primary grade [grade three], and no pupil was allowed to begin in the C Intermediate grade [grade six]. The success attending the instruction caused a great many English-speaking children to enter the German classes. It therefore became necessary to change the method of instruction and also to change textbooks."[49]

This was clearly a prosperous period for German FLES in Indianapolis. "During the year 1877 German was being taught in ten district schools to 2,432 pupils, but, oddly enough, it was taken out of the first year in high school and kept in the last three years only."[50]

[46] Ellis cites these regulations (*ibid.*, pp. 254–255), noting in brackets the minor changes made in 1874. See Appendix H, Part 2.
[47] Ellis, "Historical Account of German Instruction," pp. 257–258.
[48] *Ibid.*, p. 258.
[49] *Ibid.*, p. 258.
[50] *Ibid.*, pp. 258–259.

In 1878 twelve of the thirty-three high-school graduates were enrolled in German in their senior year. "Two of the twenty-seven essays that were read at the exercises were in German, even though German was not the native tongue of the young ladies who read them."[51]

At the end of the school year in 1883, German was taught in thirteen district schools in addition to the high school. The total number of pupils from grades 2A through 8A was 2,460, of whom 1,402 were of German parentage. "One noticeable and deplorable fact in the table of statistics of those studying German for the year 1882–1883 was the great decrease of pupils in the upper grammar grades. There were two reasons for this, namely, withdrawal from school and dropping the subject because it was too hard, although many other reasons were offered as excuses. By the fourth grade, for instance, only 37 per cent of those who had studied German remained in the schools, whereas 50 per cent of those not studying German continued."[52]

EDUCATION AND POLITICS. In 1886, when the German instruction seemed to be improving and was well regarded by the board of education, one of its members suddenly introduced a resolution to suspend the teaching of German for one year. It failed to pass, but only a week later another trustee moved a resolution that the office of supervisor of German be abolished and "that the teaching of German be suspended in the Primary Grades for one year and until the Board shall have recovered from its present financial embarrassment."[53] This too failed to pass but was symptomatic of the harassment suffered by the program from time to time.

In 1890 the board of trustees, taking advantage of the absence of two members favorable to German, voted to discontinue German in all schools except the high schools. Despite protest meetings and editorials in the *Telegraph* it proved impossible to persuade the board to reverse this decision. Therefore, the matter was taken to court, and the Circuit Court of Marion County, sustained in 1891 by the Indiana Supreme Court, found that "the board of school commissioners can not set up a lack of funds as an excuse for their re-

[51] *Ibid.*, p. 259.
[52] *Ibid.*, p. 261.
[53] *Ibid.*, pp. 262–263.

fusal to introduce the study of German, where it appears that studies not named in the statute as required studies are taught at an expense greater than would be necessary for the teaching of German."[54]

ROBERT NIX, SUPERVISOR OF GERMAN, 1894–1910. During the term of Robert Nix, beginning in 1894 and continuing until his death in 1910, German instruction prospered in Indianapolis. "By 1902, it was being taught in thirty-four district schools and in both high schools. There were 375 German classes with 6,170 pupils in the district schools; twenty-five classes with 458 pupils in the high schools. Five teachers of German were employed in the latter, and thirty-seven, including two substitutes, in the former."[55] In 1909 the number of classes in the district schools had increased to 404 and in the high school to 47. There were forty-two German teachers in the grades whereas eight taught in the high schools. The total number of pupils studying German in the public schools was 7,496, of whom 2,094 or 28 per cent were of German parentage. "The total cost of instruction in German in the district schools for the year 1908 was $28,142.58. Based on the February enrollment this made the expenditure per pupil $4.33."[56]

SUPERINTENDENT PETER SCHERER, 1910–1918. The last report before World War I was that submitted by Superintendent Peter Scherer in June of 1916. The program it describes had had its ups and downs but generally enjoyed the support of the community. The teaching of German sounds quite modern. The "direct method" predominated, which means that German was used as the language of the classroom during the twenty-five- or thirty-minute daily lesson. In the fifth grade the systematic study of grammar began. The aims of the program included not only language and literature but also the history, customs, and ideals of the German people. Other features of the program were the frequent singing of German songs, the celebration of German Christmas, and the staging of the annual German play.

German was introduced as an elective subject in the second year and continued to the eighth. In February of 1916 there were 476 German classes in the elementary schools and 85 in the high schools,

[54] *Ibid.*, p. 276.
[55] *Ibid.*, p. 359.
[56] *Ibid.*, p. 361.

and in June of the same year 332 of the elementary-school graduates had completed the German course. Of these, 273 received high-school credit, and 271 enrolled in the advanced German high-school course. The work in the high school was a continuation of the instruction in the grades and progressed to the point of giving the students a real *Sprachgefühl.* Thanks to the wide range of vocabulary developed, instruction in other subjects could be conducted in German. The best of the high-school graduates took oral and written examinations and were licensed to teach German in the elementary schools. Those who went on to college received advanced standing in German there.[57]

THE ROLE OF BOOTH TARKINGTON. Peter Scherer's report was in reality the swan song of German instruction in Indianapolis. War was declared in April of 1917. The first indication of trouble came in May, when the school board received a letter from the American Rights Committee. This letter, signed by ten men, including Booth Tarkington, protested the singing of the Star Spangled Banner and other patriotic songs in the German language.

On January 29, 1918, at the meeting of the board of trustees, Commissioner Clarence E. Crippin introduced the following resolution:

Whereas, The second semester of the public schools of the city of Indianapolis will meet again as soon as the fuel situation will permit; and

Whereas, The beginning of the school semester is the natural and most favorable time for the commencement or discontinuance of studies by the pupils,

Whereas, For many years the German language has, to the exclusion of all other modern foreign languages, been ordered by law to be taught in the grade schools of Indianapolis; and

Whereas, A state of war exists between the Government of the United States and the Imperial Government of Germany, and in consequence thereof many of the pupils have asked to be excused from the further study of German and parents of pupils have expressed a desire that the teaching of the German language be discontinued in the graded schools of Indianapolis; therefore be it

Resolved, By the Board of School Commissioners of the City of Indianapolis that the teaching of the German language in the graded schools of the school city of Indianapolis be and hereby is discontinued from and

[57] *Ibid.,* pp. 369–371, see Appendix H, Part 3.

after the date of the adoption of this resolution by the said Board of
School Commissioners, and be it further

Resolved That the Board of School Commissioners of the City of Indianapolis subscribes to the belief that the public schools should teach our
boys and girls the principle of one nation, one language, and one flag, and
should not assist in perpetuating the language of an alien enemy in our
homes and enemy viewpoints in the community; and be it further

Resolved, By the Board of School Commissioners of the City of Indianapolis that the teachers now employed and under contract to teach the
German language in the graded schools of Indianapolis be assigned to
other duties by the superintendent of public schools until such contract
shall have expired; and be it further

Resolved, That because and in consequence of the foregoing resolutions,
the position of director of languages in the grade schools be and hereby
is discontinued, and that the occupant of this position shall be assigned
by the Superintendent of Schools to other duties during the life of his
contract.[58]

The resolution was adopted with only one dissenting vote. This
courageous dissenter was Theodore Stempfel, whose reasoned reply
to the resolution has been vindicated by the history of the succeeding decades. As FLES succumbed to the unpatriotic patriotic pas-
sions of 1918, Theodore Stempfel expressed an attitude that is gradually regaining acceptance and that has made possible the rebirth
of FLES during the period examined in the next chapter.

This resolution has been introduced on account of the present political
and international situation. It is my opinion that this makes it more than
otherwise important that we, as school commissioners, should be absolute-
ly free from bias and passion and treat the large question involved from
a broad and constructive educational standpoint. Any radical change we
make in the curriculum of our schools will affect the education of the
children of our city, not only for the present time, but also for the future.
It is the easiest thing in the world to destroy. It would not require any
thought whatever, but only a prearranged vote of three members of this
board, to eliminate with one stroke from the school curriculum any subject which for years has been taught in our schools with good results. By
passing this resolution offered, you are heartlessly destroying what has
been successfully built up by the conscientious work of teachers for half
a century. . . . You are doing precisely the opposite of the advice given by

[58] Ellis, "Historical Account of German Instruction," pp. 373–374.

the United States Commissioner of Education, and by leading educators of our own country and abroad.[59]

Evaluations

HANDSCHIN'S CONCLUSIONS, 1911. Writing in 1911, Handschin finds that "The outlook for German instruction in the elementary schools is good in the sections of the country having a dense German population, although the number of cities where such instruction is given fluctuates from year to year. The Germans are very insistent in their claims, and instruction in German in the elementary school is indeed excellent in most of the cities, and from a pedagogical point of view has fully justified itself.

"The plan of teaching certain branches, e.g., Geography, History, Arithmetic, and Nature Study, by the medium of the German language has been tried successfully in some schools. However in a number of States there is a law prohibiting the teaching of the common branches in any language except the English."[60]

EVALUATION BY BAGSTER-COLLINS, 1930. Bagster-Collins' conclusions, published in 1930, have the advantage of greater historical perspective. "Although German in the course of time became strongly entrenched in a number of cities, it had constantly to act on the defensive. A number of arguments were periodically brought forward against and for the study of German in the grades. One was that the children in the earlier years of their training had quite enough to learn in their English studies without burdening them with a second language. Another was the factor of expense, which is so often advanced as the argument against foreign languages in the elementary school. There were naturally champions of the German cause who maintained that, far from being a burden to the pupils, the study of German was an aid to good work, that the children of the German-English schools commonly stood higher, especially in the English branches, and entered high school better prepared."[61]

Bagster-Collins quotes the Cleveland *Annual Report of the Board of Education* for 1876 to support his contention that early language study has a beneficial effect on other parts of the curriculum: "Three hundred and fifteen pupils examined for admission to the Cleveland

[59] *Ibid.*, pp. 374–375.
[60] Handschin, *Teaching of Modern Languages*, p. 73.
[61] Bagster-Collins, "History of Modern Language Teaching," p. 66.

high schools for the year 1875 were rated as follows: of those who had studied German, 157, or 86¼ per cent, passed; of those who had not studied German, 101, or 76 per cent, passed."[62]

Conclusion

Despite examples of successful teaching of German and other foreign languages in the elementary grades, the reasons advanced for the study of foreign languages were not always quite proper. FLES was urged predominantly as a matter of expediency and special interest rather than for its purely educational value. More often than not the quality of teaching was not assured: community support was often vacillating, competent supervisors were not always appointed, and teachers were often underpaid and incompetent. The benefits were, therefore, far short of what they might have been. To be sure, a million Americans or more received some early instruction in German and other languages, which served them as well as or better than the traditional high-school instruction in foreign language. Of these, many were descendants of families who spoke foreign languages and were thus able to perpetuate the use and tradition of another language and culture a little longer than would otherwise have been possible. However, the teaching of foreign languages in the elementary grades never came to be highly valued by the mass of the population. The place of language learning in a liberal education was never fully understood, nor did the need of widespread communication outside the limits of one's mother tongue receive strong acceptance. On the contrary, at the very time when knowledge of German would have seemed to be especially important in the national interest, during World War I, we took pains to destroy it. Therefore, the only real benefit of this first stage of language instruction in the elementary school is the clear demonstration that, when it is well taught, it produces good learning results and that the learning of a second language in the grades, far from interfering with the other common learnings, seems rather to produce better results there, too.

[62] *Ibid.*, p. 17.

5. History of Foreign-Language Teaching in the
Elementary School: 1920–1967

THE EIGHTY YEARS that constituted the first stage of FLES in the United States witnessed a series of halting efforts crowned by occasional periods of success before FLES finally collapsed completely in the midst of war hysteria. The second chapter of the FLES story covers some forty-five years, and its development is sufficiently different from the first experiment to deserve separate consideration.

Despite the extensive teaching of German in elementary schools the *idea* of FLES was by no means universally accepted in the nineteenth century and the first two decades of the twentieth. The banishment of German during World War I merely confirmed the isolationist and anti-intellectual philosophy that pervades much of our popular thinking. Individual educators, defending the value of foreign languages in our school program, continued, however, to maintain that children learn foreign speech more easily than older students and sought to translate this advantage into practice. Almost immediately, therefore, isolated new FLES programs began to appear, though not in German.

Rebirth of FLES, 1920–1952

The history of FLES from 1920 to 1952 is well described in the "Report on the Status of and Practices in the Teaching of Foreign Languages in the Public Elementary Schools of the United States," revised to July 1, 1953, prepared by a committee of five under the chairmanship of Emilie Margaret White, supervisor of foreign languages in Washington, D.C.[1] This report was submitted to the National Conference on the Role of Foreign Languages in American Schools, January 15–16, 1963, sponsored by the United States Office of Education and directed by the United States Commissioner of Education Earl J. McGrath.

According to the White Report, there were, in 1952, eighty-nine communities in twenty-seven states and the District of Columbia which offered some instruction in a modern foreign language at some point between kindergarten and grade six. Sixty-two of these programs reported the teaching of Spanish, forty-three French, nine German, and one Italian. Instruction began in various grades: four programs reported a beginning in kindergarten, eight in grade one, five in grade two, nineteen in grade three, twenty-two in grade four, sixteen in grade five, and seven in grade six. An adequate teaching staff was maintained in various ways. Forty-one programs used secondary-school language specialists; twenty-seven, regular classroom teachers; seven, native speakers from the community; six, professors from nearby universities; five, student language majors; and one, Cleveland, specially prepared and certified elementary-school language teachers. In some cases children in the class who already spoke a foreign language were used as helpers by the classroom teacher, and in a few cases foreign parents were called on to help. Forty-two of the programs were open to all children; in eighteen the children were selected on the basis of intelligence or reading ability; and in eleven the children were given the opportunity to choose whether or not to participate in the program.

[1] This committee, consisting of Ruth R. Ginsburg, Marjorie C. Johnston, Ralph M. Perry, Josette E. Spink, and Emilie Margaret White, chairman, published a brief "Report on the Status of and Practices in the Teaching of Foreign Languages in the Public Elementary Schools of the United States," *The Modern Language Journal*, Vol. XXXVII, No. 3 (March, 1953), pp. 123–127. Concerning other conference papers Dr. Marjorie C. Johnston, director, Instructional Resources Branch, Division of State Grants, Office of Education, United States Department of Health, Education, and Welfare, (now retired), has reported that "The supply of papers presented at the McGrath conference has long since been exhausted. We mimeographed them several times but finally gave up the effort to make them available. I shall always regret that the Office of Education did not publish a comprehensive report of that conference."

Answers to a questionnaire indicated that the programs were started on the initiative of parents, community organizations, elementary-school teachers, secondary-school curriculum directors, school administrators, or college professors. Miss White reported that:

The program does not at present involve additional expense because in this experimental stage teachers already in the system do the instruction. . . .

Languages taught as a special subject are correlated with the regular course in a given grade wherever the opportunity to do so is present, which occurs mainly in arithmetic, art, health, language arts, music, and social studies. . . .

The method is all oral, with emphasis on dialogue, songs, games and activities. . . .

Actual instruction as *language* is given from fifteen minutes to twenty minutes three or four times a week or daily, with incidental use of the language in various ways during the day. . . .

There is wide-spread enthusiasm for the program. . . .

The results are gratifying.[2]

Miss White listed the following beneficial outcomes: "an increased interest on the part of the children, a desire to read and to learn about foreign people and their backgrounds, a new sense of pride and assurance for children of minority and ethnic groups, personality growth and a sense of satisfaction for the slow learner who achieves success, an increased sense of language in general and new interest in their own language, help in some cases in overcoming speech defects, an encouragement to do better in the regular work, and a stimulus for teachers to study and broaden their cultural knowledge."[3]

The White Report showed that secondary-school language teachers used their free periods to teach an elementary-school class, taught before or after school, or filled out programs that were not quite full by teaching in the elementary schools. "A few communities reported classes in which the regular teacher and the children are learning the language together with help from a language spe-

---

[2] White, "Report on the Status of and Practices in the Teaching of Foreign Language," pp. 123–127.

[3] *Ibid.*, pp. 123–127.

cialist."[4] In a small number of cases language instruction was confined to clubs or extracurricular activities.

Growth of FLES was slow through the twenties, thirties, and forties. Miss White lists—on the basis of incomplete information—the number of programs beginning in each year: "one in 1920, one in 1921, two in 1925, two in 1927, one in 1929, one in 1931, one in 1936, one in 1939, three in 1940, three in 1942, three in 1943, two in 1944, two in 1945, two in 1948, five in 1949, six in 1950, seven in 1951, and eighteen in 1952."[5] This sudden increase in the early fifties foreshadows the great expansion of the fifties and sixties.

THE CLEVELAND PROGRAM. Before studying the prospering of the FLES idea in the next decade, brief examination of two early FLES programs is necessary. Despite a generally equivocal public attitude toward languages, a few programs managed to take root in the isolationist twenties and thirties. The oldest of these was the Cleveland program, whose genius was Emile B. de Sauzé. This pioneer language educator came from France shortly after World War I and settled in Cleveland. As professor of French in Western Reserve University and director of foreign languages in the Cleveland Public Schools, he was able, with the collaboration of the Women's City Club of Cleveland, to give substance to his dream of a strong French program starting in the first grade and continuing through high school.[6] Included in the Major-Work Program provided for gifted children in the Cleveland schools,[7] French has been taught from grade one or two through grade six since 1921–1922, and any attempt to yield to the impulse of economy and eliminate it from the school curriculum would now meet with overwhelming resistance from parents. It is interesting to note, however, that the excellent example of Cleveland was not emulated by the affluent suburbs of the city until 1957. Success in these relatively sterile decades re-

[4] *Ibid.*, pp. 123–127.

[5] *Ibid.*

[6] Dr. Emile Blais de Sauzé told this story in a paper entitled "Foreign Languages for the Gifted in the Cleveland Elementary Schools," contributed to the National Conference on the Role of Foreign Languages in American Schools, Washington, D. C., January 15, 1953, and published in *The French Review*, Vol. XXVI, No. 5 (April, 1953), pp. 371–376, under the title "Teaching French in the Elementary Schools of Cleveland."

[7] For an account of the Major-Work Program see Theodore Hall, *Gifted Children: The Cleveland Story.*

quired a well-informed and convinced public as well as the enlightened guiding spirit of de Sauzé.[8]

The Cleveland program, which continues to follow essentially its original pattern, is designed for motivated children of an IQ of 115 and over who are judged suitable by the school authorities and whose parents are interested. Children admitted to this program attend special schools. Their work in French occupies half an hour daily and is completely audio-lingual, or aural-oral, which was the term more commonly used until recently.[9] The materials used were developed by de Sauzé and his associates.[10] French is the medium of instruction in the class, and a rapid tempo is maintained as the teacher presents material, illustrates the meaning with objects, pictures, or action, makes the class repeat and practice numerous times, and finally uses questions and answers, games, and dramatic skits. The children learn to understand and reproduce the speech contained in the *Course of Study*. There is no reading or writing. Graduates of this program may continue their French as a separate group in grade seven and in grade eight join the stream of those who have begun in grade seven. Instruction in the high school, though based on a conventional grammar approach, is also conducted in French and stresses speaking. The basic text is de Sauzé's *Nouveau cours pratique de français pour commençants,* written entirely in French.

The Cleveland program is the classic program of this second stage of FLES development. In its formative years it enjoyed a unity and firmness of direction in the person of de Sauzé, who, until his

[8] Those interested in more information are referred to Sister Mary Lelia Pond, S.S.N.D., "The Multiple Approach Method of Teaching French Versus the Grammar Method," *The French Review,* Vol. XIII, No. 6 (May, 1940), pp. 475–482; to Emile Blais de Sauzé, "An Oralist Looks at the Results," *Education,* Vol. LVII, No. 7 (March, 1937), pp. 422–427, and *The Cleveland Plan for the Teaching of Modern Languages, With Special Reference to French;* and to William McClain, "Twenty-Five Years of the Cleveland Plan," *Education,* Vol. LXV, No. 9 (May, 1945), pp. 541–547. For a recent retrospective description see "The Cleveland Program," pp. 112–116, in Marguerite Eriksson, Ilse Forest, and Ruth Mulhauser, *Foreign Languages in the Elementary School.*

[9] The pronunciation of "aural-oral" has always given difficulty, for, despite the fact that some American speakers distinguish—in a variety of ways—between the two words, most do not. The new term "audio-lingual," suggested by Nelson Brooks of Yale, filled the need.

[10] Cleveland Public Schools, *Course of Study for French in the Elementary School (Grades 1–6).*

retirement in 1949, not only directed the foreign-language program but also prepared most of its teachers.

NEW YORK PUBLIC SCHOOL 208 IN BROOKLYN. Another notable experiment has since 1931 permitted the teaching of Spanish and since 1936 the teaching of French in New York's Public School 208 in Brooklyn.[11] The founder and guiding spirit of this program was Miss Elsa Ebeling, pioneering principal of the school. Sensitive to an interest on the part of the parents in her school district, she obtained permission to engage teachers, one for Spanish and one for French, to be paid out of a modest monthly fee contributed by parents. The teachers were usually teacher candidates in a neighboring college. They would circulate from room to room conducting lessons of about fifteen minutes in each room from grade one through grade eight. There was not much continuity, for the teachers improvised materials from day to day. Also they took all interested children, whether they had had any instruction in previous grades or not. Unfortunately no analysis exists of the influence of this program on later study in high school or college.

THE EFFECT OF FOREIGN POLICY ON FLES. The occasional programs that began in the twenties and thirties aimed to provide academic enrichment in the elementary-school course of study. The Good Neighbor Policy enunciated by President Roosevelt in 1938 and elaborated in the Hemispheric Solidarity Policy, aimed to encourage closer relations with our neighbors to the south and resulted in a great emphasis on programs in Spanish, the purpose of which was to provide future citizens able to communicate in Spanish. In the early forties dozens of communities began Spanish programs in the grades, especially in Texas, Florida, and New Mexico. Classroom teachers who had had some Spanish and who wished to provide instruction were furnished with a state course of study but were given no other assistance.[12] Since the vast majority of these teachers were not adequately prepared and since the methods used were often more appropriate to secondary-school teaching, it was

[11] For an account of this program and a classroom picture, see "New York Public School 208 in Brooklyn," *New York Times*, June 3, 1953, p. 33.

[12] See, for example, Texas Department of Education, *Tentative Course of Study for the Teaching of Spanish in Grades 3 to 8 Inclusive*, Bulletin No. 426, 1943.

inevitable that most of these programs should fail. This they did, so quickly that they left no trace in the White survey. This fiasco undoubtedly retarded the development of FLES.

World War II, however, made us as a nation acutely aware of our great linguistic deficiencies; and it became necessary, if we were to communicate with either our allies or our enemies, for us quickly to prepare specialists able to understand and speak other languages. This was done in Army Specialized Training Programs at an estimated cost of forty million dollars.[13] These programs, in which American linguistic scientists played a prominent role, were an admirable improvisation, and they made many Americans realize that other languages could be learned, even by adults. Indirectly, the emphasis on speaking a foreign language benefited FLES, because greater numbers of Americans came to realize the natural advantage that children have in learning foreign speech.

In May of 1945, the *Woman's Home Companion* published the results of a survey in which more than two thousand carefully selected readers, considered a cross section of many millions, had been asked: "'Do you think our schools should make the study of at least one foreign language compulsory?' Only six per cent had no opinion; seventy-three per cent answered yes; twenty-one per cent no. Moreover, forty-three per cent thought that this teaching should begin in the grade schools."[14] No doubt the war situation publicized our linguistic shortcomings and may well have accounted for the overwhelmingly affirmative reply, but what is surprising is that in 1945, with the German FLES program long since forgotten and only a sprinkling of FLES programs in existence, there should be 43 per cent of respondents in favor of starting languages in the elementary schools.

[13] For reports on this program see the Modern Language Association of America, *A Survey of Language Classes in the Army Specialized Training Program,* Report of a Special Committee Prepared for the Commission on Trends in Education of the Modern Language Association of America, New York, 1943; Paul Angiolillo, *Armed Forces Foreign Language Teaching: Critical Evaluation and Implications;* Melva Lind, "Modern Language Learning: The Intensive Course as Sponsored by the United States Army and Implications for the Undergraduate Course of Study," *Genetic Psychology Monographs,* Vol. XXXVIII, First Half (August, 1948), pp. 3–82.

[14] *Woman's Home Companion,* May, 1945.

LOS ANGELES PROGRAM. A large program in Los Angeles,[15] which began in 1943 through the initiative of Dr. Vierling Kersey, superintendent of schools, reflected this favorable public opinion. California has, of course, a special need to develop citizens capable of communicating with its neighbors near and far, for it is situated next door to Mexico, and its approximately 1.5 million Spanish-name citizens constitute approximately one-tenth of the total population.[16] Moreover, its Chinese and Japanese speakers are a natural link with our overseas neighbors.

In June of 1943, Dr. Kersey announced that Spanish would be taught in the grades of the Los Angeles schools that fall. Preparatory steps included a Mexican workshop for two weeks in July, a survey of teachers with preparation in Spanish as well as of secondary-school specialists in Spanish willing to assist in the program as sponsors and advisers, the organization of committees to set up objectives and prepare materials, and the planning of meetings to inform the school personnel about the project. As a result of the survey, eighty-five secondary-school teachers, seventy elementary-school teachers, and fourteen teachers of adult classes offered their services and to these were apprenticed the elementary-school teachers. An elaborate program of organization, instruction, and in-service training was set up under the supervision of Mrs. Ruth Ginsburg, a Spanish teacher in the Abraham Lincoln High School, who was soon appointed supervisor of foreign languages. Materials prepared by committees included an instructional guide,[17] a set of recordings, and other aids, which were made available to all elementary-school teachers.

Since the program was planned to include all children from kindergarten through the sixth grade on a city-wide basis, it was thought necessary to use the classroom teachers to provide instruction. The vast majority did not possess the knowledge of Spanish essential to perform competently, so the program was conducted on

[15] Described by Grace M. Dreier, assistant superintendent of schools, in a report entitled "Developing and Introducing a Program of Conversational Spanish in the Elementary Schools of Los Angeles, California," submitted to the National Conference on the Role of Foreign Languages in American Schools, Washington, D. C., January 15, 1953.

[16] U. S., Department of Commerce, Bureau of the Census, *United States Census of Population: 1960.*

[17] Los Angeles, City Schools, *Instructional Guide for Teaching Spanish in the Elementary Schools*, Publication No. 414, 1946.

the principle that the teachers would learn along with the pupils. Recordings of model speakers were provided. Because of this situation, the goals set were extremely modest. Mrs. Dreier reported the following achievements: "Ability of children to respond spontaneously to greetings; ability of children to carry on simple conversation about their school, their friends, the home, and the community; increased appreciation of and greater interest in the cultural contributions of our neighbors as evidenced by the many fine programs reflecting the life and customs of Latin Americans presented by children's groups during the Christmas season, at Parent-Teacher Association meetings, during Public Schools Week, and on similar occasions."[18] Mrs. Dreier concluded her presentation by observing that "additional help of special teachers, facile in the use of Spanish, who could serve several schools were needed for teacher help, would be of great assistance in advancing the program to serve all children more adequately with greater equality of opportunity."[19] She also pointed out that teacher-training institutions could be of help in providing larger numbers of teachers trained in spoken Spanish, and she noted the promise of radio and television as a way of extending language learning to more children. The urgent need for more language specialists to give this very ambitious program greater substance has not to this day been met because of eternal financial reasons.

SOMERVILLE, NEW JERSEY. The Somerville, New Jersey, program, modest in scope, but of superior quality, represents what was possible in the early fifties. In the fall of 1949 French instruction began in the third grade of the Somerville Public Schools, to be followed by Spanish the following year. Thereafter French and Spanish have alternated in grades three through six. Children beginning with French continue their French study through the sixth grade and those beginning with Spanish continue their Spanish study. Continuity has also been provided in the junior and senior high schools. Margaret C. McCormack, supervisor of elementary schools in Somerville, explained how the program began.[20]

[18] Dreier, "Developing and Introducing a Program of Conversational Spanish."
[19] *Ibid.*
[20] Margaret C. McCormack, Report submitted to the National Conference on the Role of Foreign Languages in American Schools, Washington, D. C., January 15, 1953.

"Six years ago, our Supervising Principal and I sat down to discuss the possibility of including the study of one or more foreign languages in our elementary schools. From our own experiences, observations, and research, we were convinced that a foreign language, to become functional must have its beginnings much earlier than the difficult adolescent years." These two enterprising school administrators considered how to elicit the interest and support of parents and teachers in both the elementary and secondary schools, at what grade level to begin instruction, how to obtain qualified teachers, how to finance the program, and how to find time in the already crowded elementary-school curriculum. Among parents they found no lack of interest. The teachers were more skeptical but willing to cooperate. They decided to begin instruction in the third grade because children of this age "had acquired a working knowledge of the tools of learning" and because the third-grade course of study included a unit on Mexico. High-school teachers were found who were willing to contribute extra teaching without compensation until such a time as provision could be made for special FLES teachers. The following year the board of education approved the needed budget item for salaries. The plan was to start a language in the third grade and to continue through grade eight. The program was coordinated by the elementary-school supervisor and the high-school language teachers. The opportunity was extended to all children and the approach was functional. Songs, games, and various other activities were used to hold the interest of the children and to make the language usable. Materials were prepared by the local staff. In the initial stages no books or writing were used. In grades five and six the children were permitted to copy material from the blackboard in Spanish in their notebooks. At the conclusion of her report Miss McCormack noted the following problems: How to articulate the elementary and secondary programs; how to revise the secondary-school program in the light of the FLES program; whether to provide in high school two kinds of language instruction, one for the general student and one for the college-preparatory student; whether the high-school enrollment in French and Spanish would greatly increase as a result of the FLES program; how to measure achievement and aptitude at the end of the eighth grade; whether to weed out those pupils who did not succeed and in the eighth grade teach only a selected group; whether to

continue to offer language instruction to all children at the lower
levels in the elementary schools; how to work out satisfactory
arrangements with the state Department of Education for the certification of teachers with a liberal arts background.[21]

A description and evaluation of the Somerville FLES courses in
French and Spanish in 1962[22] reveal a well-articulated program in
grades three through twelve.

Immediate stress is placed upon building comprehension of words, sentences, and ideas expressed by the teacher. The children are encouraged
to repeat in chorus and individually; and from the first day . . . they are
expected to reply and are encouraged to gain confidence. . . . The goal is
active participation and involvement of all students. . . .

The core of the FLES program in Somerville is the basic dialogue. . . .
The basic dialogue represents some realistic situation related to the experiences and interests of most children of the age group, often correlat-
ing with some other area in the school curriculum, such as hygiene or
geography.[23]

Articulation between elementary and high-school grades is arranged as follows: At the end of grade six a screening takes place
based on Modern Language Association Cooperative Tests and on
the teacher's recommendation. The Modern Language Aptitude
Test is given in the eighth grade together with the Otis Mental
Ability Test and the Iowa Test of Basic Skills. The pupil's placement in grade nine depends on the results of these tests and on the
teachers' grades and recommendations. Three choices are available:
an accelerated group, a regular college-preparatory class, or a
general, terminal class for pupils of less than average ability. The
first of these is a specially designed transitional course leading to a
Level III course in grade ten. Here the FLES graduate joins
eleventh-grade students from the area surrounding Somerville who

[21] *Ibid.*

[22] Somerville Public Schools, *Evaluation of the Effects of Foreign Language
Study in the Elementary School Upon Achievement in the High School*, (NDEA
Title VI Research Project Number SAE 9516), pp. 13–51. The former superintendent of Somerville also gives a personal appraisal of this unpretentious but
substantial program (John B. Geissinger, "Foreign Languages in the Elementary
Schools," *The American School Board Journal*, Vol. CXXXIII, No. 2 [August,
1956], pp. 27–29).

[23] Somerville Public Schools, *Evaluation*, p. 13.

have not had FLES but who have had Levels I and II in grades nine and ten.

Somerville seems to be happy with its ten-year sequence of foreign-language study. Here, for example, quoted from the same evaluation study, is a subjective report on the program: "The pupil of low I.Q. apparently learned as well as the pupil of high I.Q.— sometimes better because his most important equipment is a good ear. A second language even did something for stutterers: They did not stutter in Spanish! Too, the enthusiasm of the third-grader was never matched in a high-school class. A point was also made of having every third-grade parent visit the program sometime during the year. The most frequent comment was: Why didn't they do this when I was in school?"[24]

Somerville is one of the few FLES programs to have evaluated itself in any but an impressionistic way. Below are the more significant conclusions:

The FLES pupil does as well as the non-FLES pupil in subjects other than language; the time and effort required by the FLES program apparently does not impede learning in other areas.[25]

FLES pupils can advance at least one year in their high-school language study without harmful effect. In fact, the students themselves would favor acceleration of a year and a half. . . .

Currently, the advantage which FLES students may anticipate in high school is a college-level course in their senior year. This course leads to the Advanced Placement examination; therefore, the successful passing of this examination carries the further advantage of possible higher college placement and/or college credit, or for some the advantage of having met the college language requirement. . . .

Although the analysis of teachers' marks incorporated in this research indicates neutral findings, a pilot study completed in 1960 by STACO, Statistical Consultants, 188 Highland Avenue, Moorestown, New Jersey, and incorporated into the Somerville evaluation is significant. The STACO report indicated that at mid-term FLES students in a Spanish 3 class achieve approximately ten percent higher grades than did other pupils in the class who were in the traditional language pattern group, even though the FLES students were one year younger. A ten-per cent difference is mathematically significant.[26]

[24] *Ibid.*, pp. 2–3.
[25] *Ibid.*, p. 3.
[26] *Ibid.*, p. 9.

Also considered noteworthy is the fact that 70% of the non-college-bound FLES students—free from the dictates of college entrance requirements—did elect some foreign language during their four years in high school. In fact even among the non-FLES non-college-bound students at Somerville High School 62% elect a foreign language. The difference is significant at 13 to 1 odds (90% level of significance). In New Jersey in the fall of 1959, 48.2% of all pupils were enrolled in foreign language, and in the fall of the previous year 43.7% were enrolled.[27] The national percentages at the same time were 27% in 1959 and 24.3% in 1958.

As might be expected, a very significant difference favored the Somerville pupils in continuation from Language Two to Language Three. Of 973 pupils enrolled in Language Two and 322 in Language Three, the FLES continuation was 47% and the non-FLES 24%.[28]

In June of 1964, Miss Dorothy E. Chamberlain, chairman of the Foreign Languages Department, described her first-hand impressions in a personal letter: "We know that our fifth year classes are bigger—next year's French class [1964–1965] is eighteen. It started with four ... We know that we are doing a better job in the grades and the product we are getting [in high school] is better. We know that more students stay with the program through their junior year —fourth year [level] of the language. We know that so far we are the only department in Somerville that gets 5's [highest rating] in the Advanced Placement exam ... We get fantastic reports from our students in college and they are being placed very high in such schools as Smith, Wellesley, Cornell, etc. In the smaller schools some of them are placed high and are still using texts or reading books they had read here. Some of the parents are very vocal about their opinions of the program and I think it would be impossible to remove the program from the curriculum."[29]

Growth of FLES, 1952–1966

McGRATH's CALL TO ACTION. Clearly the idea of FLES was in many people's minds; it only awaited the necessary leadership to be realized. This leadership was fortunately furnished by Earl J. McGrath, then United States commissioner of education. Dr.

---

[27] See, The Modern Language Association of America, *Reports of Surveys and Studies in the Teaching of Modern Foreign Languages, 1959–1961*, p. 21.

[28] Somerville Public Schools, *Evaluation*, p. 11.

[29] Dorothy E. Chamberlain, letter to author, June, 1964.

McGrath had gradually come to the position that "unless a student shows a marked lack of aptitude in the study of a foreign language, he ought to gain at least an elementary knowledge of one language other than his own as a part of his general studies," and in 1952 he was ready to take the giant step to FLES. He had just returned from an international education meeting in Beirut which had opened his eyes completely to the humiliating inability of even educated Americans to communicate in languages other than English. Shocked into action, he requested permission of the Central States Modern Language Teachers Association to address their annual meeting. In St. Louis on May 3, 1952, he electrified a large audience of language teachers by confessing that he, like many other professional educators, had been skeptical about the necessity of languages in the American school curriculum but that he had been completely converted by his experience in Beirut. There he had, for example, observed an Egyptian delegate address the conference on one day in fluent English and on the following day in equally fluent French. Between sessions he saw the same Egyptian delegate converse with the West German delegates in German. Dr. McGrath was one of five American representatives, all holders of the Ph.D. degree, of whom not one was able to use, formally or informally, any language except English. His urgent proposal was couched in the following words:

The social, the political, the international reasons for the study of languages deserve the thoughtful consideration of all who determine the character of American education. There are, of course, other arguments for the study of languages . . . [but] for the average citizen the basic consideration . . . is our world position as a nation. . . . This small world is one in which . . . our children will live even more intimately than we with their contemporaries in other lands. Whether we discharge our world responsibilities well or poorly . . . will be determined by our ability to understand other people and their ability to understand us. . . . Only through the ability to use another language even modestly can one really become conscious of the full meaning of being a member of another nationality or cultural group. It is in our national interest to give as many of our citizens as possible the opportunity to gain these cultural insights. . . .

Educators from the elementary schools to the top levels of the university system ought to give immediate attention to this matter. . . . The citizens of other nations excel ours in using foreign languages, and the principal reason for this superiority is that they have the opportunity to study languages early in their lives in the school system. . . . Only a small percentage of American children have an opportunity to begin the study or use of a language other than their own before they enter high school. Yet it is a psychological fact that young children learn new languages easily and idiomatically. . . . My . . . proposal then is that there be complete reconsideration of the place of foreign language study in American elementary education. Such a reappraisal, I should hope, would lead to the offering of foreign language at least on an optional basis in many of our schools beginning in the fourth, fifth, or sixth grades. . . . Much could be done at once in many places. . . . I am not proposing that *every* child in *every* elementary school in *every* American community should be required to begin the study of a foreign language. I am suggesting that as many American children as possible be given the opportunity to do so. . . . With a little ingenuity and determination this opportunity could be extended to hundreds of thousands.[30]

Dr. McGrath followed up his call to action by organizing the National Conference on the Role of Foreign Languages in American Schools, held in Washington on January 15 and 16, 1953. This conference brought together about 350 educators who were almost equally divided between Education and foreign languages. In addition to listening to the presentations of Emilie Margaret White, Grace Dreier, Emile B. de Sauzé, Margaret C. McCormack, and others who described the background and status of FLES, the conferees had an opportunity to discuss in smaller groups such topics as the education of elementary-school language teachers, problems of aims and objectives, curriculum, administration, and needed research. The conference stimulated much enthusiasm and expressed agreement with the Commissioner that educators should seek ways of introducing FLES programs where conditions were favorable.

SURVEYS BY MILDENBERGER.[31] The year 1952 also saw the launching of the Foreign Language Program of the Modern Language Association, under the direction of its executive secretary, William Riley

[30] Earl J. McGrath, "Language Study and World Affairs," *The Modern Language Journal*, Vol. XXXVI, No. 5 (May, 1952), pp. 205–209.

[31] Kenneth W. Mildenberger, then assistant director of the foreign language program of the Modern Language Association, conducted surveys in 1953, 1954, and 1955, issued in mimeograph form by the United States Office of Education under the title "Status of Foreign Language Study in American Elementary Schools." These are unfortunately now unavailable.

Parker. This program, which was supported by the Rockefeller Foundation until 1958, did much to stir the conscience of the modern-language teaching profession. Impressive improvements were made which prepared the stage for the inclusion of modern foreign languages with mathematics and science in the National Defense Education Act of 1958. Assisting Parker in the Foreign Language Program was Kenneth W. Mildenberger, who undertook to study the status of foreign-language teaching in the elementary schools. His first survey, conducted in 1953, showed that in 1952 seven new FLES programs had been organized before the Commissioner's address in St. Louis and that twenty-eight more were organized later in the same year. In the following year, 1953, ninety-three programs began. The survey of 1954 reported that a hundred new programs were started in that year. Figures from the 1955 survey suggest that there were seventy-seven new programs in 1955. Mildenberger commented in his 1954 survey that "only fifty-two of the 280 cities and towns were involved in 1951; thirty-three in 1949; nine in 1939. In 1939 probably fewer than 2,000 pupils were studying foreign languages in the public elementary schools."[32]

Interesting innovations reported by Mildenberger in his 1954 survey were the teaching of Spanish by radio in Miami since 1953 and the teaching of French in Schenectady by television since 1952. Twenty-four stations in nine states in the Midwest offered the fourteen-lesson French series (called, in good Americanized French, "Visitons Mimi"), and station directors reported an estimated 119,222 participants. In Kansas a thirty-three–lesson German series was offered by two stations, and 300 children participants were reported.

Mildenberger's 1954 report contains a significant paragraph on suspended programs. FLES was still far from having official endorsement or being accepted as a regular part of the "common learnings." Without adequate provision for financing, for finding qualified teachers, or for guaranteeing continuity, one would expect a large number of suspended programs—but the contrary seemed to be true. Mildenberger wrote that

In the fall of 1953 survey, 145 cities and towns were found to have language ventures. All of these places were sent questionnaires in the current survey. Only eight did not reply (four of these in 1953 had their

[32] *Ibid.*, 1954, p. 1.

classes in grades seven–eight, information about which was not requested in this survey), and one would not give out information. Of the remaining 136 communities covered by replies, only eleven had suspended all language teaching in the fall of 1954. Nine blamed the suspension on overcrowded conditions and consequent pressure on teachers . . . ; one reported the preliminary experiment successful and a fuller program in preparation; one merely reported the venture ended. Six of the eleven expected to resume instruction in 1955. While no assessment of the ventures was requested, a surprising number of questionnaires carried gratuitous comments of satisfaction. No adverse remarks were received.[33]

An analysis of Mildenberger's reports reveals these interesting conclusions.

In what grade was FLES begun? Table 2 shows a wide distribution from kindergarten through grade six, with a certain concentration in grades three, four, and five. In 1955 there is perhaps a slight trend toward beginning in grade one, with sixty-eight as compared to thirty-seven in 1954. There is no indication that either experimentation or theoretical considerations have determined the best point for beginning instruction. It is tempting to conclude that it was rather chance, the availability of teachers, and curricular convenience that played the decisive roles.

There was also a great range in the number of classes per week. In view of the fact that language educators recommend frequent short classes, it is both encouraging to see the preponderance of programs meeting five times a week and discouraging to note that a considerable number met only once or twice a week.

The lessons varied in length from five minutes to ninety minutes. Table 2 reveals that the most popular length of time was thirty minutes, followed by twenty, followed by fifteen. The predominance of the thirty-minute period is undoubtedly due to the large number of two- and three-lesson programs a week. It is interesting to note that thirty-one programs in 1953, thirty-eight in 1954, and thirty-seven in 1955 required as much as two hours a week or longer. Since one of the principal alleged difficulties in instituting a FLES program is finding time in the curriculum, there is an indication that in at least this number of programs lack of time was not an insuperable obstacle.

[33] *Ibid.*, 1955, p. 2.

TABLE 2. *Mildenberger FLES Surveys, 1953, 1954, 1955*[a]

Figure 1. In What Grade Is FLES Begun?

Grades	K	1	2	3	4	5	6
1953	8	18	26	32	49	38	15
1954	26	37	29	63	87	53	33
1955	35	68	38	99	116	69	63
Totals	69	123	93	194	252	160	111

Figure 2. Number of Classes Per Week

Times	1	2	3	4	5
1953	16	45	34	1	75
1954	67	75	36	24	122
1955	74	92	61	17	176
Totals	157	212	131	42	373

Figure 3. Length of Lessons

Minutes Per Week	5	10	15	20	25	30	35	40	45	50	60	75	90
1953	0	3	32	42	15	52	5	9	6	5	10	0	0
1954	0	6	61	72	22	94	4	18	16	13	26	1	1
1955	2	12	87	100	26	115	6	13	20	20	18	0	1
Totals	2	21	180	214	63	261	15	40	42	38	54	1	2

[a] Kenneth W. Mildenberger, "Status of Foreign Language Study in American Elementary Schools, Fall Term 1953, 1954, 1955," Washington, 1954, 1955, 1956. (Mimeographed.)

An examination of Mildenberger's reports to discover the basis for selecting pupils shows that, in 1953, all pupils in a given grade were without question included in the instruction in 133 programs, that in 32 programs the pupils volunteered, and that in 29 programs the pupils were selected on some objective basis, such as high IQ, reading maturity, rank in class, or a combination of these. In 1954 the corresponding numbers were 240, 99, and 28; and in 1955 they were 326, 64, and 40. It is quite possible that many of the volunteer programs turned out to be similar to the all-inclusive programs. It has been the experience of many FLES teachers that if children are given an opportunity to volunteer for such instruction they all avail themselves of it. Whether or not the question is raised, therefore, seems to be somewhat academic. Between 1954 and 1955 the marked reduction from 99 to 64 in the number of programs that called themselves voluntary is perhaps an indication of this fact. These reports show that volunteer or selective programs are much more frequent in the intermediate grades than in the primary grades, and, indeed, the principle of selectivity is more defensible at this level.

Where do the teachers come from? On this point Mildenberger's reports disclose great resourcefulness. During the three years in question the majority of FLES teachers were traveling specialists (520), followed by the regular classroom teacher (444), college students (70), parents and other citizens (23), native speakers from the community (20), superintendents or principals (5), and others (5). In this latter group were a dean of women, a supervisor, a music teacher, and a librarian. One trend is worth recording: Whereas in 1953 the classroom teachers outnumbered the specialists 104 to 77 the opposite was true in 1954 and 1955, when the specialists predominated 179 to 155 and 264 to 185 respectively.

It is clear that there is no single pattern. It seems, however, that the ideally qualified teacher, the one who has a native or near-native command of the language and demonstrated skill in guiding the learning of children, is rare. The classroom teacher may be deficient in language control, and the specialist may be deficient in elementary-school theory and practice. Most communities take their teachers where they can find them. This, of course, accounts in part for the lack of stability in FLES programs. Many of these teachers volunteer their services, often because they believe in such a program and are willing to demonstrate this belief for a reasonable length of time. However, if after one or more years of such successful demonstration the public, school board, and school administration do not act on the evidence—and this has happened many times—the teachers discontinue their services, and, often enough, the program either stops or is continued on a makeshift basis.

FLES IN CATHOLIC ELEMENTARY SCHOOLS. In his 1955 report Mildenberger refers to a survey of FLES in Catholic elementary schools conducted during 1955 by Sister M. Annunciata, O. P., of Edgewood College of the Sacred Heart, Madison, Wisconsin. According to this survey 156,700 children were studying foreign languages in 483 Catholic elementary schools in 285 cities and towns of 27 states and the District of Columbia. Principal languages studied were French, 88,379, of which nearly 80,000 were in 155 New England communities where much of the Catholic population is of French descent; Polish, 39,999; Italian, 15,510; Lithuanian, 9,991; Slovak, 2,924; Ukrainian, 1,984; Spanish, 708; and Latin, 105. A majority of the programs reported instruction to begin in grade one and to continue through grade eight. Several of the French programs in New England began generations ago, but the recent FLES movement has, nevertheless, had an impact on Catholic schools. Mildenberger says that "During the past five years, instruction in French was introduced in Catholic schools of twenty-four communities; Italian in nine; Polish in four; and Spanish in eleven."[34]

AASA-NEA RESEARCH DIVISION SURVEY, 1955. Another valuable document for the recent history of FLES is a report published by the American Association of School Administrators (AASA) and the Research Division of the National Education Association (NEA) in its Educational Research Service (Circular Number 6, August, 1955).

This report resulted from an inquiry sent to 650 urban and suburban school districts throughout the country. Of the 400 replies received (62 per cent), 53 (13 per cent) reported formal FLES programs. These programs are described in some detail, as are 19 additional programs of informal foreign-language activities such as radio and out-of-school programs.

In the 53 formal programs described Spanish ranks first as the language most frequently taught (37 school systems), French ranks second (32 school systems), German comes third with 10, followed by 2 in Italian, one in Polish, and one in Latin in grade VI. Less than half of the school systems are reported as beginning below the fourth grade. Less than one-third of the systems reported the use of special teachers. The attitude of parents and general public was reported to be "favorable" or "enthusiastic," while that of the respondents ranged from favorable to definitely opposed.[35]

[34] _Ibid._

[35] National Education Association, American Association of School Administrators, and Research Division, _Foreign Language Programs in Elementary Schools_; see also, Appendix H, Part 4.

Extent of FLES in 1955. In the fall of 1955 at least 271,617 public elementary-school children (kindergarten through grade six) were receiving instruction from the classroom teacher or from visiting language specialists. This represents an increase of 62,000 pupils over the fall of 1954. It is estimated that in 1941, fifteen years before, fewer than 5,000 pupils were receiving such instruction. As late as 1952 only 89 communities had some kind of FLES program as compared with 357 in 1955. In this three-year period the number of communities involved quadrupled. In the fall of 1955 the number of public elementary-school children learning a foreign language was more than one-third the enrollment in modern foreign languages in the high schools and was fast approaching the number of students studying modern languages in all our colleges and universities.

Cincinnati Survey. In order to determine the feasibility of FLES, the Cincinnati Public Schools in February 1959 sent out questionnaires to the 50 cities in the United States with a population of 200,000 or more. Forty-five replies were received, of which 32, or 71.1 per cent, reported some kind of FLES program. Of the 13 cities that considered FLES to be a regular part of the elementary program, 11 reported teaching Spanish, 8 French, 4 German, and 1 Russian. Programs beginning below the fourth grade and above the third grade were about equally divided. Of the 18 cities that considered FLES not to be a regular part of the elementary program 14 reported the teaching of French, 11 Spanish, and 4 German, with a little Italian and Polish.

"Foreign Languages in the Elementary Schools of the United States, 1959–60."[36] In 1959–1960 the Modern Language Association again surveyed the status of FLES. This study reveals that 1,227,006 pupils were enrolled in a FLES program in more than 8,000 elementary schools (public, non-public, independent, and laboratory) in all 50 states and the District of Columbia. Of this total, public elementary schools reported 1,030,097 or 84 per cent "of the total elementary school FLES enrollment; 692,716 (67.2 per cent) were in regular classroom programs and 337,381 (32.8 per cent) were receiving instruction by television."[37] These figures, when compared with those

[36] This is the title of a report prepared by Marjorie Breunig as one of the Modern Language Association *Reports of Surveys and Studies in the Teaching of Modern Foreign Languages, 1959–1961* (see pp. 1–14).

[37] See Figures 1, 2, and 3 for enrollment details (*ibid.*).

of the Mildenberger report of 1953, show that the number of public schools offering foreign-language instruction increased from 644 to over 4,000 or more than six-fold while the number of communities in which this instruction was given increased from 145 to 1,217 or about eight-and-one-half–fold. Dr. J. Wesley Childers, then director of research for the Modern Language Association, writing the foreword to this report, commented: "This growth may indicate that FLES has passed the experimental stage and is destined to become a regular part of the elementary school curriculum,"[38]—an overly optimistic comment.

These surveys suggest the rapid growth of FLES, but what of the quality of the programs? Throughout the modern period of FLES, as in the earlier period, individual educators[39] have been concerned lest poor quality bring disrepute and the risk of failure to an otherwise promising educational venture. Feeling concern for the quality of FLES programs, the Modern Language Association in 1956 convoked its Foreign Language Program Advisory Committee to draft an important policy statement as a guide to educators interested in FLES.[40]

MODERN LANGUAGE ASSOCIATION EVALUATION OF FLES, 1961. In the five years between 1956 and 1961, the spread of FLES programs was dramatic but the improvement in quality did not keep pace. This conclusion is inescapable after reading the report of Nancy V. Alkonis and Mary B. Brophy, "A Survey of FLES Practices," written after these two experienced FLES teachers had visited sixty-two communities with reportedly good FLES programs in the spring of 1961. Reading their conclusions is sobering:

"Conclusions: If the 62 school systems that we visited are representative, we are forced to conclude that the state of FLES in the United States needs a lot of improvement, because:
    "1) A majority of the FLES programs that we observed do not fulfill the primary aim of such a program—teaching the four language skills—even when this is clearly stated as their ob-

---

[38] *Ibid.*

[39] See William Riley Parker, "Foreign Languages in the Grades: A Caution," *The National Elementary Principal*, Vol. XXXVI, No. 5 (February, 1957), pp. 4–6.

[40] See Appendix B.

jective. . . . Sometimes the teacher is weak; just as often the weakness lies beyond the teacher's control, in the materials or the scheduling.

"2) Many programs emphasized such aims as 'world understanding' or 'broadened horizons' to the extent that it is a clear misnomer to call them *language* programs. We saw no evidence of effective evaluation of the teaching directed toward these objectives. . . .

"3) There is such a diversity of linguistic content that a general evaluation of results using a single test or series of tests appears to be impracticable.

"4) From the widespread emphasis upon learning lists of words, we conclude that a majority of the FLES teachers think of language as words to be learned in isolation and then strung into 'conversation.' They showed no awareness of the interacting systems of structure or pattern that are basic to each language.

"5) Many programs, started without planning and provision for the materials, the instruction, and the eventual integration with junior- and senior-high-school courses, are considered 'experimental,' but there is no clear statement of the conditions and terms of the experiment and no provision for an evaluation of its results.

"6) The most obvious weakness is lack of teachers with sufficient skill in the language and training in methods. (This is no reflection on the sincerity, the enthusiasm, or the good will of the instructors. How many of us, with no knowledge of music and unable to play the piano, could successfully teach a roomful of little children to play that instrument?)

"7) In many schools—certainly in the majority of those we visited —FLES is conceived of as merely a preview or prelude to 'real' language learning (which will begin in the high school) rather than as a serious, systematic attempt to develop attitudes and skills.

"8) Few programs are planned as an unbroken, cumulative sequence from the primary through the junior high school, partly because of the lack of appropriate teaching materials for the junior high school, but more because of the inadequacy of the FLES work itself.

"Before further encouragement is given to an increase in the number of FLES programs or to any kind of quantitative expansion, there is a clear need, among teachers, administrators, professional organizations, and state and national departments of education, for a qualitative improvement of FLES. Nevertheless, and despite the eight-point indictment above, one conclusion is inescapable:

"9) The evidence—scattered in bits and pieces throughout the country—makes it perfectly clear that with an enthusiastic teacher who has an adequate command of the foreign language, materials that reflect the nature of language and how it is learned, and expert supervision, American youngsters can learn and are indeed learning foreign languages very well in our elementary schools."[41]

The inadequate quality of many—indeed of most—FLES programs led the Modern Language Association Advisory Committee, after consulting with selected FLES experts, to prepare a second statement of policy in the spring of 1961 in an effort to redefine FLES and to caution educators as to the minimal conditions necessary for a satisfactory program.[42]

MILWAUKEE SURVEY, 1966. In order to compare its FLES program with those of other cities the Milwaukee Public Schools in December 1966 sent out questionnaires to the 48 cities having a population of over 300,000. Of the 42 returns, 31 indicated the presence of a FLES program. In 11 of these cities the FLES program involved all elementary schools in the system. In the remaining 20 systems the number of schools involved ranged from 4 per cent to 92 per cent. As usual Spanish is the most popular language (25 cities), French comes next (21 cities), and German follows with 5 programs. One city, New York, offers FLES in 4 languages, French, Spanish, Italian, and Hebrew; 6 cities offer FLES in French, German, or Spanish; and 10 cities offer FLES in two languages. Two-thirds of the programs begin above the third grade and one-third below the fourth grade. The average classtime is 93 minutes a week. Only 9 cities reported a formal evaluation of their program. However, 14 cities reported

[41] Nancy V. Alkonis and Mary A. Brophy, "A Survey of FLES Practices," in Modern Language Association, *Reports of Surveys and Studies*, pp. 213–217.
[42] See Appendix C.

satisfaction with their present program, and 19 reported that they did not expect any major changes in their programs in the near future.[43]

Representative FLES Programs, 1952–1966

YORK, PENNSYLVANIA, 1952. The French experiment[44] that began in September of 1952 in the second grade of the Jacob L. Devers School of York, Pennsylvania, grew out of an educational workshop. One section of this workshop set for itself the study of human relations and before long reached the conclusion that human relations involved international as well as national and local relations. This immediately brought the question of language into focus. As the committee members studied the question of language learning, they discovered in various parts of the country a growing interest in introducing languages into the elementary schools. They sent for information and materials such as guides, handbooks, and courses of study. A generous school board financed the attendance of representatives at various conferences where this question was discussed. There was much interest on the part of the townspeople. A canvas was made of the community members who had a speaking knowledge of foreign languages. Teachers with the necessary qualifications were asked whether they would be interested in teaching a language. There was, to be sure, a certain amount of skepticism. Could young children learn a second language without harmful effect on their English? What were the financial implications and would the cost be justified by the results? After extensive consultation and discussion, and with the encouragement of the superintendent, the board of education decided to start a small experiment involving two second-grade classes in one of the elementary schools. To the satisfaction of all concerned not only did the experiment produce excellent results in the classroom, but the teacher and the administrative officers also took care to inform the general public through talks at Parent-Teacher Association meetings, class demonstrations before various groups, and radio programs. As a result it was decided to expand the program, to preserve its experimental nature, and to con-

[43] Anthony Gradisnik, "A Survey of FLES Instruction in Cities Over 300,000," *Foreign Language Annals*, Vol. II, No. 1 (October, 1968), pp. 54–57.

[44] For a more detailed description see Eriksson, Forest, Mulhauser, *Foreign Languages in the Elementary School*, pp. 116–119.

tinue the experiment long enough to get a definitive answer based on ample data.

By 1955–1956 this tentative beginning had expanded to eight schools and involved approximately seven hundred children in grades three, four, and five. By this time the FLES program was outgrowing the schools; it was affecting the whole community. One explanation of this unusual result is that York had become twinned with the historic city of Arles in Southern France. This twinning had resulted particularly from the efforts of Dr. Victoria Lyles, supervisor of elementary education, who was invited along with Miss Marguerite Eriksson, the French teacher, to Arles for the Fourth of July, 1954. In September of 1955, a French delegation of six, including the mayor of Arles, returned the visit and spent ten festive days in York. In addition to this exchange of official visits there sprang up a lively correspondence between school officials and other citizens of Arles and York. Newspapers between the sister towns were exchanged, as well as pictures between camera clubs and business and industrial information. There was also an exchange of letters and tapes between the school children in each town, the York children writing or speaking in English and the Arles children in French.

Here, for example, are two letters from Arles:

"Cher Ami,
"Je m'appelle Tony Boyer. J'ai 10 ans. Je vais à l'école Emile Loubet. M. Gros est mon maître. Il est très gentil avec nous et je l'aime beaucoup. Ce qui nous plaît le plus à l'école c'est le calcul. Comme jeu celui que j'aime le plus c'est de jouer au taureau. J'ai une petite soeur de 5 ans qui s'appelle Bernadette que j'aime bien et que je taquine souvent.

"Votre ami
"Tony Boyer"

"Je suis content de recevoir une lettre d'un petit Américain— J'aimerais savoir comment vivent les écoliers Américains, comment est votre ville, quelles sont les distractions que vous aimez. Moi j'aime la bicyclette et le cinéma. Si vous voulez, nous échangerons des timbres, des pièces de monnaie et des photos de nos pays. J'ai commencé les compositions [exams], je n'ai pas encore les résultats.
"Mes jeux préférés sont le ballon, je joue aussi avec des petits autos

—j'en ai quatre. J'ai un ping-pong, un jeu carré,[45] un jeu de loto, un jeu de chevaux, et des jeux de cartes pour jouer en famille; mais je préfère jouer aux Indiens et aux cow-boys avec mon frère qui a le même âge que moi. J'ai aussi une grande soeur qui apprendra l'Américain avec moi. J'ai aussi un aquarium avec des poissons. J'ai un train électrique et j'aime aussi jouer au soldat. J'aime beaucoup la ville de'Arles avec ses beaux monuments anciens.

"Ton ami Arlésien
"Yves."

In the spring of 1956, an American *assistante* went to Arles to help formally organize the first program that had begun informally in the elementary schools and to volunteer her services to two high-school teachers of English. Since that time, there has been a regular exchange of FLES teachers between Arles and York. As a fitting climax, the mayor of Arles, a bachelor, married one of the York *assistantes*.

After an evaluation in May of 1957, the board of education voted to extend the teaching of French to all schools in the city but in the interest of economy decided to begin instruction in grade five, to limit it to the better pupils, and to provide a continuing program in the junior and senior high schools. In 1964 instruction was given three times a week by five traveling specialists to sixty-two classes totaling approximately 1,950 children and was supplemented by a weekly television program. Continuity, on a selective basis, was provided in the junior high school. A further selection took place at the end of the first semester in the ninth grade, as a result of which some 200 pupils continued in the tenth grade, a majority at level III. The best of these were selected to go on to college French. Enrollment in this honors class in 1962–1963 was ten, in 1963–1964 seventeen, and in 1964–1965, thirty-one. All of these pupils received advanced placement in college.[46] This program appears to have acquired stability.

"THE HACKENSACK STORY: A LONG SEQUENCE IN SPANISH, 1955."

[45] A game played by hitting with rackets rubber balls at the end of a heavy elastic that is attached to a heavy concrete block.

[46] Data obtained from a report in York (Pennsylvania) Public Schools, "York Schools Pioneer in Elementary French," *Spotlight on Schools*, Vol. VII, No. 5 (May, 1964); and from Miss Marguerite A. Eriksson, coordinator of elementary French, letter to author.

This is the title of an account written by Conrad J. Schmitt, the former coordinator of foreign languages in Hackensack, New Jersey.[47] The Hackensack FLES program, which was deliberately not called experimental, began in 1955 as a result particularly of the interest of Philip J. Audino, former president of the Hackensack Board of Education. Starting in September of that year, six language specialists taught some 1,700 pupils in five elementary schools, moving from class to class for fifteen-minute lessons. Originally FLES began in grade one, but now instruction begins in grade three, and at the end of grade six 40 to 90 per cent of the pupils, depending on the school, are selected, on the basis of their performance, interest, IQ, and reading level in English for a continuing program in the junior high school. This program consists of three forty-minute classes a week in grades seven and eight. Nearly all students from grade eight continue in grade nine. From grade nine through grade twelve these FLES graduates follow a course of study which is completely distinct from the four-year sequence followed by those students who begin Spanish in grade nine.

In the early grades dialogs that present a real life situation are taught audio-lingually and the basic language patterns are thoroughly drilled. Cultural units are presented and great care is taken to provide continuity from unit to unit. A particular feature is the opportunity for pupils, after they have thoroughly mastered the material, to talk about what is happening in the dialog and even to combine materials from several dialogs. Reading recognition begins in March of the fifth grade, and in the sixth grade the children begin to read short stories consisting only of vocabulary and patterns that have previously been learned audio-lingually.

In the junior high school the reading and writing skills are developed but without de-emphasizing oral practice, which must continue. The transition to reading is accomplished by using at the beginning only material that has been already learned by ear. Slides are used for a visual presentation of printed materials.

Sequence and progression also mark the senior-high-school program. The second-year course presents a study of the history of Spain, and the students discuss—in Spanish, of course—the geogra-

[47] Conrad J. Schmitt, "The Hackensack Story: A Long Sequence in Spanish," *The DFL Bulletin*, Vol. III, No. 1 (May, 1964).

phy, history, customs, and characteristics of the people of each region. There is included also a brief study of the development of the Spanish language with some attention to the dialects of Spain. The various literary forms are introduced as a preparation for more advanced study in future courses. Students prepare oral reports on each unit and write a short composition each week.

The third-year program consists of selected poems and short stories of Spain and Spanish America as well as of continuing structure drills. Two plays and two novels are read in class, and an additional novel is read outside of class. The oral reports and weekly written compositions continue. A special feature of the third year is an additional elective course in Spanish given in response to pressure from highly motivated students. These students, most of whom plan to major in Spanish in college, meet twice a day in Spanish and study one phase of Hispanic culture in greater detail, for example, the nineteenth century in Spain. Political and sociological questions are studied in such authors as Larra, Valera, Galdós, Ganivet, Unamuno, and Baroja. At least one work of each author is read.

The fourth year presents the major writers of both Spain and Spanish America, and in addition the students read a variety of magazine articles and prepare oral and written reports.

Schmitt states that "the fluency of many of our students is such that seven of them are presently [1965] working as bilingual and trilingual guides at the World's Fair."[48] His report goes on to say that in 1962–1963 there were fifteen students in Spanish IV; in 1963–1964 this number increased to sixty-two out of a total high-school enrollment of 1,230 of whom 25 per cent are college preparatory. "The enrollment in every language has increased because more students are studying more than one foreign language."[49]

FLES IN NEW YORK CITY, 1957.[50] In 1957 an experimental program for selected children was initiated in the fourth grade of four selected elementary schools. The program grew rapidly and in June

[48] Conrad J. Schmitt, letter to author.

[49] Schmitt, "The Hackensack Story."

[50] Data in this section were submitted by Dr. Emilio L. Guerra, in June 1964 while he was acting director, Bureau of Foreign Languages, Board of Education of the City of New York, and by Gladys Lipton, acting assistant director of the bureau. See also New York City, Board of Education, Division of Elementary Schools, *Foreign Languages in Elementary Schools*, November, 1964.

of 1961 it was decided to permit no further expansion before the completion of a three-year evaluation. Tests were administered in June of 1961, 1962, and 1963, which showed that the addition of a foreign language did not interfere with progress in the basic subject areas. "Because of the favorable results in these tests, the Board of Education officially established foreign languages as an optional curriculum area for elementary schools on March 25, 1964."[51]

The following table shows the scope of the FLES program as of June 1, 1964.

TABLE 3. *Organization of Foreign-Language Classes, June 1, 1964*

	French	Spanish	Italian	Hebrew	Total
No. of schools	52	24	5	2	83*
No. of classes	154	53	8	2	217
No. of teachers	97	31	5	2	135
No. of children	5155	1748	275	74	7252

* 10 of which combine French and Spanish

In the school year of 1964–1965, the FLES program was expanded to include eighty-three schools and 7,725 children, 5,308 in French, 1,749 in Spanish, 431 in Italian, and 237 in Hebrew. And in September of 1966, a further expansion took place. In fourteen pilot intermediate schools the FLES program was opened to all pupils in grade five. The FLES program begins in grade four and is completely audio-lingual (ninety minutes a week). In the fifth grade it increases to one hundred minutes a week; audio-lingual instruction continues and reading activities are introduced. There is no time increase in grade six. Instruction continues to emphasize hearing and speaking. Emphasis on reading is increased and writing activities are introduced.[52]

Concerning FLES teachers, Dr. Emilio L. Guerra reported that "Heretofore, at the request of principals of elementary schools, FLES teachers were authorized by the Elementary School Division after being certified by the Director of Foreign Languages. Beginning with the school year 1964–1965, regularly licensed teachers of

51 New York City, *Foreign Languages in Elementary Schools.*

52 *French in the Elementary Schools, Grades 4–5–6; Italian in the Elementary Schools; and Spanish in the Elementary Schools, Grades 4–5–6,* have been developed as syllabi for the guidance of teachers.

common branches will be tested by the Board of Examiners and will obtain certificates of competency to teach foreign languages. Those common branch teachers who hold licenses to teach foreign languages on the secondary school level will be granted certificates of competency without further examination."[53] The FLES teachers are assisted by foreign-language specialists, who visit the various schools in order to give demonstrations in classroom teaching and in the use of audio-visual equipment, to hold conferences with teachers and supervisors, to evaluate materials and help prepare supplementary materials, and to teach in-service courses. A teacher-training film has been prepared to demonstrate audio-lingual techniques for FLES teachers. Language laboratories are in operation in seven elementary schools. Guerra also reported that some progress has been made to promote articulation between FLES and the junior-high-school program.

Experiments of particular relevance to the FLES program are the Gifted Child Project, a joint New York State and New York City project to study the relative effectiveness of the classroom teacher and the specialist, and the Program for Bilingual Instruction for Kindergarten Children, in cooperation with Hunter College.

Future plans for the Hunter College FLES program include:

1. Ancillary certificates for foreign-language teachers.
2. Expansion of the program (particularly in Spanish, Hebrew, and Italian).
3. Extension of the program to other classes not classified as intellectually gifted.
4. Provision for articulation with the junior-high-school program.
5. Follow-up of continuing FLES classes in the junior high schools.
6. Evaluation of French and Spanish bulletins and plans for revision.
7. Preparation of Hebrew and Italian bulletins.
8. In-service courses for teacher-training.
9. Preparation of other teacher-training films on teaching other foreign-language skills.
10. Evaluation of language laboratories in elementary schools.
11. Writing of scripts for tapes.

[53] Dr. Emilio L. Guerra, letter to author.

12. Tape production in four languages.
13. Development of supplementary drills.
14. Preparation of tests for Levels A (4th grade), B (5th grade), and C (6th grade).

The tone of Dr. Guerra's report suggests satisfaction with this FLES program.

BELLEVUE, WASHINGTON, 1959. In 1958–1959 a committee of third-grade teachers worked out plans for a FLES program in the Bellevue Public Schools. Starting experimentally in 1959–1960 a half-time specialist, assisted by some linguistically prepared classroom teachers, taught Spanish for twenty minutes twice a week in the third grades of four of the eleven schools. In addition the Seattle Educational Television series "Rosita y Panchito" was used once a week. The Spanish consultant also conducted an in-service class in Spanish FLES for third-grade and other interested teachers and adapted or prepared tapes and other materials. After further experimentation the FLES program was stabilized in 1962–1963 under the leadership of Edward Matkovick, foreign-language coordinator for both elementary and secondary schools.

It is worth recording the scope and some of the main features of this program as of 1964–1965. Seven Spanish specialists, including one television teacher, taught some 5,500 children in grades three through six in all elementary schools. The Bellevue Television series "Se Habla Español," revised in collaboration with the Foreign Language Department of the Seattle Public Schools, became a King County-wide program for elementary Spanish, available to all cooperating schools in the KCTS-TV viewing area. The following schedule prevailed in Bellevue:

Third and fourth grades—2 television lessons; 1 lesson with a specialist
2 follow-up classes with classroom teachers
Fifth and sixth grades—2 lessons with a specialist
3 follow-up classes with classroom teachers

In 1967–1968 the Bellevue Foreign Language Program was reorganized, with some losses and some gains. The services of Edward Matkovick were lost as foreign-language coordinator, but those of

Lester McKim, formerly of Central Washington State College at Ellensburg, were acquired. The beginning of the FLES program was delayed to the fifth grade, but instruction was increased from twice to three times a week. For the first time French was introduced in the FLES program in 1966–1967 in three elementary schools. The program, involving 350 fifth-graders, proved successful and was continued in 1967–1968.[54]

Despite the general satisfaction of children and parents, storm clouds began to gather. The expense of an expanding program mounted conspicuously. Foreign-language teachers in high school, finding the problem of articulation troublesome, took the easy alternative and started the FLES products over from the beginning. Parents assumed, therefore, that their children's learning had been insignificant. Teachers of other subjects saw general salary increases endangered and voted against FLES. Tax payers felt the financial burden to be increasingly heavy in a residential area where there was no industry. It was therefore decided to phase out the fifth-grade program in 1968–1969 and the sixth-grade program in 1969–1970.

The Bellevue experiment exemplifies what can happen, even to a quality program. What started so hopefully and seemed for several years to prosper so well now stands as a failure that began, flourished, and died all within a decade.

BEVERLY HILLS, CALIFORNIA, 1960. The Beverly Hills FLES Program,[55] the youngest of those selected for description, appears also to be one of the most promising. Blessed with adequate means, Beverly Hills offers its children a well-planned twelve-year sequence of foreign-language study.

Parents may at the outset choose French or Spanish, which is continued through the eighth grade, and the child is encouraged to remain with his language choice until he graduates from high school, because the general objective of the program is bilingualism. French and Spanish are taught for twenty minutes every day in grades one through six and for thirty minutes daily in grades seven and eight. Specialist traveling teachers are divided into teams: Team One, re-

[54] Superintendent John W. Brubacher, letters to author, June 5, 9, 16, 1967.
[55] Described by the head of the FLES Department, Albert W. JeKenta, "FLES: Foreign Language in the Elementary School," Beverly Hills, California, July, 1964. (Mimeographed.)

sponsible for the primary grades, one to three; Team Two, for the intermediate grades, four to six; and Team Three, for the departmental grades seven and eight. Teachers on Team One teach eight twenty-minute classes daily in grades one and two; teachers on Teams Two and Three teach three twenty-minute classes daily in grades three to five and four thirty-minute classes in grades six to eight. Extra time for FLES was made by lengthening the school day by ten minutes and by reducing slightly the time devoted to other subjects.

In addition to nineteen traveling teachers, in 1964, the FLES program had the benefit of two traveling teacher-interns from neighboring University of Southern California, one French specialist, one Spanish specialist, and the foreign-language coordinator. All of these teachers collaborate on the preparation and constant revision of teaching materials and evaluation instruments and procedures. They gather in frequent department, grade-level, or committee meetings that reflect their concern for improving their work, for keeping up with advances in the profession, and for explaining their program to other educators and the public. Their professional growth is encouraged through work in professional organizations, through the opportunity to visit one another's classes or other FLES programs, and through participation in a required four-year professional-growth program and an elective incentive-growth program.

Other valuable features of this program are before- and after-school and summer programs for transfer students or others needing special help, the assignment of a student helper to another student in need of assistance, self-teaching materials for use at home or in the library, listening posts in the library, the grouping of students for more effective progress, a six-week summer study-travel session abroad for pre-senior-high-school students, and a flexible schedule of foreign-language study.

An ingenious arrangement of tracks and levels is meant to provide maximum benefit to the individual, who may move freely from one track to another. The arrangement, as envisioned in 1964, is reflected in Table 4.

Perhaps the most hopeful aspect of the Beverly Hills Foreign Language Program is that, despite the very considerable development it shows already, its administrators and teachers seem to be acutely aware of the problems that still need to be solved. Through frequent

TABLE 4. *Track Levels in Beverly Hills FLES*[a]

Track A		Track B		Track C High School	
Grade	Level[b]	Grade	Level	Grade	Level
1					
2					
3	I				
4					
5					
6		6			
7	II	7	I		
8		8			
9	III	9	II	9	I
10	IV	10	III	10	II
11	V	11	IV	11	III
12	VI	12	V	12	IV

[a] Albert JeKenta, "FLES: Foreign Language in the Elementary School," p. 30. (Mimeographed.)

[b] For an explanation of the concept of levels, see Nelson Brooks, *Language and Language Learning: Theory and Practice*, pp. 119–138.

and friendly dialogs FLES teachers and high-school teachers, who so often work at cross purposes, here seem to be elaborating a coherent and progressive program. Time only will tell whether it will be spared the mishaps that overtake so many FLES programs.

TELEVISION. In her report on "Foreign Languages in the Elementary Schools of the United States, 1959–1960," Marjorie Breunig estimated that there were 337,381 children, or 32 per cent of the public elementary-school FLES enrollment, who were studying FLES by television that year. On June 27, 1963, William N. Locke, chairman of the Modern Language Project (MLP) Steering Committee, reported to the MLP National Advisory Committee that, "In June of 1962 approximately 75,000 students of 'Parlons Français' (usually in grades four, five, and six, but occasionally in other grades—one through nine) in Eastern Massachusetts, Southern New Hampshire, and Northern Rhode Island completed the first three-year cycle (180 student lessons) over educational television. At the same time approximately 350,000 students (generally in grades three through six) in six areas—Chicago, New York, Washington, Charlotte, St. Paul, and Calgary (Alberta)—were completing the first year (sixty student lessons) of the newly produced film edition over TV." The immensely popular Modern Language Project "Parlons Français," a Spanish television FLES program called "Una Aventura Española," as well as numerous other television programs, have added a whole new dimension to FLES which requires careful consideration.[56]

Our American fondness for gadgets predisposes us to television. The scarcity of qualified teachers adds to its attractiveness, as does the thought that television teaching is less expensive than "live" teaching. The real question is not whether FLES *can* be taught satisfactorily by television, for I believe it can be, but whether FLES *is* satisfactorily taught in this way. Fortunately there is some evidence on this subject.

MODERN LANGUAGE PROJECT EVALUATIONS. Between September and December of 1963, Anne Slack and Jacqueline Gadoury of the Modern Language Project staff visited eighteen areas using the Level II film edition of "Parlons Français." They found that most Level II teachers were not familiar with the content of Level I, did not view the teacher-training film that is provided, and did not use the teacher's recordings. Some conducted their classes in English; put undue emphasis on the teaching of nouns, numbers, and songs; and displayed bad pronunciation and bad teaching techniques. Fortunately, however, a large proportion of the teachers displayed good FLES techniques.

From 1959 to 1962 Dr. Ralph Garry of Boston University and Dr. Edna Mauriello of Salem Teachers College conducted an evaluation of various aspects of the "Parlons Français" program.[57] Below are some of their findings:

1. Televised language instruction without classroom following is ineffective. Classes having thirty minutes or more follow-up each week score significantly better than those with less.
2. Listening-comprehension test scores indicate that the average student understands and can distinguish between 50 and 55 per

---

[56] The rapid expansion of commercial Spanish-language stations may open still another channel for language learning (see John Tebbel, "Newest TV Boom: Spanish-Language Stations," *Saturday Review*, June 8, 1968).

[57] Ralph Garry and Edna Mauriello, *Evaluation of "Parlons Français" Program*. This report was issued by the Modern Language Project, 9 Newbury Street, Boston, Massachusetts 02116.

cent of the vocabulary and structural items covered at the three levels of the course.

3. Achievement in all areas at the three levels of the course indicates that "Parlons Français" provides an effective means for teaching French—not alone, but in conjunction with classroom follow-up practice conducted by skilled teachers, regardless of their previous language background.

4. Children who take "Parlons Français" perform at least as well in other subject areas as those who do not.

UNIVERSITY OF ILLINOIS EXPERIMENT. In 1963 four investigators reported the results of a three-year experiment by the University of Illinois "to determine the effectiveness of non-specialist teachers in helping elementary school pupils learn a second language when the instructional program is especially designed and presented by newer educational media."[58] Two classes beginning in the fourth grade and continuing through the fifth and sixth grades were taught by Spanish specialists (control group). Two other comparable classes were taught one day a week by television and four days by teachers unfamiliar with Spanish but using tape recordings by native speakers (experimental group). Below are the major findings:

The differences between the mean Spanish achievement test scores of the control and experimental groups tended to consistently and accumulatively favor the control group over the three-year period.

At the end of the three years, the control group received higher mean scores than the experimental group on all Spanish achievement tests. However, their mean scores on these tests ranged from 69% to 94% of those obtained by the control group. The differences in means for the composite scores and for four of the sub-tests (immediacy of response, appropriateness of response, pronunciation, and oral reading) were regarded as significant. The differences in mean scores on the listening and reading comprehension sub-tests were not regarded as significant.[59]

Among other findings the authors noted that, "Pupils who devoted twenty minutes of the school day to the study of a foreign language

[58] Charles E. Johnson, Joseph S. Flores, Fred P. Ellison, and Miguel A. Riestra, "The Development and Evaluation of Methods and Materials to Facilitate Foreign Language Instruction in Elementary Schools," summary of the report by the same name. See also their article, "The Non-Specialist Teacher in FLES," *The Modern Language Journal*, Vol. LI, No. 2 (February, 1967), pp. 76–79.

[59] Johnson, *et al.*, "Non-Specialist Teacher in FLES," p. 77.

earned average achievement test scores in other subjects which were not regarded as significantly different from those earned by pupils who did not engage in foreign language study, but distributed the twenty minutes of time among various subjects."[60]

Finally, the investigators reported the following conclusions:

When the study was begun the co-directors anticipated that at the end of the three-year period the group taught by specialist teachers would obtain higher mean scores than the group guided by non-specialists. It was therefore necessary to decide in advance what level of achievement would have to be obtained by the experimental group for results of the experiment to be regarded as either successful or unsuccessful. The decision was that if the experimental group obtained mean raw scores which were at least sixty per cent of the mean raw scores earned by the control group, then the experiment would be regarded as successful in that the use of the instructional program would be warranted in situations where qualified specialist language teachers were unavailable. On the other hand, it was decided that if the results yielded mean raw scores below the sixty per cent level, the experiment would be regarded as unsuccessful in that the use of the instructional program would not be recommended. The findings revealed that in all tests the experimental group obtained mean raw scores substantially above the established sixty per cent level.

The co-directors thus arrived at the following generalized conclusion: General elementary school teachers with no special training in a particular foreign language can, with a minimum of daily preparation, successfully guide their pupils in learning that language *provided*: (1) that the instructional program be of a particular design, (2) that efficient use is made of newer educational media, and (3) that the level of achievement expected of the pupils is relatively lower in some aspects of language learning than that which would have been achieved had the pupils received instruction over the same content by well-qualified specialist teachers.[61]

MODERN LANGUAGE ASSOCIATION TELEVISION SURVEY CONDUCTED BY J. RICHARD REID, 1961.[62] In 1960–1961 Professor J. Richard Reid

[60] Johnson, *et al.*, "Development and Evaluation of Methods and Materials," p. 2.

[61] Johnson, *et al.*, "Non-Specialist Teachers in FLES," pp. 78–79.

[62] J. Richard Reid, "An Exploratory Survey of Foreign Language Teaching by Television in the United States," in Modern Language Association, *Reports of Surveys and Studies in the Teaching of Modern Foreign Languages, 1959–1961*, pp. 197–211. See also a list of other evaluations, *ibid.*, pp. 205–206.

of Clark University conducted for the Modern Language Association an extensive personal survey of foreign-language teaching by television. This was done as part of a contract with the United States Office of Education under the National Defense Education Act to make quantitative and qualitative surveys of foreign-language learning in the United States.

Reid's judgment is a reasonable assessment of the value of teaching by television.

> . . . A single, skillful, inspired teacher, on a city-wide or nation-wide network, can not and will not be able to do the work of several hundred, or a hundred, classroom teachers—or of one classroom teacher. Such a television teacher can, however, do *a significant part* of the work of several hundred teachers.
>
> Television is not *the answer* to the shortage of teachers, but insofar as TV teaching of foreign languages is done by skillful, inspired teachers, backed by sound advice from linguists and producers, and by a sound program in the schools, television can be *a major part* of the solution to this problem. The virtue is not in the TV tube or in any one person in the studio. It is in all the people who collaborate in its use.[63]

INDIANAPOLIS SURVEY, 1966.[64] In an effort to provide a better transition to foreign-language study in the junior high school, the Indianapolis Public Schools surveyed FLES practices in forty-five large cities of the United States. Only three school systems reported no foreign-language program below the ninth grade. It was found that eight languages are being taught: Spanish in thirty-six school systems, French in thirty-four, German in eighteen, Latin in eight, Russian in five, Chinese in two, and Italian and Hebrew in one each. Rather surprisingly, eight schools offer four or more languages, thirteen three languages, and nine two. Only two schools begin in grade one and one in grade two. As usual, most programs begin in grade three (10), grade four (9), or higher. Thirty-two of the programs are continuous from their inception through grade twelve. The weekly instruction averages from 69 minutes in grade three to 184 minutes in grade eight. Time is made for language instruction by taking time from other subjects, redividing the day to provide an extra period,

---

63 *Ibid.*

64 Reported by Edith M. Allen, "Foreign Language Below the Ninth Grade: What Are We Doing?" *The Modern Language Journal*, Vol. L, No. 2 (February, 1966), pp. 101–104.

or lengthening the school day. Unlike earlier programs, a majority of these reported using commercially published rather than locally prepared teaching materials. Testing materials, however, are prepared locally rather than commercially. Problems of articulation apparently remain largely unsolved. The largest single number of schools (9, or 20.9 per cent of the total) report that all students enter the first semester in high school regardless of previous work. Others (7, or 16 per cent of the total) equate one year in junior high school with half a year in senior high school. The various other arrangements all indicate a failure to assure a satisfactory progression from FLES to high school. Despite this dubious observation, it can be noted with satisfaction that an overwhelming majority of large cities support a FLES program of varying degrees of quality.

Bilingual Programs

A new departure in American education, the development in the nineteen-sixties of numerous bilingual programs, especially in the primary grades, seems certain to exert an influence on FLES. Experimental bilingual programs of varying patterns have been reported in Arizona, California, Colorado, Florida, New Mexico, and Texas.[65]

[65] See Southwest Council of Foreign Language Teachers [name changed in 1967 to Southwest Council for Bilingual Education], Second Annual Conference, November 13, 1965, *Reports: Our Bilingual: Social and Psychological Barriers* (P. O. Box 47, University of Texas, El Paso, Texas); Appendix G; National Education Association, Department of Rural Education, *The Invisible Minority: Report of the NEA Tucson Survey on the Teaching of Spanish to the Spanish-Speaking*; National Education Association, The Commission on Professional Rights and Responsibilities, *Las Voces Nuevas del Sudoeste/New Voices of the Southwest*; Southwest Council of Foreign Language Teachers, Third Annual Conference, November 4–5, 1966, *Reports: Bilingualism*, Charles Stubing, ed.; Southwest Council of Foreign Language Teachers, Fourth Annual Conference, November 10–11, 1967, *Reports: Bilingual Education: Research and Teaching*, Chester Christian, ed.; *The Journal of Social Issues*, Special Issue on Problems of Bilingualism, Vol. XXIII, No. 2 (April, 1967); Dwain N. Estes, and David W. Darling, eds., *Improving Educational Opportunities of the Mexican-American: Proceedings of the First Conference for the Mexican-American, April 13–15, 1967, San Antonio, Texas*; Texas Education Agency, Regional Educational Agencies Project in International Education, *Addresses and Reports Presented at the Conference on Development of Bilingualism in Children of Varying Linguistic and Cultural Heritages*, January 31–February 3, 1967, Austin, Texas, 1967; Theodore Andersson, "The Bilingual in the Southwest," *The Flori-*

DADE COUNTY, FLORIDA, 1963.[66] The Dade County Schools, Miami, Florida, introduced in 1963 a bilingual program in one school, the Coral Way Elementary School, for the benefit of both the native English-speaking and the Spanish-speaking Cuban children who attend it. In 1966 this program was extended into Leroy Fienberg Elementary School. During half of the school day, subjects are taught in the children's vernacular—in English by English-speaking teachers to English-speaking children and in Spanish by Cuban teachers to Spanish-speaking children. During the other half of the school day, the concepts introduced in the vernacular are reinforced in the child's second language. After the children have sufficient control of their second language, concepts are introduced in the native language of the teacher regardless of the native language of the student. And on the playground and at lunch, in music and art, the children from the beginning are mixed and are free to speak in either language. A 1968 evaluation shows satisfactory results.[67]

---

da FL [Foreign Language] Reporter, Vol. X, No. 2 (Spring, 1967); U. S. Congress, Senate, Committee on Labor and Public Welfare, *Bilingual Education. Hearings* before the Special Subcommittee on Bilingual Education of the Committee on Labor and Public Welfare, Senate, on S. 428, Parts 1 and 2, 90th Cong., 1st sess.; Eleanor Wall Thonis, *Bilingual Education for Mexican-American Children: An Experiment in the Marysville Joint Unified School District, October 1966–June 1967*; A. Bruce Gaarder, "Organization of the Bilingual School," *The Journal of Social Issues,* Vol. XXIII, No. 2 (April, 1967).

[66] See A. Bruce Gaarder and Mabel W. Richardson, "Two Patterns of Bilingual Education in Dade County, Florida," in Thomas E. Bird, ed., *Foreign Language: Research and Development: An Assessment.*

[67] Mabel Wilson Richardson reports in her D.Ed. dissertation, "An Evaluation of Certain Aspects of the Academic Achievement of Elementary Pupils in a Bilingual Program" (The University of Miami, January, 1968), results of an evaluation of the bilingual program at the Coral Way Elementary School, Miami, Florida. Her principal conclusion, within the limitations of her study, is the following:

"The bilingual program of study was relatively as effective for both English and Spanish-speaking subjects as the regular curriculum in achieving progress in the language arts and in arithmetic. In other words, the experimental subjects were not handicapped in academic achievement in English by studying and learning through a second language for approximately half of each school day.

"It must be noted here, that in addition to performing as well as the control group in the regular curriculum, the English-speaking pupils were learning a second language and the Spanish-speaking pupils were learning to read and write their native language."

SAN ANTONIO, TEXAS, 1964. The San Antonio Language Research Project of the San Antonio Independent School District, which has attracted national attention, began in 1964 as an experiment in teaching oral language and reading to children of Mexican-American descent. This carefully designed experiment, initiated by Dr. Thomas D. Horn of The University of Texas, is bilingual to the extent that children in one experimental group have from the beginning been taught in Spanish for at least half an hour in the morning and half an hour in the afternoon. By September of 1967, this project, begun in the first grade of selected schools, had reached grade four. Beginning in 1967 the bilingual approach was emphasized in grades one and two in two of the experimental streams. In one, English and Spanish are each taught intensively forty minutes a day by a bilingual teacher. In another, English is taught for forty minutes by an English speaker and Spanish for forty minutes by a Spanish speaker.

UNITED CONSOLIDATED INDEPENDENT SCHOOL DISTRICT, LAREDO, TEXAS, 1964. This program, begun in the first grades of the Nye Elementary School in 1964 and extended in 1966 to the other two schools in the district, is, like the Dade County project, completely and equally bilingual but uses only one set of teachers. These teachers, some of whom were born in Mexico, are fluent in English and Spanish and are fully prepared elementary-school teachers. For half of the children English is the mother tongue and for half Spanish is the home language, but within a few weeks both groups are using both languages comfortably and are proud to be learning two languages. The program is not experimentally designed, partly because everyone connected with it—school board, administrators, teachers, and parents—is so convinced of the superiority of this bilingual program over the traditional monolingual system that they do not wish to sacrifice children to a control group. It would be interesting, however, to compare the achievement of these children who are taught bilingually with that of children in earlier classes.[68]

[68] As though in answer to this wish, I have received a copy of Bertha Alicia Gámez Treviño's doctoral dissertation (The University of Texas at Austin, January, 1968) entitled "An Analysis of the Effectiveness of a Bilingual Program in the Teaching of Mathematics in the Primary Grades." This study reveals that children, both English-speaking and Spanish-speaking, learn mathematics better bilingually (in English and Spanish) than they do in English alone. This result

EDINBURG, TEXAS, 1965. Begun in January 1965, the Edinburg program is conducted in grades one through six in ten schools, in which 70 per cent of the children are Spanish speakers. The forty-minute daily instruction in Spanish is meant primarily to provide a bridge to English and secondarily to encourage a degree of literacy in Spanish.

HARLANDALE INDEPENDENT SCHOOL DISTRICT, SAN ANTONIO, 1966. During the second semester of 1965–1966 in one first-grade class of the Stonewall Elementary School, located in an all-Spanish-surname neighborhood, instruction was conducted in both English and Spanish by a completely bilingual teacher assisted by a teacher's aide. The teacher provided a bilingual environment "in which the Mexican culture was not devalued or repressed but appreciated and used as a source of experiential enrichment." The other three first grades were taught in English only, the prevailing traditional method. In his objective evaluation, Dr. Guy C. Pryor, associate professor of Education, Our Lady of the Lake College, found no significant difference in ability among the four sections.[69] Testing for reading readiness and for reading for meaning in English, Dr. Pryor found no significant difference, but in testing for social adjustment he found that the experimental section tested much higher than the control sections. In his unpublished report he concludes that: "The finding that the bilingual group exceeded the other sections in personal and social adjustment was very important to this project. It was an important hypothesis of the designers of this project that teaching pupils from Spanish-speaking homes in both English and Spanish gives the pupils a better sense of belonging, increases their

---

is no longer surprising, however, for similar results were reported in the Iloilo Experiment in the Philippines (United Nations, Economic and Social Council, *The Use of Vernacular Languages in Education*, 1953, pp. 125–131). More recently Nancy Modiano has found that Mexican Indians "learn to read with greater comprehension in the national language when they first learn to read in their mother tongue than when they receive all reading instruction in the national language" ("National or Mother Language in Beginning Reading: A Comparative Study," *Research in the Teaching of English*, Vol. I, No. 2 [Spring, 1968], pp. 32–43).

[69] Guy C. Pryor, "An Evaluation of the Bilingual Instructional Project for Spanish-Speaking Children in the First Grade of the Stonewall Elementary School in the Harlandale Independent School District, San Antonio, Texas." June, 1966. (Mimeographed.)

feeling of acceptance, enhances their self image, makes them happier in their school life at this important developmental stage, and brings all the concomitant values that accompany wholesome social and personal adjustment."[70]

ZAPATA, TEXAS, 1966. In 1966 the Zapata County Independent School District launched a bilingual preschool program "to enable all preschool children, both English-speaking and Spanish-speaking, to gain skill in understanding and speaking English and Spanish." The main purpose of this program is to provide the children, most of whom are Spanish-speaking, with a variety of experience as part of a reading-readiness program in both English and Spanish.

DEL RIO, TEXAS, 1966. A bilingual program conceived to be experimental in design was launched in September of 1966 in the first grades of the Garfield Elementary School of Del Rio, Texas, by its principal, R. J. Waddell, and a staff of fluently bilingual, experienced teachers. Special tests are being designed, thanks to which it is hoped that the soundness of the bilingual approach may be objectively evaluated.

EL PASO, TEXAS, 1966. Under Title III of the Elementary and Secondary Education Act of 1965, El Paso, Texas, is conducting a pilot study in the education of bilingual children whose mother tongue is Spanish and in training programs for their teachers. The El Paso "bilingual" project began in four first-grade classes in two schools, Beall and Roosevelt, in September 1966. The program includes the daily use of a language laboratory and various other "innovational" approaches.

The first-grade curriculum centers around the teaching of English as a second language. In the language laboratory of the Applied Language Research Center, to which the children are bussed daily for a thirty-five–minute lab session, the children receive intensive oral English practice. Instruction throughout the morning and throughout most of the afternoon is in English. In the afternoon a few teachers make limited use of Spanish in teaching aspects of social studies. Occasionally Spanish is spoken during the day to facilitate the children's understanding.

The primary goal of this program is fluency in a standard dialect of English, but an effort is made to help the children feel at home in

[70] *Ibid.*

Spanish and to help them develop a respect for their ancestral culture. To facilitate the achievement of these educational goals, the non-Spanish-speaking teachers are encouraged to study Spanish, Mexican culture, contrastive linguistics of English and Spanish, and audio-lingual methods for teaching English as a second language.

An elaborate program of evaluation is under way but has not as yet given measurable results.

CREEDMOOR BILINGUAL SCHOOL, DEL VALLE, TEXAS, 1967. In September of 1967, the Del Valle Independent School District, located near Austin, the capital of Texas, launched the Creedmoor Bilingual School Project with sponsorship under Title III of the Elementary and Secondary Education Act of 1965. This school with its five classrooms and one hundred children, of whom about sixty-five are Spanish-speaking, is located in a low-income area and enjoys no natural advantages except the usual dedication of teachers and administrators. The teaching staff consists of bilingual teachers and English-speaking teacher aides assisted by consultants from other Texas bilingual programs and from The University of Texas. The plan calls for teaching all subjects as much as possible in both English and Spanish. It is hoped that by welcoming the children in their home language and by using freely the two languages spoken in the community the children will, as a result of a newfound feeling of confidence, feel a greater incentive to learn the school subjects. Informally, the children themselves are learning both English and Spanish from one another on the playground. And perhaps more significant than the improvement in confidence and ability to learn is the gain in pride, both personal and cultural. With a change of administration (1968) and the inevitable reappraisal, it remains to be seen how much of this promising bilingual program is retained.

OTHER BILINGUAL PROGRAMS. As I write these lines, reports reach me of a few tentative bilingual Spanish-English programs in such places as Marysville and Calexico, California; Las Cruces, New Mexico; and Tucson, Arizona. It is not rash to declare that before this book is published there will be a great expansion of bilingual programs. I only wonder what their quality will be.

THE POSSIBLE IMPACT OF BILINGUAL EDUCATION ON FLES. The President's War on Poverty and the passage of the Bilingual Education Act of 1968 have given bilingual education a powerful boost since the relation of literacy to economic opportunity has become

obvious. Equally promising are the psychological and social benefits
to be enjoyed by Americans of foreign origin or background who are
beginning to find themselves no longer handicapped and rejected
but suddenly appreciated and sought after. Bilingual programs usually begin in the first year of school and sometimes even in the preschool years, when children are of an age to learn languages without
toil. Is it not possible that those responsible for FLES programs in
monolingual areas may take the hint and provide FLES programs
for children at an earlier and more favorable learning age? These
rapidly expanding bilingual programs may indeed be blazing new
trails, the story of which will have to be reserved for future books
on FLES.

Summary

This chapter has analyzed the remarkable growth of FLES, particularly in the last decade and a half. Almost immediately after the
debacle of World War I new FLES programs began springing up,
the first important one in Cleveland. The early programs were in
French, but gradually the number of Spanish programs caught up.
The twenties, thirties, and forties were a relatively sterile period,
toward the end of which the Good Neighbor Policy and the Hemispheric Solidarity Policy caused considerable expansion of Spanish
teaching in the elementary schools, particularly in the South and
Southwest. Only a few of these programs were of sufficient quality
to endure, however, for most of them were taught by unprepared
classroom teachers unprovided with adequate materials. Toward the
end of the forties FLES programs began slowly to multiply, increasing more rapidly in the early fifties. Only in this decade did German
begin to win back some of its former prestige. The disaster of our
isolationist policies had become evident in World War II, and our
need to communicate with all parts of the world grew even more apparent after the war. Commissioner Earl J. McGrath called eloquent-
ly in 1952 for a much greater knowledge of languages by more Americans; he was the first prominent educational official to propose the
teaching of languages in the elementary school. The conference that
he organized in January of 1953 gave further impetus to this movement, which was in turn endorsed in 1956 by the Modern Language
Association.

In addition to establishing guidelines to help school administrators, the Modern Language Association organized teams of volunteer teachers to prepare FLES materials, soon to be followed by commercially produced texts. The lack of materials was thus gradually overcome, but FLES still suffers from a great dearth of qualified teachers. Teacher-training institutions have done little to prepare competent FLES teachers. Even the Language Development Program of the United States Office of Education failed to emphasize FLES, perhaps because it was still considered somewhat controversial or because the great deficiencies in secondary-school language programs were thought to need first attention.

FLES in the late sixties is in a precarious situation. Generally accepted as axiomatic is the fact that young children are capable of learning languages more effectively than adolescents and adults. Most citizens are convinced, therefore, that the teaching of modern languages should begin in the grades—preferably in the early grades. But we are now, as we have been throughout our educational history, bedeviled by a lack of quality and of discipline in our education. Before we are able to put our house in order in secondary schools and in colleges, we are called on to organize an extensive FLES program. For example, impressed by the need to remedy our language deficiencies, the California state assembly mandated a program in grades six, seven, and eight, which went into effect in 1965 but without adequate financial support. It has also legalized bilingual education.[71] The Texas legislature, too, is considering (1969) a bill authorizing instruction through a foreign language whenever it is educationally advantageous.

As this book goes to press, other states are amending laws that forbid use of languages other than English in school instruction. These changes augur well since they promise to give free rein to curriculum improvements like those provided by the Bilingual Education Act of 1968. Originally sponsored by Senator Ralph Yarborough, this act will, when adequately funded, provide financial assistance to local school districts wishing to promote bilingual education.

Characteristically we display imagination and resourcefulness—in

[71] California, Assembly Bill No. 2564, 1961, prescribed the mandated program. Senate Bill No. 53 has amended Sections 71 and 12,154 of the *Education Code,* making it legal to use languages other than English as media of instruction.

devising ingenious programs, in discovering teachers, in developing materials—but we still falter before the essential task of insuring the quality of our FLES programs and so risk ultimate failure. The theoretical and practical steps that need to be taken to guarantee success will be explored in succeeding chapters.

6. Preparing for a FLES Program

✥✥

A BACKWARD GLANCE over a century and a quarter of FLES history shows that many FLES experiments have survived only a few years and that even the more durable programs of the last century and the first two decades of this century were brought to an abrupt halt through a sudden change in national values. Many of the more recent failures, notably those which characterized the Spanish FLES programs in the early forties in California, Florida, New Mexico, and Texas, can be attributed in large part to lack of adequate preparation. It behooves us, therefore, to prepare for a FLES program so carefully that it has a reasonable chance of success.

Programs in the past have usually been promoted by one or more dedicated persons. Such promoters may be members of a school board, superintendents, principals, supervisors, college teachers, high-school teachers, elementary-school teachers, education committee, Parent-Teacher Associations, or other citizen groups. In Cleveland the program was started by a gifted language teacher who was vigorously supported by the Women's City Club. In Los Angeles the initiative was taken by the superintendent of schools. In York, Pennsylvania, the FLES program grew out of an education workshop. In Jamestown, New York, a high-school teacher offered to train elementary classroom teachers in Spanish. In Somerville, New Jersey, the elementary-school supervisor and the superintendent collaborated on initial plans. In Washington, D. C., the first program resulted from the interest of the foreign-language supervisor and the willingness of a high-school teacher to volunteer her services for an experimental program in the grades. In Hackensack, New Jersey, the first step was taken by the president of the school board.

Background Study by a Committee

Whoever takes the initiative—and it matters little—it is, of course, the school board that has the final responsibility. Many school boards, consisting of public-spirited citizens who serve without compensation, are much taken up with such practical matters as the study of bids, the letting of contracts, and the authorizing of payments. Under the circumstances, it is unlikely that school-board members will themselves be able to make the detailed study necessary to reach an informed and judicious decision on such a complex question as the establishment of a FLES program. Once the question has been raised and it has been decided to consider seriously the *possibility* of FLES, the school board should appoint a broadly representative committee to study the question and to assemble the relevant information, with the clear understanding that the findings of the committee will be given careful consideration. Although it is not possible to detail the composition of such a committee, for local conditions vary, it should include both educators and lay members of the community, representing all shades of opinion from enthusiasm to skepticism. The committee should be provided with consultant services, with travel expenses to visit representative programs, and with a secretary. Ideally, such a study should be combined with a comprehensive curricular review, for decisions taken will necessarily affect other parts of the curriculum. The committee will need from half a school year to a year and a half to do a thorough investigation. And once the committee has made its recommendation and the board has approved a proposal to launch a FLES program, no less than six months should be allowed between this decision and the actual beginning of classes in September.

WHAT IS LANGUAGE AND HOW IS IT LEARNED? Before the committee begins its work, it should make sure that each member understands the nature of language and the process of language learning, both of a native tongue and of a foreign language. Widespread misconceptions concerning these fundamental points account for much of the inefficiency that has brought language teaching into disrepute and for the lack of public understanding and support. The committee should also make certain that these basic facts and principles are understood by the school board, school administrators, teaching staff, and general public.[1]

VALUE AND COST. A second problem the committee will wish to examine concerns the values of a well-conducted FLES program. It should early decide whether or not these values are sufficient to justify the cost. This matter is particularly delicate, for almost everyone who has been through school has had the experience—all too often the frustration—of trying to learn a foreign language. Many educated Americans will want to echo Wilder Penfield, who wrote in *The Atlantic Monthly* of July 1964: "My own studies of three secondary languages were truly remarkable, but only because so much toil, after the age of sixteen, resulted in such a pitiful harvest."[2] But individual views may well be out of date, for both theory and practice have evolved rapidly in the field of modern-language teaching and learning. Visitors to well-taught FLES classes or audio-lingual classes in a high school or college have often remarked, "Why didn't they do this when I was in school?" It is particularly important to divest oneself of a *parti pris* when it comes to the consideration of cost. Many educational innovations have been refused serious consideration, even before the matter of educational value was weighed, simply because of cost. All too often a state of mind exists in many of our communities which automatically considers an educational proposal bad if it is expensive.

The essential question is "What are its values considered in relation to its cost?" Educational values[3] are intangible and as such difficult to appraise in terms of dollars and cents. Our military expenditures, which since the middle fifties have amounted to more than half our national budget, we resent but nonetheless pay, for we understand the relation between them and our chances of survival in a still brutish world. For recreation and such luxuries as alcoholic beverages, tobacco, and cosmetics we are willing to spend some 1,400

---

[1] Authoritative books on this subject are: Nelson Brooks, *Language and Language Learning: Theory and Practice*; and Robert Lado, *Language Teaching: A Scientific Approach*.

[2] Wilder G. Penfield, "The Uncommitted Cortex: The Child's Changing Brain," *The Atlantic Monthly*, Vol. CCXIV, No. 1 (July, 1964), pp. 77–81.

[3] For a statement of the "Values of Foreign Language Study" see Appendix A.

times as much as we do for education.[4] Is this a true index of the
value that we *mean* to place on education? And how does language
education fit into the picture? Does foreign-language learning enrich
our personal lives? Is it related to our national security? Once the
values of language study are realistically appraised and generally
understood, and once the cost has been accurately determined, is the
community willing to underwrite this extra expense? These are not
easy questions to answer, but they are questions that an investigating
commitee cannot well afford to neglect.[5]

Having reached a consensus, if it is possible to do so, on the question of educational values, the committee should next investigate a
variety of practical questions. What language or languages should be
selected? What are the dimensions of an ideal FLES program and
should the committee recommend an ideal program or something
short of perfection? In what grade should such a program be started?
Can continuity and progression be assured? Can adequate time be
provided? How long should lessons be? How frequent? Should the
teachers be specialists or the regular classroom teachers? Would it be
appropriate to plan television programs? What about the availability
of teachers? Are adequate teaching materials available? What provision can be made for experimentation and evaluation? Is a language
coordinator needed?

What Language or Languages Should Be Selected?

The community should decide the language to be studied on the
basis of its particular interests, ethnic groups, or the availability of
teachers and materials.

Despite the early popularity of German, its sudden death during
World War I was such a blow that it has not to this day recovered a

----

[4] According to the *United States Digest of Educational Statistics*, 1965 edition, the estimated expenditures for public elementary and secondary education
for 1964–1965 were $23,106,854 (p. 58) and for public and private higher
education in 1963–1964, they were $9,197,400 (p. 103), or an annual total of
about $32,304,254. For the year 1964, the estimated personal consumption ex-
penditures for recreation were $23.8 billion, for alcoholic beverages $12.4 billion, for tobacco $7.8 billion (See *Statistical Abstract of the United States, 1966*,
p. 324.), and for cosmetics $2.5 billion (See *Oil, Paint, and Drug Reporter*, Vol.
CLXXXV, No. 4 [January 27, 1964], p. 7).

[5] Recommended as useful to such a committee as it ponders these questions
is William Riley Parker's *The National Interest and Foreign Languages*.

proper place in our educational scheme. According to the 1959–1960 survey of FLES conducted by the Modern Language Association, German was being studied by 25,285 children or only 2.1 per cent of the total FLES enrollment in kindergarten through grade eight. In comparison, Spanish attracted 61.5 per cent of the children and French 34.2 per cent. There is of course no relationship between this figure of 2.1 per cent and the real value of German, whether one thinks in cultural and scientific terms or in terms of simple, practical usefulness for communication in international affairs. For advanced study in many fields German is rightly considered to be, along with French and Russian, an indispensable tool. German deserves much more attention and will in due course receive it, once we recover from the self-inflicted educational wound of World War I. German is spoken by an estimated 120,000,000 people and ranks sixth among the world's languages in the number of its speakers.[6] According to the 1960 census we have over 3,000,000 speakers of German in the United States.[7] These data suggest that German deserves serious consideration among possible languages for FLES, especially in areas where German is commonly spoken. Trained teachers are, to be sure, in short supply; but, by using the considerable number of native speakers of German, we could train teachers rather quickly. In addition, it is possible to arrange teacher exchanges with the German Federal Republic, with Austria, and with Switzerland, incidentally giving our own teachers of German the opportunity to live in a German community.

After 1919 French displaced German in a few scattered FLES programs during the twenties, thirties, and forties, although French was quickly overtaken by Spanish. In 1959–1960 nearly twice as many children were learning Spanish in the grades as were learning French (754,174 as compared to 419,660). Whether we consider French from a cultural or a practical point of view, it deserves a place among the first languages to be introduced into the elementary schools. In addition to being spoken by some 74,000,000 persons, twelfth among the world's languages,[8] French has a rather wide geographical distribu-

[6] *The World Almanac*, 1968, p. 160.

[7] Joshua A. Fishman, *Language Loyalty in the United States: The Maintenance and Perpetuation of Non-English Mother Tongues by American Ethnic and Religious Groups*, p. 44.

[8] *The World Almanac*, 1968, p. 160.

tion. In our hemisphere it is spoken in Canada, Haiti, Martinique, Guadeloupe, on the islands of St. Pierre and Miquelon off Newfoundland, and in French Guiana. It is widely spoken in Algeria, Morocco, Tunisia, in various nations and territories of West Africa, in French Somaliland, in Angola, the Congo, and Mozambique, in parts of India and Southeast Asia, in Madagascar (Malagasy Republic) and Réunion, and in the New Caledonia Islands of the Pacific— not to mention in France itself. French is an official language in Belgium (along with Flemish), in Canada (along with English), and in Switzerland (along with German and Italian).[9] French is one of the five official languages of the United Nations and is often one of two working languages at international conferences. As a nation we have had close and usually friendly relations with France ever since the American Revolution. In the eastern part of our country it is only natural that French should make the greatest appeal to our school boards, for in addition to our traditional links with France we have an estimated 1,000,000 speakers of French, mostly of Canadian origin, in New England, along the Canadian border, and in Louisiana. The estimated 400,000 speakers of French in Louisiana, popularly called Cajuns, are descendants of about 4,000 Acadians who were moved by the British from Nova Scotia in 1755. The maintenance and cultivation of the French spoken by these Americans, as well as the acquisition of French by others, is vital to our communication with French-speaking peoples in other parts of the world.

Spanish enjoys a predominant place in our FLES programs, amounting in 1959–1960 to 754,174 or 61.5 per cent of the FLES enrollment in all our elementary schools, from kindergarten through the eighth grade. It is easy to account for this popularity of Spanish. First, it is widely considered to be a little more accessible to American learners than are the other common European languages because the Spanish writing system corresponds more closely to its sound system than does the French, for example. Secondly, we have a large number (approximately 5,000,000) of native speakers of Spanish

---

[9] See Henry de Torrenté, "The Role of Language in the Development of Swiss National Consciousness," *PMLA*, Vol. LXXII, No. 2 (April, 1957), pp. 29–31; and Louis E. Couillard, "The Role of Languages in the Development of National Consciousness: The Canadian Experience," *PMLA*, Vol. LXXII, No. 2 (April, 1957), pp. 43–48.

within our borders.[10] These are concentrated in the Southwest, where one in ten in California and one in seven in Texas speak Spanish, and we have similarly large proportions in the other southwestern states. In New York City one school child in four is a native Spanish-speaking American.[11] Thirdly, Spanish, which ranks fifth among the world's languages, is spoken by 174,000,000.[12] It is the language of Spain, including the Balearic and Canary Islands, of a part of Morocco, of Spanish Sahara, and of Spanish and Continental Guinea; and it is still spoken in the Philippines. A majority of Spanish speakers are concentrated in our hemisphere, where Spanish is the official language of nine South American Republics (all except Brazil and the Guianas), of Mexico and the six Central American republics, of Cuba, Santo Domingo, and the Commonwealth of Puerto Rico.

The introduction of Spanish into the elementary schools of Corpus Christi, El Paso, Houston, and many other Texas communities; of Albuquerque, Carlsbad, and other towns in New Mexico; of Tucson, Arizona; of San Diego, Los Angeles, and many other places in California, has begun to raise thousands of Americans of Hispanic origin to first-class citizenship. Little by little English speakers are coming to realize that the Spanish language and culture not only enrich the American culture but can be a valuable link in our dialog with Spanish-speaking nations; and Spanish speakers are increasingly

10 This estimate is based on the following fragmentary statistics: Senator Ralph Yarborough of Texas gives (U.S., Congress, Senate, speaking on Two Proposals for a Better Way of Life for Mexican-Americans of the Southwest. S. Res. 352–S. Res. 361 Bill S. 428, 90th Cong., 1st sess., January 17, 1967, *Congressional Record*, CXIII, 5.) the number of Spanish-speaking people of the Southwest as 3,465,000, or 12 per cent of the population of the southwestern states. According to the Department of Commerce, Bureau of the Census, (*United States Census of Population, 1960, Puerto Ricans in the United States*, p. 2), Puerto Ricans of all ages number 892,513. And according to Tom Alexander ("Those Amazing Cuban Emigrés," *Fortune*, Vol. LXXIX, No. 5 [October 1966], p. 145), "some 300,000 [Cuban refugees] have come since 1959." These fragments already add up to 4,657,513, to which must be added an unknown number of Mexican-Americans living throughout the Midwest and Northwest.

11 Of the 1,550,730 persons enrolled in school in and around New York City, five to thirty-five years old (U.S., Department of Commerce, Bureau of the Census, *United States Census of Population, 1960, New York, Detailed Characteristics*, p. 34-449), 378,135 are of Puerto Rican birth or parentage (*ibid.*, p. 94).

12 *The World Almanac*, 1968, p. 160.

sensing the fact that theirs is a glorious cultural heritage. It is, therefore, natural and proper that we should give a prominent place to
Spanish in the schools of many parts of our country.

Among the modern languages Polish comes next in FLES enrollment, with .86 per cent of the overall FLES enrollment or a total of
10,636 pupils, mostly in Catholic schools. This may surprise the reader if he does not know that the population of Poland is 33,000,000
(twenty-fifth among world languages)[13] and that we have in the
United States over 2,000,000 speakers of Polish.[14] It is reasonable to
expect that this language will become increasingly important in our
country and in our world.

Italian follows Polish in FLES enrollment, with a total of 5,374
or .43 per cent. The presence of Italian in our elementary schools
is explained by the heavy population of Italian speakers in certain
states, notably California, Connecticut, and New York. Italians, estimated at over 3,500,000, form the largest group of speakers of
other languages in our country after Spanish.[15] Italian is spoken
by some 58,000,000 people, occupying thirteenth place among the
world's tongues. Not only these statistics but the long and glorious
cultural tradition of Italy would justify a more populous Italian
FLES program.

According to the Modern Language Association survey of 1959–
1960, Russian is studied by only 3,197 children in kindergarten and
in grades one through eight, or .26 per cent of the total FLES population. Russian deserves a much more prominent position than it so
far enjoys. The present enrollment figures do not remotely correspond to the political and cultural importance of Russian but rather
indicate how far our language instruction is from reflecting world
realities. In future FLES programs, Russian should rank with French,
German, and Spanish.

At least two other languages deserve consideration by virtue of the
number of their speakers: Chinese and Japanese. Nearly 700,000,000
persons or one quarter of the world's population speak a Chinese
language or dialect.[16] Chinese is one of the official languages of the
United Nations; and China, whatever its political destiny, is bound

13 *Ibid.*
14 *Language Loyalty in the United States*, p. 44.
15 *The World Almanac*, 1968, p. 160.
16 *Ibid.*, p. 160.

to be increasingly important in the world of the future. The establishment at the University of Hawaii of the East-West Center is a recognition of the fact that we should be able to talk directly with the Chinese and other oriental neighbors. Fortunately we have on our west coast and in Hawaii many native speakers of the Chinese languages who could form a natural link between the United States and the Far East. The Modern Language Association survey records only 214 pupils as studying Chinese in the elementary school in 1959–1960. The fact that Chinese is less closely related to English than are French, German, Italian, Russian, and Spanish is at once an advantage and a disadvantage. The Chinese tones make it less accessible to adult English speakers than the European languages, but small children do not encounter the same difficulties. For this reason the study of Chinese in the elementary grades promises greater return than in high school or college.

Japanese, seventh among world languages, had 873 pupils in Hawaiian elementary schools in 1959–1960. Japan is a progressive nation with a population of about 100,000,000, with whom we should communicate increasingly through our Japanese speakers. To strengthen this link, it would be highly desirable to develop more extensive FLES programs in Japanese, especially in Hawaii and on the Pacific coast.

Before concluding, we should speak briefly of Portuguese, with 381 FLES pupils in 1959–1960; Norwegian, with 53; and Swedish, with 30. These, and perhaps a few others of the several dozen languages that are spoken in the United States, deserve preservation and cultivation through instruction in the elementary schools in areas where the population consists prominently of speakers of these languages. It will be argued that these languages cannot compare in international importance with those already discussed. However, in the case of Portuguese, which ranks tenth among world languages, with some 93,000,000 speakers, in Portugal and Brazil principally, this is patently not the case.[17] In the early days of the National Defense Education Act it was labeled by the United States commissioner of education as one of the six most critical languages. This classification has been reaffirmed in the United States commissioner's more recent decision to emphasize both Portuguese and Spanish in a

[17] *Ibid.*

new Latin American studies program. For these reasons among others, communities in which there is a concentration of Portuguese speakers might well consider the desirability of establishing Portuguese FLES programs. Incidentally, Parker predicts that one day "Portuguese will vie with Spanish in popularity at all levels."[18]

In the case of Polish, the Scandinavian languages, and perhaps some others we have large number of potential spokesmen for the United States in our relations with the various countries in which these languages are spoken. Unless we preserve and cultivate these languages, we shall continue to find our international representatives linguistically deficient.

The Dimensions of an Ideal FLES Program

Many communities, enchanted by the promise that a FLES program offers, set out with a minimum of preparation, only to find later that, to endure, a FLES program requires hard work, time, money, and expertise. A minimum commitment—a late start, doubtful continuity, too little class time, overloading the teacher, leaving the teacher to work in isolation—leads to almost certain disenchantment.

Should a FLES study committee recommend an ideal program or something more modest? To what extent can the community economize without endangering the success of a program? Even if the community decides in favor of a quality program and is willing to guarantee financial support, can adequate personnel, materials, and cooperation be assured? These are inescapable questions for the committee, and they deserve closer consideration.

IN WHAT GRADE SHOULD A FLES PROGRAM BEGIN? Here I believe the evidence, as it has been adduced in an earlier chapter, indicates that ideally a FLES program should start in nursery school, in kindergarten, or in the first grade at the latest.[19] I say "at the latest" because if in a given community there should be an opportunity for a preschool program involving one or, indeed, several languages the school board may wish to consider an experimental program and propose it for support under Title III of the Elementary and Second-

18 Parker, *National Interest and Foreign Languages*, p. 153.

19 More and more the magic learning capacities of the young child are coming to be recognized. Typical is the survey article entitled "Kindergarten is Too Late," by Esther P. Edwards of the Eliot Pearson Department of Child Study, Tufts University, in *Saturday Review*, June 15, 1968, pp. 68–70, 76–79.

ary Education Amendments of 1967. In the past we have had exploratory language programs in junior high school based on the fallacious assumption that language learning depends primarily on analysis rather than on practice and that it is possible to acquire proficiency in a foreign language in two years. It is now well established that understanding and speaking a language are primarily skills. Therefore, the proper time to introduce the exploratory idea would be during the preschool years, when the learner's skill in perceiving and reproducing sounds is still keen, or, as Wilder Penfield expresses it, when the child's cortex is still uncommitted.[20]

MULTILINGUAL NURSERY SCHOOL. Let me, therefore, propose,[21] for communities large enough to have the resources, the organization of an experimental international nursery school. In such a school the children could be introduced to as many languages as there are days in the week. The teachers should be native speakers of the languages concerned and should also be well-trained and skillful nursery-school teachers. The exact procedures should be worked out carefully in collaboration with nursery-school experts and child psychologists, but the general features of such a program might be somewhat as follows. Since there is no known limit to the number of languages a small child can learn in a natural cultural setting, a program might start with five languages. For practical purposes I should select Chinese or Japanese, French, German, Russian, and Spanish. On Monday from nine to twelve the Spanish-speaking teacher would be in charge and would conduct her work in Spanish. On Tuesday the Russian teacher would direct the activities in Russian. On Wednesday the German teacher would take over, as would the Chinese or Japanese teacher on Thursday and the French teacher on Friday. While observing the basic principles governing the conduct of an American nursery school and thus maintaining a uniform policy under the direction of the English-speaking American nursery-school expert, each teacher would represent, as naturally as is possible in this necessarily artificial setting, her own culture. She would behave with the children—two, three, or four years old—as one does in her country and she would urge them to behave as children do in her

[20] Penfield, "The Uncommitted Cortex," pp. 77–81.

[21] As I did in my article "The Optimum Age for Beginning the Study of Modern Languages," *International Review of Education*, Vol. VI, No. 3 (1960), p. 306.

country. She would speak only in her own language—except in an emergency—and would use action and gestures to help convey meaning. The children would be instructed initially by the directress to respond in English or in any way that seemed natural—or not at all, until they feel ready. It is my guess, subject to verification, that the children would by the end of the school year understand everything that is said in this limited setting in all five languages. The experiment should if possible be continued into a second, third, and fourth year; for children, who learn incredibly fast at this age, forget just as rapidly unless habits are reinforced by continued exposure.

Such a plan naturally poses a problem of articulation. What happens when these children reach kindergarten or the first grade? Hopefully the community will, if this program proves successful, establish in kindergarten or grade one a regular FLES program in which the children may continue learning one of the five languages. In the other four, recorded materials—children's dialogs, games, songs, sayings, verses—should be made available to those children who continue to be interested. By hearing and responding in their own way—singly, in pairs, or in groups—they can perhaps maintain their auditory acuteness long enough to acquire permanently a good ear for languages.

In deciding at what level to begin FLES the committee will have to weigh advantages and disadvantages. It seems clear from the evidence that from the viewpoint of effectiveness in learning, particularly in learning to understand and to speak with a good accent, the earliest possible start is best. It is sometimes urged that children need a year or two to get accustomed to school, but there is no evidence that the presence of a second language in the kindergarten or first grade interferes with the adaptation of children to school life.

A decision *not* to begin in kindergarten or in the first grade must, therefore, rest on purely expedient grounds, such as lack of funds or of teachers able to staff such a program. It is well at this point to remind ourselves of the Modern Language Association suggestion that if a community can afford only one of two possible language sequences, one in grades seven through twelve and the other in the elementary school, it might well give priority to the secondary-school program, for without a continuation in high school a FLES program would wither. Even if the committee decides to urge a long sequence of language study, beginning with the child's initial schooling and continuing through the twelfth grade, it may for practical reasons consider it more desirable to extend a six-year high-school sequence downward a grade at a time, into the sixth, then the fifth, the fourth, and so on, than to begin with the child's first school year and move up a grade at a time. The former arrangement has the advantage of easing the articulation between the elementary and the secondary school.[22]

IMPORTANCE OF CONTINUITY. It is now generally agreed that a FLES program should not be started unless it can be continued throughout the elementary and secondary grades. In the words of the Modern Language Association Advisory and Liaison Committee, "We believe that FLES . . . is an essential part of the long sequence, ten years or more, needed to approach mastery of a second language in school."[23] The local planners should, therefore, most earnestly consider the chances of continuity and progression. The community, school board, school administration, and teaching staff should all be firm in their resolution to support the program long enough for it to articulate with the secondary-school program. If there is not a clear consensus on this subject, the program should not be attempted.

ADEQUATE TIME PROVISION. Most FLES lessons are fifteen to twenty minutes long and occur from two to five times a week. That many FLES programs have been able to achieve worthwhile goals in such a limited time is a tribute to the ingenuity of their teachers. The short lessons have two justifications: (1) A teacher who maintains a fast tempo finds it difficult to hold the attention of young children for longer than twenty minutes at a time. (2) Since FLES should not displace other subjects but rather should be accommodated by compressing already scheduled activities, a minimum period of time should be requested. More important than long lessons are frequent ones. For this reason a FLES program of high quality should consist of five short lessons a week.

Overburdening FLES teachers often results in lowering dangerously the quality of a program. The FLES teacher, to be successful, must prepare special materials, must plan carefully for each class, must—especially if she is a traveling teacher—have her props in order, must know each individual child, and must know just where the classroom teacher is in each subject of the curriculum. This can-

[22] See Appendix D.
[23] *Ibid.*

not be done without an adequate time allowance. A traveling teacher working in one school can attend to a maximum of three classes in an hour and not more than ten in a day. If she visits two or three schools, the number of classes would have to be correspondingly fewer, certainly no more than eight. The specialist teacher who is allowed time to keep informed about the children's progress in other subjects and to reinforce the classroom teacher's work while teaching the foreign language is also more likely to be welcomed rather than resented by the regular teacher.

Teachers and Materials

SHOULD THE FLES TEACHER BE THE REGULAR CLASSROOM TEACHER OR A SPECIALIST? Theoretically the classroom teacher, who knows the children and can best correlate FLES with the rest of the curriculum, is best qualified, provided she is a native speaker of the language she teaches and an authentic representative of its culture and provided she is a trained and skillful language teacher. More often than not, however, this is expecting too much of the classroom teacher—as it is expecting too much that she be a scientist, a mathematician, and sometimes even an artist and a musician. For this reason the prevailing trend in FLES is to use a traveling specialist teacher. FLES teaching *is* a specialized task, but the FLES teacher must nevertheless avoid playing a star role in the classroom. She must get and hold the attention of the children for the fifteen to twenty minutes that she is present, but her teaching should fit into the regular program and contribute to it as much as possible.

FLES BY TELEVISION. Economy-minded school boards and administrators are sometimes tempted to subscribe to a FLES program by television. Why, indeed, should a gifted FLES teacher not be made available at the same time to all the children at a given grade level? There is no necessary reason why this arrangement should not succeed if it is carefully planned and executed, but the truth seems to be that it fails more often than it succeeds. The most successful French television course, "Parlons Français," has proved itself admirably when classroom teachers carry out the prescribed preparations or follow the television lessons with related classroom work. However, this coordination is not always present, and, therefore, results often fall short of expectations.[24] Dr. J. Richard Reid, after con-

[24] See Chapter 5.

cluding a survey of foreign-language teaching by television, found that "Television is not *the answer* to the shortage of teachers, but insofar as TV teaching of foreign languages is done by skillful, inspired teachers, backed by sound advice from linguists and producers, and by a sound program in the schools, television can be *a major part* of the solution to this problem. The virtue is not in the TV tube or in any one person in the studio. It is in all the people that collaborate in its use."[25]

FINDING TEACHERS. There remains the critical question of finding qualified teachers.[26] A fully qualified teacher of FLES should possess a native command of the language he teaches, should be an authentic representative of its culture, and should be skillful in guiding the learning of children of a particular age and background. Unfortunately our present certification policies are far from guaranteeing competence. As recently as 1960 not a single state required that a teacher of modern languages be able to understand and speak the language he teaches. At the same time, the method of certification often barred qualified native speakers from teaching because they lacked certain course credits or sufficient hours in an American institution of higher learning to meet technical requirements. Ironically, the coordinator of a FLES program that was moved out of the regular school schedule for lack of time expressed a wry satisfaction because he could now find qualified teachers in great plenty since they did not have to satisfy technical certification requirements.[27] School administrators find themselves in a quandary. If they wish to include FLES among the common learnings in a regular school day, as it should be, they are certain to have difficulty finding teachers in ample supply who are both qualified and certifiable. The greater ease, at least in some parts of the country, of finding enough qualified teachers to teach before and after school provides a certain temptation to favor this arrangement. If the committee reaches the conclusion that FLES merits a place in the curriculum, it should, of course,

[25] J. Richard Reid, "An Exploratory Survey of Foreign Language Teaching by Television," *Reports of Surveys and Studies in the Teaching of Modern Foreign Languages, 1959–1961*, p. 207.

[26] See my chapter on "The Teacher of Modern Foreign Languages" in Ernest Stabler, ed., *The Education of the Secondary School Teacher*.

[27] See my article "Do We Want Certified Teachers or Qualified Ones?" *The Modern Language Journal*, Vol. XLVII, No. 5 (October, 1963), pp. 231–235.

be a part of the regular school program, whatever the difficulty may be in finding enough qualified teachers.

The committee may have to consider new sources of teacher supply. State teacher-training institutions are usually willing to cooperate in a search for well-educated native speakers who would be interested in undertaking a training program in order to become FLES teachers. Exchanges of American and foreign elementary-school teachers would provide a valuable source of qualified personnel. On both sides it would be necessary to set up arrangements for the careful selection of exchangees and to organize an orientation program during the summer preceding the year in which the exchangee would teach. Such experimental exchange programs might be financed under one of the national education acts.

Still another possible source of supply would be students from neighboring universities. Almost every college and university has its complement of foreign students. Some of these, particularly if they plan to be teachers, might be suitable for teaching in a FLES program if they could be carefully oriented and closely supervised.

ARE ADEQUATE MATERIALS AVAILABLE? Not long ago the answer to this question would have been negative; but as FLES programs began to multiply in the early fifties, the Modern Language Association invited the most experienced FLES teachers of French, German, and Spanish to join with linguists and other foreign-language specialists to form teams for developing FLES materials. Booklets entitled *Beginning French (German, Spanish) in Grade Three, French (German, Spanish) in Grade Four, French (German, Spanish) in Grade Five,* and *French (German, Spanish) in Grade Six* filled the early need and provided valuable guidance to inexperienced FLES teachers. Many school districts preferred to develop their own materials, which, though often amateurish, fitted the local situation. Finally, commercial publishers subsidized teams of talented and experienced FLES teachers and other professionals, who have produced some of the best available FLES materials for the upper elementary grades. For the three common languages there is now no dearth of materials for the intermediate grades, but for other languages and for the primary grades materials will have to be adapted or developed.

THE NECESSITY OF A FOREIGN-LANGUAGE COORDINATOR. This description of the many aspects of a sound FLES program, sketchy though it is, serves to show that no single FLES teacher nor any team of FLES teachers can hope without solid support to succeed in a teaching task that is still relatively unstandardized and, to many, unacceptable. Competent leadership is needed. The board of education is well advised to find a highly qualified language teacher to serve as coordinator of the entire foreign-language program and to defend and interpret this program to educators and public. Full responsibility should be delegated to the foreign-language coordinator, subject of course to the usual procedure of reporting to the director of instruction or superintendent.

Experimentation and Evaluation

Any well-run FLES program provides an opportunity for experimentation. For example, although observation and theoretical considerations lead to the assumption that the younger the child is the better he learns to understand and speak (especially pronounce) a second language, this assumption should be verified objectively. Sensitive tests of listening comprehension and speaking (with emphasis on pronunciation) are needed to determine whether the achievement of learners who have begun in kindergarten or the first grade is superior to the achievement of those who have begun in the third or fourth grade.[28] It is also important to discover whether the addition of a foreign language to the elementary course of study detracts from the rest of the program. Does time taken away from the other common learnings result in lowered achievement? Present research does not support this conclusion.[29]

Planning for evaluation is an important part of the preparation for a FLES program; yet few of the present programs have had ade-

[28] See Chapter 3, at note 57, for a report on this subject.

[29] In addition to the Somerville, Illinois, and "Parlons Français" evaluations already mentioned, important studies include Ralph C. Geigle, "Foreign Language and Basic Learnings," *Elementary School Journal*, Vol. LVII, No. 8 (May, 1957); Alice L. Foley *et al.*, *Impact of Elementary Foreign Language on Secondary Program: Final Report*; Walter B. Leino and Louis A. Haak, *The Teaching of Spanish in the Elementary Schools and the Effects on Achievement in Other Selected Subject Areas*; Evelyn Brega and John M. Newell, "High School Performance of FLES and Non-FLES Students," *The Modern Language Journal*, Vol. LI, No. 7 (November, 1967); and Joseph M. Vocolo, "The Effect of Foreign Language Study in the Elementary School Upon Achievement in the Same Foreign Language in the High School," *The Modern Language Journal*, Vol. LI, No. 8 (December, 1967). For the impact of FLES on college majors see Chapter 3, note 29.

quate provision for evaluation built into them. The primary purpose of such evaluation is to determine to what extent the program is accomplishing the objectives defined at the outset. This means that the objectives must be defined very clearly. Language educators are generally agreed on basic objectives; however, their goals do not always correspond to those of elementary-school educators, social-studies teachers, and supervisors.[30]

Objectives stated by some elementary educators tend to stress first and perhaps exclusively such matters as awakening interest in and respect for other people, their culture, and country, and the creation of better international understanding.[31] Such a point of view seems to assume that language is an introduction to culture, but educators must, in the words of William Parker,

understand that language is not just a convenient door opening on another culture but a *significant and inseparable part of that culture* . . . This does not mean teaching children the foreign words for American things; it does not mean teaching isolated words at all. It means, basically, helping young children to make, through a form of play acting and imitation, the foreign verbal and nonverbal responses to real situations, both familiar and strange. Thus the child does not sit passively and hear about another culture. Rather, in a measure he experiences that culture. As the experience grows, the foreignness, of course, fades away. At the same time a genuine and lasting understanding begins to dawn—deep in his sympathies, not in scribbled notebooks.[32]

To summarize, the objectives of any FLES program should include the language skills, first hearing and speaking, and later reading and writing, and the creation of cultural understanding and sympathy through the learning of language in culturally authentic situations.

[30] See Appendix C for the redefinition of FLES by the Modern Language Association.

[31] Elizabeth Engel Thompson and A. E. Hamalainen (*Foreign Language Teaching in Elementary Schools: An Examination of Current Practices*) stress the social studies values of foreign languages and for this reason even suggest the desirability of introducing into the elementary grades words and expressions from several languages.

[32] William Riley Parker, "Foreign Languages in the Grades: A Caution," *The National Elementary Principal*, Vol. XXXVI, No. 5 (February, 1957), p. 6. Kenneth W. Mildenberger ("Research Findings on Teaching a Second Language in the Elementary School") has distinguished clearly between these two sets of objectives, the one evolving from the language point of view and the other from the social-studies point of view.

It is easiest to evaluate the acquisition of language skills. Listening comprehension is simplest of all to test; and although there is a paucity of tests for FLES, the general pattern for listening-comprehension tests exists. Testing speech is more difficult and involves listening by well-trained language educators who select in advance particular linguistic features and check them as they listen directly to a child speaking or as they listen to a tape recording of a child's speech. Testing reading and writing in the later stages provides less difficulty, for language teachers have long experience in this field.[33]

Particularly difficult to evaluate is the quality and extent of attitude change. Some attitude-inventory tests exist, but they have not as yet been applied very scientifically to FLES, and there is still much development needed in this area. FLES teachers speak enthusiastically of their pupils' increasing tolerance of and sympathy for foreign children and grown-ups, but this subjective observation should be corroborated by objective measurements as well.

Conclusion

Initial enthusiasm for FLES may spring from a variety of sources. Whatever the source, enthusiasm, however contagious, is not enough. Those ultimately responsible, the school board and school administrators, must be sure that they and the general public understand thoroughly what is involved. They should insist on a clear idea of what language is, how it is learned at different age levels, what its relation is to culture and intercultural understanding. Especially should they be assured of the willingness of the community to support a long-range program. And they should not give their approval to a FLES program until they feel certain that all the necessary preparations have been made: a supply of interested and qualified FLES teachers, adequate materials at each grade level, articulation with the rest of the study program and with the language program in the secondary school, specific plans for continual evaluation, and, above all, assurance, in advance, of ungrudging support by all concerned. FLES is very promising in theory, but in practice its success depends on careful and expert planning and execution of plans.

[33] For guidance in foreign language testing, see Robert Lado, *Language Testing: A Scientific Approach*; and Rebecca M. Valette, *Modern Language Testing: A Handbook*.

7. The Course of Study

❖❖❖

IN USING THE TERM "course of study" I refer to the written document that spells out, at times sketchily but often in great detail, the values of a particular subject, a suggested way of looking at it, ways of learning it, objectives, a course outline, materials, methods, and suggestions for evaluation. Sometimes called a teacher's guide,[1] this material is often presented in outline form, usually called a scope and sequence chart. The FLES course of study in any given community should emerge from the cooperative effort of the FLES staff and other teachers and administrators. Inevitably it reflects the prevailing philosophy of foreign-language learning and teaching.

Without losing sight of the importance of other subjects in the school program, the language teachers who have primary responsibility for the course of study in foreign languages should have very clear ideas concerning the values of foreign-language study and the nature of language and the language-learning process. Language teachers in a given community might well start with a critical analysis and discussion of the Modern Language Association statement

[1] The MLA calls its series Teacher's Guides: *Beginning French (German, Spanish) in Grade 3, French (German, Spanish) in Grade 4 (5, 6)*. The most detailed courses of study in the field of languages are those contained in Margit MacRae's series: *Spanish in the Grades*, I, II, III, IV; and *Mi cuaderno de español* (Houghton Mifflin and Co.); and the Holt, Rinehart and Winston FLES series in Spanish.

on Values of Foreign Language Study,[2] add to it in any way that seems appropriate, and decide upon a definition for inclusion in the course of study on which they can all agree.

The New Philosophy

As has already been suggested, the new generation of modern-language teachers is likely to differ somewhat from its predecessors in its outlook on language and, therefore, in its teaching objectives. Teachers today concern themselves more with language as talk and with talk as a form of behavior characteristic of a culture. In affirming the primacy of the spoken word, the new generation does not value the importance of writing or of literature less than the older generation did. Rather it aspires to help bring about both improved literary and linguistic study by preparing students in the rudiments of all aspects of language: understanding, speaking, reading, writing, applied linguistics, and culture, including literature.[3]

The concept of language as a form of behavior characteristic of a culture is also more widely and consciously accepted by the new generation than by the old. Not only linguistic but cultural authenticity is the new aim of language teachers. According to this view, language has structure and this structure is determined by the culture of those who speak it. Language is in its very form and fabric as well as in its content the expression of a culture. Too often in the past, language instruction has been more concerned with learning *about* language, that is, studying grammar, than with acquiring language skills. Similarly, it is possible to learn *about* a culture without learning to sense the culture by developing for the language expressing it a "feel" approximating that of a native speaker. Though a given culture expresses itself in a variety of ways—in art, music, literature, drama, social institutions, among others—social scientists are agreed that language is the medium that best expresses and reflects culture.[4]

2 See Appendix A.

3 See Statement of Values (Appendix A) and Statement of Qualifications (Appendix D).

4 See, for example, Clyde Kluckhohn, *Mirror of Man: The Relation of Anthropology to Modern Life*; Edward T. Hall, *The Silent Language*; Benjamin Lee Whorf, *Language, Thought, and Reality: Selected Writings*; Ruth Benedict, *Patterns of Culture: An Analysis of Our Social Structure as Related to Primitive Civilizations*; Margaret Mead, ed., *Cultural Patterns and Technical Change: A Manual for the World Federation of Mental Health*; and Francis Debyser, "The

Many language teachers say, "Yes, yes, that's obvious," without fully understanding the implications of these simple-sounding statements. Yet nothing is more difficult than to break out of a monocultural shell. An example or two may help to clarify the point. When an American radio announcer who has not studied French or any other foreign language pronounces De Gaulle to rhyme with Paul, he reveals his limited view. For him, it is perfectly natural to give to the letters of foreign names the phonetic values of the same letters in English words. "Obviously we know how to pronounce the French President's name. Isn't it spelled . . . ?" Why should we stop to inquire whether he and 74,000,000 other French speakers pronounce it differently? Occasionally a Cuban, Venezuelan, or Mexican joins one of our ball teams. Do most of us make an effort to approximate the pronunciation of his name? Not at all. Those "z's" in González and Hernández are Anglicized without any regard for the fact that in the Spanish of this hemisphere they are pronounced like "s", a sound that is perfectly easy for the American tongue. How many radio and television announcers resist their monolinguistic impulses when they pronounce such a foreign name as Khrushchev? Few pronounce the former Russian Premier's name or that of U Thant, the Secretary General of the United Nations, as though they were anything but American.

Language also expresses differences in habits and attitudes. The Hispanic obliviousness to time in contrast to the American passion for punctuality has given rise in Mexico to a dual time system called *hora mexicana* and *hora americana*. Too easily Americans assume that Mexicans are merely unreliable. Hall points out that, even within a culture, individuals have different built-in systems. Failure to realize that the other fellow is not "tuned in on the same wave length" is often a cause of conflict.[5]

It is interesting to speculate on the relation of intercultural understanding to humanity's struggle for peace. The Latin official who

Relation of Language to Culture and the Teaching of Culture to Beginning Language Students," *The CCD Language Quarterly: The Chilton-Didier Foreign Language Newsletter*, Vol. VI, No. 1 and No. 2 (Spring/Summer, 1968).

[5] See Edward Hall, *Silent Language*; Martin Joos, *The Five Clocks*; and Wilmarth H. Starr, "Foreign-Language Teaching and Intercultural Understanding," *School and Society*, March 19, 1955; Lee Sparkman, ed., *Culture in the FLES Program*, no. 1769.

keeps the American diplomat "cooling his heels" in the outer office for half an hour and the American businessman who plunges into the heart of his mission abroad without taking time for preliminaries would perhaps both be shocked to be told that they are preparing for war rather than for peace. In our relations between nations as between individuals we have so far depended more on the uncertain qualities of individual tact, sensitiveness, and good judgment—all of which are needed—than on the insights of cultural anthropologists. Is it not time for modern-language teachers, who are responsible for teaching language skills—both for linguistic communication and for intercultural understanding—to emphasize more consistently the use of language as a means of communication and understanding —and to seek more help from colleagues in the social sciences?[6]

Another difference between the older and younger generations of teachers has to do with the process of language learning, whether of the mother tongue or of a second or foreign language.[7] The present generation of teachers is perhaps more willing to recognize the distinction between natural and artificial language learning. All school learning of foreign languages is necessarily artificial since it cannot take place in the cultural environment in which the language is spoken naturally. While admitting inevitable limitations, the modern FLES teacher tries as much as possible to create a learning situation that comes close to the natural situation.

Another mark of the new generation is a better understanding by language teachers and by educators generally of the young child's special capacity for foreign-language learning. The common misconception that this remarkable process is simply a matter of imitation, as educators and laymen alike have formerly assumed, makes it advisable to include some clarifying statements on this subject in the course of study.

PSYCHOLOGY OF LANGUAGE LEARNING. Psychology has been called the basic science of education, and it is scarcely possible to exaggerate the importance of a sound knowledge of this discipline. Language teachers of the past have had little or no initiation into the psychology of language learning, a subject that has lately received

[6] See Chapter 2, note 26.

[7] See Albert H. Marckwardt, "English as a Second Language and English as a Foreign Language," in Harold B. Allen, ed., *Teaching English as a Second Language: A Book of Readings*, pp. 3–8.

considerable attention.[8] It would, therefore, be well to reserve a section of the course of study for this subject.

The more a FLES teacher knows about learning theory and its application to language learning, the better. Slowly we add to essential knowledge in this as in every specialized area. I shall quote extensively from two significant studies since they are unpublished and therefore relatively inaccessible. In one of these the late Donald Snygg[9] points out the tragic consequence of the lag between theory and practice. "The first continued, systematic investigation of learning by experimental methods, carried out by Thorndike between 1898 and 1925, greatly enriched the authors and publishers of textbooks and workbooks, but, in the opinion of many observers, made school readers less interesting and arithmetic teaching even less meaningful than it had been. The later work of Thorndike and the work of the other connectionist experimentalists (Howe,

[8] Social Science Research Council, Committee on Linguistics and Psychology, *Psycholinguistics: A Survey of Theory and Research Problems* (report of the 1953 Summer Seminar Sponsored by the Committee on Linguistics and Psychology of the Social Science Research Council, by John B. Carroll, Charles E. Osgood, ed., and Thomas A. Sebeok, assoc. ed., with a foreword by John W. Gardner); Sol Saporta, ed., *Psycholinguistics: A Book of Readings*, prepared with the assistance of Jarvis R. Bastian; Tatiana Slama-Cazacu, *Le problème du langage dans la conception de l'expression et de l'interprétation par des organisations contextuelles*; Wallace E. Lambert, "Psychological Approaches to the Study of Language," Part I: "On Learning, Thinking, and Human Abilities," *The Modern Language Journal*, Vol. XLVII, No. 2 (February, 1963), pp. 51–62; Part II: "On Second-Language Learning and Bilingualism," *The Modern Language Journal*, Vol. XLVII, No. 3 (March, 1963), pp. 114–121; Ursula Bellugi and Roger William Brown, eds., *The Acquisition of Language* (reports of the Fourth Conference Sponsored by the Committee on Intellective Processes, Research of the Social Science Research Council); John B. Carroll, *Language and Thought*; and "The Contributions of Psychological Theory and Educational Research to the Teaching of Foreign Languages," *The Modern Language Journal*, Vol. XLIX, No. 5 (May, 1965), pp. 273–281; Wilga H. Rivers, *The Psychologist and the Foreign Language Teacher*; and Charles E. Osgood, ed., *Psycholinguistics: A Survey of Theory and Research Problems*; E. H. Lenneberg, *Biological Foundations of Language*.

[9] Donald Snygg, "Learning Theory as It Influences Instructional Materials and Resources," 14 pp. (report to the Association of Supervision and Curriculum Development Commission on New Media of Instruction, 1960). A summary of this paper was published in *Audiovisual Instruction*, Vol. VII, No. 1 (January, 1962), pp. 8–12, under the title "The Tortuous Path of Learning Theory."

Spence, and Skinner), who have dominated the experimental laboratories since, has, so far, had no effect at all on school practices."[10]

Snygg comments particularly on a grave error concerning transfer of training. "The mistake Thorndike made was this. When he disproved the faculty explanation of transfer he believed that he had disproved the existence of transfer. It was an educational disaster that he persuaded a whole generation of educators to agree with him."[11] One of the most serious of educational consequences has to do with learning how to read. All too often teachers of reading concentrate all their efforts on the direct teaching of individual words repeated *ad nauseam* in different but restricted contexts, instead of cultivating the child's inherent ability to work out from what is already known the sound and sense of new words. Since the average American six-year-old child has a recognition vocabulary of some sixteen thousand words, he could, if he were encouraged to, sound out words according to systematic principles and quickly learn to transfer large numbers of words from his passive to his active vocabulary.[12] This process could be further speeded through a replacement of the present stultifying readers by much more exciting ones, written by literary artists rather than by us unimaginative academics.[13]

Snygg correctly points out that there are different kinds of learning. "The implications of the S-R [stimulus-response] concept of learning, in its present stage, are promising and [yet] profoundly disturbing. If the object of education is to teach what is already known, to promote conventional, conforming behavior, to prepare pupils to live in a world exactly like the one in which they are educated, a crash program for S-R type research should be undertaken at once."[14] Curiously enough, language learning in its early stages is, to a considerable extent, precisely this kind of learning.

[10] Snygg, "Learning Theory," p. 3.

[11] *Ibid.*, p. 4.

[12] See Chapter 3, note 22. This process of discovering in writing or print words already known by their sound, this "cracking the code," so to speak, was clearly understood by the great linguistic scientist Bloomfield (Leonard Bloomfield and Clarence L. Barnhart, *Let's Read: A Linguistic Approach*) and by another eminent linguist, Charles Carpenter Fries (*Linguistics and Reading*).

[13] *The Wonderful Adventures of Nils* by the Swedish Nobel Laureate, Selma Lagerlöf, was written to fill the need for a Swedish geography textbook.

[14] Snygg, "Learning Theory," p. 6.

Snygg continues, "If, on the other hand, what is desired is a creative, adaptable citizen able to deal with problems his teachers could not have envisaged and with problems they were unable to solve, another model for learning must be used."[15] Having acquired language as a medium of communication in strict conformity to the patterns of his culture (de Saussure's *langue*), it is even more important for a child to be encouraged to develop this medium as an instrument of individual thought and expression (de Saussure's *parole*). This would seem to mean that in the later stages of language teaching another approach should be emphasized.

The approach that Snygg would recommend is based on what he calls the cognitive or perceptual field theory of learning. "The basic assumption of this alternative approach is an assumption that behavior is always appropriate to the situation as perceived by the behaver at that instant. If he perceived his behavior as inappropriate he would change it. Behavior is determined by the behaver's perceptions, not directly by reality. The hunter mistaken for a deer is shot at, the deer mistaken for a bush goes free. Learning is therefore the result of the learner's achieving a clearer, more realistic perception of the situation with which he is dealing and takes place in the following steps:

"(1) The learner becomes aware of a need or goal whose achievement will enable him to satisfy the need. (Goal)

"(2) The existence of an obstacle makes it necessary for him to perceive the situation. (Interpretation$_1$)

"(3) He attacks the problem (attempts to reach the goal) in terms of his perception of the situation. (Act$_1$)

"(4) This act has consequences. If it results in the achievement of the goal and the satisfaction of the need the process is complete. If the result is not the one sought and expected. (Result$_1$)

"(5) A re-interpretation of the situation takes place. (Interpretation$_2$)

"(6) The second attack (Act$_2$) is appropriate to this new interpretation.

"(7) The consequent result (Result$_2$), if it is the achievement of the goal, brings the search and re-interpretation to an end, or if it is not the result expected, causes a

15 *Ibid.*, p. 6.

"(8) re-evaluation of the situation. (Interpretation$_3$)"[16]

Snygg goes on to spell out in detail the implications of the cognitive field theory for each of these steps. This theory is related to the general theory of learning, but it would be useful for FLES teachers to consider carefully its specific application to the language-learning situation, taking into account the age of the learners.

Memory is one important aspect of the psychology of language learning. The subject is usually divided into four phases: impression, retention, recall, and recognition. In an interesting study entitled "Some Psychological Aspects of the Teaching and Learning of Languages," James E. Wicker analyzes the application of these concepts to language learning.[17] He particularly emphasizes the following points:

(1) Knowledge of results, i.e., tangible evidence of reaching the goal.

(2) The advantage of meaningful over rote learning.

(3) Pauses between learning sessions to enhance the learning.

(4) Advantage of recitation over continued re-reading aloud.

(5) The advantage of rote learning when learning nonserial material (such as vocabulary).

Although Wicker is concerned primarily with language learning by adults, the same principles are in part applicable to FLES, and he makes certain recommendations for the organization of a FLES course.

Since it has been demonstrated that the average college freshman uses less than one hundred words for more than 60 per cent of his speech,[18] Wicker proposes a vocabulary of not more than one hundred words to be used as a basis for the first twenty lessons. Thus each lesson for a period of one month would introduce only five new words.

[16] *Ibid.*, p. 7.

[17] James E. Wicker, "Some Psychological Aspects of the Teaching and Learning of Languages" (unpublished paper for The University of Texas at Austin). Wicker is now a psychologist engaged in the study of human factors at the General Dynamics Corporation, Fort Worth, Texas, Branch.

[18] H. Fairbanks, "Studies in Language Behavior: II, The Quantitative Differentiation of Samples of Spoken Language," *Psychological Monographs*, Vol. LVI, No. 2 (1944), pp. 19–38.

"In the class, the instructor should explain each of the words, attempting to give the students a vivid impression of each one so that recall will be easier. All of this work should be done aurally, with no reference made to the written language.

"During the listening session, these five words are to be thoroughly *overlearned*.[19] All possible combinations of these words are to be used. All usages of the verb (in the present tense) all variations of the adjectives, all forms of the nouns, etc. This listening session should be in sections of five minutes each, with a two-minute rest between sessions. During these two-minute rests, the students should not be mentally reviewing the words they have heard. It should be a definite break so that distributed practice (rather than massed practice) can take place. The format should be as varied as possible between the sections. In other words, each five-minute section should be different, and not a carbon-copy of the one before.

"The next class period, the procedure should be one of repetition, coupled with a great deal of conversation, or as much as the vocabulary will permit. A tape recorder should be used so that the students can gain an understanding of just what they sound like. This feedback process[20] will greatly improve the pronunciation of the language. Tests should be used each day.

"The next listening session (which should contain spaces for recitation as well as for listening), five new words should be given, and *in addition*, all of the words in the previous lesson should be used. The student should be aware that the words used in any one day's lesson will have to be known for all the lessons to come. Then the words will not be memorized just for the next day's lesson, but will be put in the permanent memory bank. The vocabulary should be overlearned to such an extent that the student *at once recalls any word from any lesson*. In other words, the foreign language vocabulary should be as familiar as English.

[19] Robert S. Woodworth and Harold Schlosberg, *Experimental Psychology*, p. 278. "Overlearn" means "to learn . . . so thoroughly that an automatic response habit is achieved" (Donald D. Walsh, *What's What: A List of Useful Terms for the Teacher of Modern Languages*).

[20] Charles E. Osgood, *Method and Theory in Experimental Psychology*, p. 688.

"The next two weeks (ten lessons) the student should read prepared lessons containing the words they have learned. Each lesson should contain ten new words, plus those of the lesson preceding it. These ten lessons should not follow the order the words were learned in the previous month, but should be in some other order. It will only take two weeks to learn the spelling of the basic vocabulary, since the words themselves are already well known. Recognition is easier than recall.

"At the end of these two weeks, any normal student in the class will find he has enough of a grasp of the language to be able to understand speech and written material in that language, at least as far as his basic vocabulary goes. He should be able to speak and write the language extremely well within the vocabulary he has learned.

"After this preliminary training, the lessons for the following weeks will each day take up more of a basic five hundred word vocabulary. Rare constructions, unnecessary synonyms, and the like should be avoided. This vocabulary should contain as many cognates as are in common usage and are basic words. The more common tenses of the verbs should be taken up at this time. The idea still is to acquire a little of the language thoroughly, rather than a lot poorly learned. As the students acquire a larger vocabulary in the language, conversation should be used more and more. The tape recorder should be used freely at this time to help the students acquire a correct pronunciation. Rote learning should be avoided. The fact that a student can parrot back a series of sounds that mean nothing to him proves nothing. It should be again noted that the idea of this training is to implant firmly a basic vocabulary of the language. If a person knows a thousand or so words of basic English, he can get along quite well and pick up more of the language as it becomes necessary. In too many cases, foreign-language textbooks use obscure or rare forms in teaching beginners in the language. The purpose of teaching a foreign language is to help students acquire the usage of the language, not to test the mental abilities of the student or to strengthen his mind for other studies. This simply does not happen.

"At the end of four semesters of this type of training, the student should have acquired about 1,500-2,000 words of the language (the basic vocabulary) and be able to use the verbs in this vocabulary in all necessary tenses. This material will be in the permanent memory bank, and will not be forgotten, any more than learning to ride a bicycle can be forgotten. After this, as a student uses the language, any rarer words and constructions that may be needed can be acquired."[21]

The reader of the foregoing should not be disturbed by the author's lack of linguistic sophistication. He is discussing *psychological* principles. The fact that he stresses vocabulary rather than structures is unimportant. It is generally recognized that the learner needs first to manipulate structures, using a sufficient but very limited vocabulary in order to do so. Wicker is of course right in stressing the necessity of limiting the amount of material strictly and learning it thoroughly, "overlearning," to use what has become a well-recognized technical term. This is what Wilder Penfield means by the "acquisition of speech units," that is, the sound system and forms of a language which constitute its structure. This is also what Aage Salling means by "the little language." According to Salling's theory, "However small the vocabulary of a pupil may be, you can find that he will be able to express something personal in it."[22] Like Wicker and Penfield, Salling also stresses the need of going beyond rote learning and giving children the opportunity to indulge in original expression on the basis of each advance made in the acquisition of language materials. In order to illustrate his meaning, Salling reproduces two compositions written by his pupils one month after the beginning of the English course:

(1) "I am a girl. My name is H. My sister's name is J. I live in a house. My sister also lives in a house. My father has a garden. There are big trees and small trees.

(2) "I have a little dog and her name is Silly and she is five years old. My dog's hair is white and her legs are shorter than Jacob's.—signed, Jacob."

Salling comments: "In the former composition you will find only phrases copied from the textbook, whereas in the latter there is the

21 Wicker, "Psychological Aspects," pp. 7–8.
22 Aage Salling, *Det Lille Sprog: En Sprogundervisningens Teori*, p. 133.

very element of something personal which is so important for all progress in language learning."[23]

Another important aspect of learning theory has to do with motivation. Snygg's comments on this subject are useful:

"Teachers have traditionally used praise and blame, prizes, marks, gold stars, certificates of merit, smiles, frowns, detention, and, till recently, the rod, to promote learning. On the common sense level almost everyone expects that acts which are punished are less likely to be repeated, that acts which are rewarded are more likely to be repeated. But what is rewarding? Pleasure? And what is punishment? Pain? Perhaps. But what is pleasant to one person may be painful to another, a fact well known to most families who have only one TV set. Some pupils work hard for high marks; others try to avoid them. A good conduct award in the fourth grade may cause more misconduct than it prevents. Experiments on animals show that under conditions of high motivation strong rewards and punishment *interfere* with learning. In some maze experiments animals given an electric shock every time they made the *correct* response have learned faster than comparable animals who did not suffer shock. . . . The S-R theorist, in his own experience, sees his learner as a pigeon or white rat in a box where he has only two choices. The learner is not lazy or uninterested. He is highly motivated, usually by hunger. When he makes the 'right' choice it is 'reinforced' by the experimenter (teacher) who, in person or by way of a pre-programmed machine, hands him a pellet of food. In this conceptual model the active agent is obviously the teacher. All the decisions are in his hands. All the learner has to do is to be hungry. . . . But Harlowe, after seeing one of his monkeys go for more than nineteen hours without food or rest in order to manipulate a puzzle whose only reward was the opportunity to see what the experimenter was doing for a few seconds, postulated a subjective 'curiosity' drive. . . . White . . . has presented a cogent and well-documented argument for supposing that the basic need is for 'competence' and Snygg and Combs, on both psychological and biological grounds, contend that all behavior is an effort to maintain and enhance the individual's concept of himself, to give him a greater feeling of personal worth and dig-

[23] *Ibid.*

nity. Maslow, Rogers, and many others have advanced similar concepts. . . . Since the postulated needs are for 'greater worth and value,' 'greater competence,' the learner is always motivated. His needs are not satiable. It is assumed that a desire for learning and self-improvement is a basic aspect of human nature."[24]

The teacher's central task then is not so much to teach as to induce the student to learn. It is not the statement of this task but its accomplishment which is difficult. The teacher's art rather than his science enables him to help each one of thirty differently constituted students in a class to discover his greatest capacities and to select goals which are self-enhancing and yet not discouraging. It has been found that a student may safely select his own goals and that, left to himself, he will select goals that are just within his capacity. The idea that children can be made to like school by making the work easy is false. Like everyone else children want to be worthy, and they are especially proud of difficult achievements. A great teacher will call his students to sweat and tears.

TEACHER ATTITUDES. The course of study should not only specify ways in which the teacher can skillfully adjust the learning task to the capacity of the learner but should also show how teacher attitudes can increase the motivation of children to learn. A basic principle is respect for the individual pupil. No outstanding teacher can falter in his overriding belief in the infinite worth and potentiality of the children committed to his care—if only for fifteen minutes a day. With this essential faith in human dignity anything is possible. Without it the teacher greatly reduces the goals and limits the achievement of his pupils. This does not mean, of course, that each student challenged by such faith will achieve superiority, but it does mean that he will be inspired to achieve something near *his* maximum achievement. And the teacher imbued with this respect for human worth will gain as much satisfaction from a modest achievement as from a superior performance, if it represents a pupil's best effort.

The teacher's concern reaches beyond his class to humanity itself. If a teacher whose education or experience has been limited restricts the outlook of his pupils to his own narrow horizon, he will

[24] Snygg, "Learning Theory," pp. 9–10.

hobble them in their development. In contrast, the imaginative teacher opens vast horizons to his pupils. Thus, the FLES teacher should show that he values people who know foreign languages and represent foreign cultures, and he should be able to cite interesting examples of such knowledge. These people may include the day laborer who by the luck of birth understands and speaks a language other than English though he may not read and write it. A teacher endowed with a respect for knowledge no matter how acquired is in a position to help create a proper sense of values in a whole community. By his attitude a teacher can show clearly his conviction that, everything else being equal, a person who can use two languages is worth more than a person who can use only one, that a person who can use three languages is more valuable than one who can use only two, and so on progressively. A sense of scholarly responsibility will, of course, induce him to combat the kind of popular ignorance which finds expression in such reckless remarks as "He speaks twelve languages." However, he must avoid feelings of resentment and defensiveness in the face of the anti-intellectuals who pervade our society—including our schools—and who condone ignorance of languages other than English. A steady, balanced sense of values concerning languages and their users is part of the professional responsibility of the language teacher.

Objectives

After the general section on the philosophy and psychology of language learning, comes the more specific statement of objectives. Below are a few suggestions for consideration by the committee drafting the course of study.

Language Objectives.

In general, to help children acquire the basic skills of understanding and speaking in another language.

Specifically, to train the ear while it is at its keenest.

To help children perceive speech sounds produced at a natural speed by native speakers and to discover the correspondence between speech patterns and meaning.

To enable children, preferably while they still have a large repertory of sounds, to harness the relatively small number of these sounds which are native to the foreign language by learning to reproduce them accurately in appropriate situations or dialogs.

To present in orderly fashion the basic speech patterns and to enable the children by means of intensive and varied practice to learn these structures to the point of converting them into unconscious habits and of using them for direct communication and original self-expression.

As soon as the basic skills of understanding and speaking are sufficiently mastered, to begin reading and writing.

To lead the children to the point of wanting to read on their own and to provide them with a variety of interesting reading texts.

To provide systematic writing practice: copying, labeling, taking dictation, doing written pattern practice, rewriting, and—as soon as it is feasible—expressing oneself in writing.

Cultural Objectives.

To help children break out of their monolingual and mono-cultural shell.

To enable them to participate directly or vicariously in another culture by learning to use the language in linguistically and culturally authentic situations.

To help them become aware of cultural differences, to acquire positive attitudes toward members of another culture, and to develop an appreciation of contributions made by others to our own.

Educational Objectives.

To enable the children, through direct experience in learning a second language at an age when they are more conscious than when they learned their first, gradually to acquire a new perspective on their own language, on the nature of language in general, and on the process of language learning.

To help children acquire a better ear and a better-trained tongue than would otherwise be possible, thus creating a greater "readiness" to learn other languages later.

To enable children, at an age when they are open-minded, to acquire the concept of cultural relativity, to lay the groundwork for the kind of understanding that will better enable them to resist cultural prejudices rooted in ignorance, and to help them to work rationally for intercultural and international understanding and ultimately, it is hoped, for a peaceful human existence. To use FLES to reinforce learning in other subjects. Specifically:

To reinforce children's learning in English by the acquisition in a second language of an understanding of language structure and of habits of attentive listening and of effective self-expression.

To reinforce children's learning in social studies by means of direct or vicarious participation in foreign culture and through the acquisition of cultural awareness.

To reinforce children's learning in arithmetic by practice in number manipulation in the second language.

To reinforce children's learning in music by using songs in the second language to enrich the regular music program in cooperation with the music teacher.

To reinforce children's learning in art by occasionally applying to FLES certain activities developed by the art teacher.

To reinforce children's learning in physical education by exploring in cooperation with the physical education teacher ways of enriching the physical education program by using foreign games, dances, and other rhythmical exercises, and by occasionally applying to the language lesson activities developed by the physical education teacher.

Public Relations.

To help create in parents and other taxpayers a greater interest in the school and in education by opening the FLES classes to visits and by organizing periodic demonstrations and special programs.

To create closer cooperation between the school and the community (1) by keeping the parents carefully informed about the FLES program and about ways in which they can help their children and (2) by making all possible use of speakers of the second language and other community resources.

The reader will readily understand that some of these objectives apply more directly to the intermediate grades than to the primary. Only very gradually do the children themselves become aware of certain of these objectives. The teacher should, however, be conscious of them from the outset and throughout the FLES program.

It is important to consider the language-learning objectives as *primary* and the cultural objectives, crucial as they are, as *secondary*. Some FLES programs have not achieved the language-learning objectives at all because of their almost total pursuit of superficial cultural goals and their neglect of basic language learning.

Outline of the FLES Course

This section in the course of study should deal with the problems of continuity, progression, and articulation. Complex as are the factors that need to be considered in initiating a FLES course and in carrying it through the first year, they are relatively simple when compared with the additional elements to be fitted into place as the learner moves on from grade to grade; for as time goes on his conceptual learning improves and teaching must respect this change.[25] As already stated, a FLES program should not be started without reasonable assurance that learning will be continuous from the beginning point through the twelfth grade. But unless there is also progression, mere continuity is not enough. The course of study should, then, review in detail the way in which each year's study broadens and deepens the language-learning experience of the pupils.

THE AUDIO-LINGUAL FIRST STAGE. Educators generally agree that the first stage of language learning, especially for children, should be entirely by ear. The pupils are not provided with written texts, but the teacher uses a manual. Insufficient experimentation leaves language educators uncertain as to how long the audio-lingual stage should continue. Some would go so far as to continue it through the sixth grade. Usually the children want to read and write by the time they reach the intermediate grades, and, indeed, sometimes in the third grade. The sensitive and experienced FLES teacher can usually judge at what point this wish can be satisfied without harm to the audio-lingual learning, which of course continues throughout. Except in bilingual programs, daily periods should last from fifteen to twenty minutes and should be taught

[25] In addition to the FLES series mentioned in note 1 of this chapter, the following will be most useful in their organization for anyone working on a FLES course outline: Republic of the Philippines, *Teacher's Guide for English in Grade I, II, III, IV*; and the Commonwealth of Australia, Office of Education, *English for Newcomers to Australia*.

either by the classroom teacher, if she is fully qualified in the language, or by a visiting specialist. The length of the lesson should be strictly limited in order not to use up an undue amount of curricular time. It is important that FLES lessons be held daily, if at all possible, so as to be a regular part of the common learnings on an equal footing with any other subject in the elementary-school program. The dialogs used should be built around the usual situations: the classroom, the school, home, family, pets, games, songs, holidays, numbers, time, days of the week, seasons, weather, colors, parts of the body, clothing, marketing, meals, wild animals. In all of this, adequate provision should be made for introducing culturally authentic situations characteristic of the country or region where the language is spoken. One of the primary objects of this first stage is to give the pupils ample opportunity to hear, understand, and ultimately express themselves, always in a context of varied activities but within the restricted limits of selected situations. The work of the first grade would enlarge the active and linguistic experience of the kindergarten children, and the second and third grades would draw slightly wider circles but would primarily intensify the children's experience in hearing, understanding, speaking, and acting with greater and greater ease, using materials of limited structure and vocabulary. Since in this early stage the training of the ear is basic, hearing might well exceed speaking in something like a 60/40 proportion. Indeed, the training of the ear has been most neglected in conventional language teaching. Therefore, a course of study should provide the pupils constantly with experiences in listening with understanding.

THE INTERMEDIATE GRADES. The progression in the intermediate grades will be marked by an enlargement of the repertory of structures and vocabulary and by an extension of the number and complexity of the situations involved in the dialogs, all in accordance with the maturity of the children. The length of the lesson might be extended slightly, to twenty or thirty minutes a day. Experience in hearing, understanding speech (controlled and free expression), and acting within the limits of the presented material will, of course, continue. But what chiefly marks the difference between the primary grades and the intermediate grades is the introduction of reading and writing, if it has not already begun in the third grade. If the children have been taught to pronounce words and pattern sentences correctly and are carefully trained to understand that writing is the way words look when pictured on the page, they can be helped to avoid the temptation of pronouncing foreign words with American sounds. Writing may well consist of a judicious mixture of copying, labeling pictures, dictation, and preparing short stories with the help of the teacher.

The FLES course from kindergarten or grade one through grade six should give the children ease in using all the sounds and the basic structures of the language within predetermined limits and a vocabulary of approximately a thousand words. By listening to numerous recordings of wholly or partially familiar material and by taking home from the school library simple but attractive readers, children in the upper intermediate grades may very well extend their recognition vocabulary considerably beyond their active vocabulary and, more important, acquire a permanent taste for reading.

What the average child will lack at the end of his elementary-school course is a conscious knowledge of formal grammar, a large vocabulary, and extensive experience in reading. He will, without knowing grammar rules, have acquired habits of correct usage in direct imitation of adequate models, so that in this sense he will know grammar. It remains for the junior high school to give him conscious control of grammatical terminology and usage. As has happened earlier with English, he becomes conscious of what he already knew, and he learns the terms current in this particular branch of knowledge. The junior and senior high school should build on this groundwork, should extend the pupil's repertory of structures and vocabulary, and should give him more intensive and extensive experience in reading, preferably within the framework of the Advanced Placement Program.[26]

MATERIALS. The FLES course of study should also contain a section on materials. A list of materials and supplementary aids, chosen from Elizabeth Keesee's selection of *Useful Materials for the Elementary School Teacher of Modern Languages*, published by the United States Office of Education, and from Jane Scott Chamberlain's *Source Materials for Teachers of Foreign Languages*, published by the National Education Association Department of Foreign Languages, serves the FLES teacher directly but is also useful for

[26] See Chapter 1, note 5.

parents and other interested members of the community. Parents will need careful guidance in their proper use, for considerable harm can be done if printed materials are put prematurely in the hands of the children themselves.

Communities would be well advised to adopt one or another of the numerous existing manuals rather than spend a great deal of time developing new materials. This is especially true since satisfactory materials require the collaboration of technically competent professionals in the fields of elementary education, child learning, linguistics, cultural anthropology, and language learning. A committee of FLES teachers would find it more useful to devote their time to adapting existing materials, elaborating satisfactory evaluation procedures, and experimenting with new techniques.

As has been suggested, most FLES materials are organized around topics or situations, such as the classroom, the school, the family, pets, colors, and so forth. These are normally introduced in order of immediacy. Thus, for example, the classroom is likely to receive first attention, for it is natural that young children should wish first to bring under linguistic control the immediate environment. They will want then to deal with each new field of experience in the same fashion—in the same way Gouin's nephew assimilated his experience on first seeing a mill.

Some manuals, like those of Margit MacRae, stress the story approach. Stories have the advantage of providing ample listening materials in interesting form and can easily be adapted to practice in speaking. Other manuals, like the Modern Language Association FLES series, use dialogs. The dialog and story approaches may be combined to good advantage, for the dialog tends to emphasize the immediate, the prosaic, while the story appeals to the child's imagination. The quality of imagination is such an important part of the child's makeup that something approaching 50 per cent of the material should in my opinion be primarily literary and imaginative. Songs, games, dances, dramatic sketches, and coloring and building materials are also effective tools of language teaching.

METHOD. As important as the materials is the method of presenting them. Most FLES manuals are explicit in providing the teacher with instructions for using the materials. Today's FLES teacher is lucky in having at his disposal a book by Elizabeth Keesee, a specialist in foreign languages in the United States Office of Education, entitled *Modern Foreign Languages in the Elementary School: Teaching Techniques.*[27] Free of a doctrinaire tone, this book is soundly conceived and gives concrete examples of good current practices. Combined with the full instructions contained in teacher's manuals, it will provide the guidance in method needed by the FLES teacher.

Among subjects not always listed in FLES manuals are the following: cooperation with the public library in the recording or reading of stories in foreign languages; correspondence with individuals or schools in another country, either by letter or by tape; participation in a people-to-people program, in a program for the preservation and cultivation of other languages in a community, or in a town-twinning project.

Evaluation

Another important and perhaps final section in the FLES course of study should provide suggestions for testing. No FLES program should be set up without an adequate plan for evaluation. Ideally, a program should be experimentally designed, that is, it should be so constructed as to place two matched groups of pupils in contrast, one to receive instruction in a foreign language and the other not. Such an arrangement would ascertain whether the FLES group, by virtue of the extra load, will achieve less in other subjects than the non-FLES group.

In practice it is not easy to persuade a community to undertake such an arrangement, for the parents of the non-FLES group would feel that their children are being deprived of something important and would protest. This being so, the next best way to measure achievement is to compare test scores in non-FLES subjects before and after the introduction of FLES.

A second element in an evaluation program is the testing of achievement in the foreign language: in listening comprehension, in speaking, in reading, in writing, in grammar, and in cultural attitudes and awareness. Such testing reveals to what extent the an-

[27] An interesting comparison of the philosophy of this book with that, say, of Otto Jespersen's *How to Teach a Foreign Language,* first published in 1904, reveals greater differences between contemporaries than between progressives separated by several generations.

nounced objectives are being achieved. Unfortunately there are as yet no standardized FLES tests, so they will have to be constructed locally. This is not altogether bad, for they can then be made to fit the local situation.

However it is done, it is essential to have a testing program. Without it, FLES teachers have no dependable way of knowing whether their objectives are realistic and to what extent they are achieving these objectives. More important, if FLES is attacked, its proponents have no objective defense unless they have established clear and reasonable goals and proved by means of a sound testing program that these goals are being achieved.

Summary

The FLES course of study represents the difference between improvisation and planning. Improvisation accounts for so many past failures in FLES. But the mere existence of a cooperatively developed course of study, provided it is constantly revised and improved, demonstrates that a school district is aiming at quality in its FLES program.

8. The Teacher of FLES

THE GREATEST SINGLE OBSTACLE to the growth of the FLES movement is the shortage of qualified teachers. This fact has emerged from every study. The deficiency is both quantitative and qualitative: there are not enough teachers and too many of those who do teach are not fully qualified. That FLES should, nevertheless, continue to expand under these inauspicious circumstances is truly remarkable.

Teacher Deficiencies

Of obvious importance is the quantitative aspect of the problem. It has already been noted that, ever since the last century, liberal arts colleges and universities have tended to shirk their responsibility for preparing teachers for the elementary and secondary schools. Their reluctance called into existence normal schools, which, though lacking the academic resources of the liberal arts colleges, nevertheless undertook to prepare teachers for the elementary schools and, to a lesser extent, for the secondary schools. One of the areas in which normal schools—and the teachers colleges and state colleges that grew out of them—were most deficient was in foreign-language instruction. Until recently, only a few scattered colleges —New York State College for Teachers at Albany and the New Jersey State College at Montclair, for example—of those specializing in teacher preparation have offered a major in foreign languages.[1]

[1] See the Modern Language Association of America survey report, "Modern

The situation is improving rapidly, however. A recent Modern Language Association survey[2] reveals that 46 teachers colleges now offer enough preparation in modern languages to qualify teachers for certification. But teachers colleges constitute only 6.1 per cent of the 758 institutions that reported teacher preparation, out of a total of 1,058 canvassed. This survey also shows that "colleges specifically designated as teachers colleges are rapidly disappearing from the educational scene in the United States" and that "institutions of higher learning are becoming more and more alike."[3]

Since specialized teacher-training institutions frequently lack programs adequate for the preparation of foreign-language teachers, a majority of these teachers has been prepared, though often without enthusiasm, by general colleges and liberal arts colleges[4] or by graduate schools of liberal arts or education.[5] However, programs specifically designed to meet the needs of teachers are still the exception rather than the rule. Instead, language departments have usually certified as ready to teach any student having a major or minor in the regular academic program, and they have normally left to the department or college of education the responsibility for providing the professional preparation needed by prospective teachers. Lack of unity and cooperation in the teacher-training program has thus contributed to the insufficient number of teachers. This regrettable situation continues to the present time although there is a trend toward more constructive collaboration.[6]

Despite the growing popularity of FLES only a minority of training institutions prepare FLES teachers. According to the 1959–1960

Foreign Languages in Teacher-Training Colleges," *PMLA,* Vol. LXX, No. 4, Part 2 (September, 1955), pp. 69–77.

[2] See Wesley Childers, Barbara Bell, and Harry Margulis, "Teacher Education Curricula in the Modern Foreign Languages," in Modern Language Association, *Reports of Surveys and Studies in the Teaching of Modern Foreign Languages, 1959–1961,* pp. 153–164.

[3] *Ibid.,* p. 156.

[4] Numbering 571 or 75.3 per cent of the teacher-preparing institutions in the survey just cited.

[5] Numbering 141 or 18.6 per cent of the teacher-preparing institutions.

[6] "Among institutions of higher learning, there is a growing practice of cooperation between modern language departments and departments of education in preparation of teachers, both on the undergraduate and graduate levels" (Childers, *et al.,* "Teacher Education Curricula," p. 156).

survey, 742 out of 758 institutions, or 97.9 per cent, reported training secondary-school foreign-language teachers and only 184, or 24.3 per cent, reported training FLES teachers as well as secondary-school teachers. A total of six colleges reported the preparation of FLES teachers only.[7]

The qualitative aspect of this question is hardly separable from the quantitative.[8] As long as teachers colleges lack foreign-language departments qualified to prepare teachers and as long as liberal arts colleges fail to play their part in preparing them, the quality of teacher training is not likely to improve. Nor is there much to be hoped for in the present licensing procedure in state departments of education. A Modern Language Association survey for 1958–1960 revealed that in not a single state was ability to understand and speak a particular language *required* as a condition of a license to teach this language.[9] In fact, requirements are still generally stated in terms of a specific number of hour credits in courses bearing satisfactory titles and offered as a part of an approved program by accredited universities. Our disregard for quality is carried even further when superintendents of schools, bedeviled in their turn by the teacher shortage, assign newly appointed teachers to teach subjects for which they are not prepared. Admittedly there are serious administrative difficulties, but it is discouraging to note how often administrative convenience takes precedence over sound educational standards.

Just as academic courses are often justly accused of being only partly related to the needs of teachers, so professional courses are sometimes said to be dull, trivial, and repetitious. Only exceptionally are students who consider themselves prepared or partly prepared given an opportunity to prove themselves by taking qualifying examinations or to demonstrate to experienced observers their ability to teach. As a result, many mature persons, for example, mothers whose children have reached a less dependent age, have been rebuffed when they offered their services. Their sense of urgency to help meet the teacher shortage is met by no similar sense of urgency on the part

[7] *Ibid.*, p. 154.

[8] For a discussion of ways to meet this need see Alfred S. Hayes, *Plans for a Ph.D. in Language and Language Learning.*

[9] Anna Balakian, "Certification Requirements for Modern Language Teachers in American Public Schools (1958–1960)," *PMLA*, Vol. LXXVI, No. 2B (May, 1961), pp. 20–35.

of admissions officers in teacher-training institutions, who merely advise enrolling in a conventional two-, three-, or four-year course. Experienced and well-educated citizens have often chosen not to endure what they consider to be a time-consuming and stultifying experience. Thus, the inflexible design and mediocre quality of some teacher-training programs have contributed to the short supply of teachers by failing to utilize a possible source of new recruits.

Fortunately plans to improve certification procedures and to streamline programs of preparation are now being implemented. Some universities are making increased use of the qualifying examination. The Harvard Master of Arts in Teaching Program has done this almost from the beginning. And recently The University of Texas has made it possible for teacher candidates to receive credit for courses by taking advanced standing examinations instead of course work for a part of their program. In 1959 the Commonwealth of Pennsylvania instituted the requirement of an examination for all foreign-language teacher candidates and also made it possible for foreign-born or foreign-educated applicants with the equivalent of a bachelor's degree to be certified provisionally on the basis of these proficiency examinations. A provisional certificate secured in this manner may be made permanent upon the completion of eighteen hours in professional education and three years of satisfactory teaching, in addition to compliance with the basic regulations. This new regulation seeks to tap a hitherto little used source of teachers. The conditions for making the provisional certificate permanent give one pause, however. If teaching has been satisfactory for three years, what is the purpose of courses in professional education? We find ourselves in direct educational competition with the Soviet Union with foreign languages as one of the especially critical areas, and yet we draw up regulations as though their object were to encourage the taking of courses rather than to prepare competent teachers.

The development of the Modern Language Association Foreign-Language Proficiency Tests for Teachers and Advanced Students extends the possibility of recruiting teachers.[10] Some states and many teacher-training institutions are requiring these tests of all candi-

[10] See the Modern Language Association of America, "Proficiency Tests for Certification," Foreign Language Program Notes, *PMLA*, Vol. LXXIX, No. 2 (May, 1964), p. A-18.

dates for teaching in the field of modern languages,[11] and it would be desirable for school superintendents to require them of their teacher candidates. This single requirement would serve to improve greatly the quality of their modern-language teachers.

The urgent need of more qualified FLES teachers makes necessary consideration of the closely related questions of recruitment, preparation, and certification.

Recruitment

What are the possible sources of qualified teachers? First, there is the great increase of student interest in languages in the last few years, which will presumably continue, perhaps at an even faster rate, as modern methods emphasizing direct communication are introduced into more of our schools and colleges.[12] Likewise, modern-language enrollments in four-year accredited colleges and universities increased from 425,404 in 1958 to 483,720 in 1959, to 569,846 in 1960, 650,560 in 1961, 743,875 in 1963, and 872,092 in 1965.[13] These increases will be augmented by new waves of secondary-school students who have had the advantage of from one to seven years of FLES. Some of these students, particularly the ones who have

[11] "FL Teacher Certification [in New York State] by Examination," Foreign Language Program Notes, *PMLA*, Vol. LXXVIII, No. 5 (December, 1963), p. vii; Texas Foreign Language Association, "Proficiency Tests in Pennsylvania," *Texas Foreign Language Association Bulletin*, Vol. IV, No. 3 (October, 1962), p. 4; "Foreign Language Teacher Preparation in New Hampshire," *Texas Foreign Language Association Bulletin*, Vol. III, No. 4 (November, 1961), p. 6; Wilmarth H. Starr, "MLA Foreign Language Proficiency Tests for Teachers and Advanced Students," *PMLA*, Vol. LXXVII, No. 4, Part 2 (September, 1962), pp. 31–37.

[12] Between 1948 and 1958 there was a 75.3 per cent increase in modern-foreign-language enrollments in high school, as compared with a 22.2 per cent increase in United States population age 14–17 and a 46.3 per cent increase in high-school population grades 9–12 (see J. Wesley Childers, "Foreign Language Offerings and Enrollments in Public Secondary Schools, Fall, 1959," in Modern Language Association, *Reports of Surveys and Studies in the Teaching of Modern Foreign Languages, 1959–1961*, p. 17, Table C).

[13] Mara Vamos, Harry Margulis, and Frank White, "Modern Foreign Language Enrollments in Colleges and Universities, Fall, 1958, and Fall, 1959," in Modern Language Association, *Reports of Surveys and Studies in the Teaching of Modern Foreign Languages, 1959–1961*, p. 51; Nina Greer Herslow and James F. Dershem, *Foreign Language Enrollments in Institutions of Higher Education, Fall, 1965*, pp. vii, 7.

learned the elements of a second language under satisfactory teaching conditions, may well be interested in becoming language teachers themselves.

A second source of teacher supply is to be found in the thousands of American children who have lived abroad and who have received language instruction under circumstances that are more favorable than are those found at home.[14] These children will not only have acquired language skills, but many will have had an opportunity, despite the regrettable isolation of American families in military compounds, to experience directly a foreign culture.

The speakers of other languages in our own population represent still another source of possible language teachers. Some of these will, of course, have to be retrained in a more nearly standard form of speech. The large number of native speakers of German, Italian, and Russian, not to mention Polish, Chinese, Japanese, Portuguese, and the Scandinavian languages can also be used in FLES programs.[15]

Lastly, an expanded exchange of teachers between the United States and the countries whose languages are taught in our public schools could constitute a fruitful source of supply. Already, every year, some six hundred American and foreign teachers in about fifty countries undertake teaching assignments abroad under the Teacher Exchange Program of the Fulbright and the Smith-Mundt Acts.[16]

How can teacher-training institutions increase their teacher supply? First and most obviously, academic and professional educators who are interested in the problem can develop cooperatively an effective teacher-training program within their institutions. Such a program should, without neglecting a liberal education, be designed

[14] As of November 1962, there were enrolled in Dependents Schools in Europe the following numbers of American children: In high school, grades 9 to 12, 10,679, of whom 7,525 were enrolled in German; in French, 2,606; in Latin, 507; in Italian, 193; in Russian, 39. In junior high school, grades 7 and 8, the corresponding numbers were 8,395, of whom 6,797 were enrolled in foreign languages. In the elementary school the total enrollment in Germany was 36,057; in France, 6,226; and in Italy, 1,172, of whom 99 out of 100 were enrolled in a foreign language (United States Army, Headquarters, 45 Army Dependents Education Group, *Statistical Report*, March 15, 1963).

[15] See Joshua A. Fishman, *Language Loyalty in the United States: The Maintenance and Perpetuation of Non-English Mother Tongues by American Ethnic and Religious Groups*, p. 44.

[16] U.S., Department of Health, Education, and Welfare, Office of Education, *Your Exchange Teacher from Abroad*, Publication No. OE–14022.

to meet the specific needs of foreign-language teachers. The Modern Language Association has defined the academic qualifications of a modern-language teacher,[17] has developed proficiency tests to measure these competencies as objectively as possible, and, in cooperation with the National Association of State Directors of Teacher Education and Certification, has prepared some "Guidelines for Teacher Education Programs in Modern Foreign Languages."[18] A first step would be the use of the Modern Language Association Foreign Language Proficiency Tests. Ideally they should be required for diagnostic purposes at the beginning of the professional training course, in the student's junior year, and again near the end of the training period as a condition of recommendation by the teacher-preparing institution.

Preparation

A definition of competencies on the professional side is lacking also. Educators have long struggled with this problem, but perhaps from the wrong point of view. It is not necessary to form comprehensive and philosophically consistent definition of a good teacher, but rather it is important to establish some simple working principles. Every school administrator—superintendent, principal, supervisor, department chairman—is accustomed to judging a teacher. An administrator visiting a classroom reaches a positive or negative judgment very quickly. He may wish to prolong his visit or repeat it in order to check and recheck his impressions, but once he has had an adequate opportunity to observe a teacher in action he rarely doubts the validity of his judgment. He has specific criteria, explicit or not. He seeks answers to such questions as these: Are the children interested? Are they learning? Is what they are learning worth learning? What is the attitude of the teacher toward the children as human beings? Is the class tempo fast enough, slow enough, varied enough? Has the teacher prepared a lesson plan? Is he resourceful and does he use a wide repertory of materials, techniques, and aids? All

[17] See Appendix D.

[18] See Appendix F. See also the special Golden Anniversary Issue of *The Modern Language Journal*, Vol. L, No. 6 (October, 1966), which is almost entirely devoted to an exposition of the guidelines together with a history of the events leading up to them. Also issued as a separate publication.

these questions and others could perhaps be summarized under three headings: What kind of a person is the teacher? How much does he know? And can he teach? Both the academic and the professional educator are interested in the first point though their criteria may differ. The academic educator is primarily concerned with the second point although the professional educator cannot afford to be uninterested in it. And the third point is primarily of importance to the professional educator although the academic educator cannot neglect it.

First, character and personality are what the teacher candidate himself brings to the task out of his heritage and early environment. To be sure, since young people are susceptible to the influence of individual teachers and to the intellectual climate in which they work, it is most important that the training staff be made up as much as possible of distinguished human beings. Only such persons can create the exhilarating atmosphere needed for creative effort.

Secondly, how much a person knows is, in some small part at least, a function of courses that he has "taken." A teacher-training institution should, therefore, have available for its teacher candidates carefully planned and coordinated courses both in the academic and in the professional areas. These courses should be well taught—if possible, brilliantly taught—for there is nothing more persuasive than example. On the academic side, the critical areas are: skill in the use of the language; knowledge of the nature, structure, and perhaps history of the language; knowledge of the history, civilization, and culture of the people whose language is being studied, with a particular emphasis on literature; and an extended personal experience of living within this culture. On the professional side, reasonable knowledge may be expected in the following fields: history and philosophy of education, especially as related to contemporary American education; human growth and learning, with emphasis on the psychology of language learning; testing, measurement, and experimental design and techniques; the school in American society; and, most important, a teaching apprenticeship or internship under adequate observation and direction by both academic and professional educators.

The above considerations anticipate somewhat the third point: Is the teacher able to teach? This again depends to a slight degree on courses taken. To a much greater extent, ability to teach is a function of character, personality, attitude, and experience. The latter includes in normal cases some sixteen years of direct personal involvement in American schools and colleges. Teacher candidates whose education has wholly or in part been acquired in other countries or who are largely self-educated will bring to bear invaluable experience of a different kind. Those who are responsible for teacher-training are naturally aware of this vast area of useful experience, and some make full use of it in their teacher-training program. In this respect, teacher education has an advantage over most other professions, into whose mysteries neophytes enter in an almost total state of innocence.

This analysis lays bare the essential elements of an adequate teacher-training program. They include (1) procedures for screening applicants and directing them in an individually planned program of preparation; (2) course content corresponding to the academic and professional areas listed; course syllabi, reading lists, and language laboratory facilities; and (3) a teaching apprenticeship or facilities for a paid internship.[19]

In most teacher-training programs there is considerable waste, since large numbers of students are admitted without possessing the essential personal qualities or motivation for becoming satisfactory teachers. If a competent committee or board is convinced that a student applying for a teacher-training program cannot reasonably be expected to win the recommendation of the institution's council on teacher education, it should discourage the applicant. In case of doubt, a student should be admitted on probation for a period of time, a semester, an academic year, or at most two academic years. During this period the faculty owes it to the student to observe him carefully in all activities before admitting him to a teaching candidacy. A final screening should take place at the end of the teacher-training course. If the previous screenings have been efficient, very few teacher candidates need be eliminated at this point. However, it is theoretically possible that a candidate, though promising in earlier

[19] These elements are spelled out and an intelligent general view is suggested by Nelson Brooks in his articles, "The Ideal Preparation of Foreign Language Teachers," *The Modern Language Journal*, Vol. L, No. 2 (February, 1966), pp. 71–78, and "Language Learning: A Multi-Discipline Approach," *The DFL Bulletin*, Vol. IV, No. 2 (May, 1965), pp. 1–5.

parts of the training course, has turned out during the final apprenticeship not to have the necessary qualities. Such a student must then, firmly if regretfully, be eliminated.

It does not fall within the scope of the present book to outline the content of specific courses in a teacher-training program. Course content is suggested by the Statement of Qualifications (Appendix D), the Standards for Teacher-Education Programs in Modern Foreign Languages (Appendix E), and the Guidelines for Teacher-Education Programs in Modern Foreign Languages (Appendix F). What does need underlining is the fact that there is nothing sacred about courses. Education is in the last analysis self-education, what an individual makes of his opportunities, whether these are provided by circumstances, by himself, or by an educational institution. Since teachers are agreed in applauding intellectual independence and individual initiative, it is ironic that, as a profession, they often do all they can to frustrate these very qualities by a seeming insistence on course credits rather than on knowledge or ability. This insidious form of anti-intellectualism needs to be overcome as quickly as possible. If a body of educators is agreed on what a teacher needs to know and do, let them set this down on paper, clearly and simply. At the beginning of a teacher-training program a teacher candidate should be handed such a statement and given a choice between acquiring the necessary knowledge and skills in course or out of course. The principle of recognizing knowledge or proficiency however acquired should be vigorously affirmed. Only in this way can educators really recognize individual differences, about which they claim to be concerned. Each course of study should have its syllabus and its list of readings, problems, and projects. In fact, though stimulating teachers will always be needed to attract students, each course should be programed for self-instruction. Courses should have their examinations at stated times and these examinations should be exacting. All of the usual facilities should be provided for the student, but it is time that higher education, and particularly teacher education, should honor independent achievement.

The teaching apprenticeship is by universal agreement recognized as one of the essential elements of teacher training, perhaps the most important.[20] No program can, therefore, neglect this aspect of a

[20] James Bryant Conant (*The Education of American Teachers*, p. 142), for

teacher's preparation. But it can be well or badly organized; and it is sometimes badly organized since we too often prefer an inexpensive program to a sound one. Guidance and observation of the apprentice teacher are alike the responsibility of the language educator, the professional educator, the principal of the school providing the opportunity for the apprenticeship, and the cooperating teacher to whose class the student is assigned. All of these persons should cooperate as a team in observing a candidate and in reaching a consensus as to his competency. The language educator judges primarily whether the candidate knows his subject; the professional educator judges primarily whether he possesses the requisite teaching skills; and all together judge whether the candidate has the qualities of character and personality necessary for success in the classroom. *Time* is incidental and varies greatly with the individual teacher candidate. Some candidates will be able to demonstrate quickly that they are completely ready to teach. Others will require a full semester to provide such demonstration, and still others will need slow, patient coaching over an extended period of time in order to become acceptable.

There are limited resources for teacher apprenticeships. Most communities have only a few outstanding cooperating teachers and in addition may not be able to reduce their teaching load. In view of this, the paid internship offers an alternate solution. The intern is often welcome when the apprentice is not, for he fills a vacancy. He also tries his wings under more nearly normal conditions than the apprentice. It is important, however, that he be carefully supervised.

By organizing a training course according to differing individual needs, a teacher-training institution is likely to attract more and better students. Those who are able, experienced, and self-confident are the ones most likely to respond to the challenge of such a program. In order to help overcome the shortage of qualified teachers an institution should consider organizing a vigorous recruitment program. Since the basic language skills—understanding, speaking, reading, and writing—are those which require the longest time to be learned, the training institution can greatly increase its efficiency by recruiting candidates who are already fully or partially qualified in a for-

---

example, says, "the one indisputably essential element in professional education is practice teaching."

eign language. Thus, if such an institution finds itself in an area where another language is widely spoken, it can make a special appeal to educated speakers of this language by offering its facilities to administer proficiency tests and to inform a prospective teacher candidate in detail concerning his proficiencies and deficiencies. It is conceivable, for example, that a native speaker of Spanish in the Southwest may need no training in listening comprehension and little training in speaking. But he may require considerable training in writing and a good deal of experience in reading. This could be determined rather quickly on the basis of the Modern Language Association Foreign Language Proficiency tests and interviews, and the candidate could be told what he needs to know by the end of a training course and how he may proceed, either in the course or on his own, to overcome his deficiencies.

Certification

All that has hitherto been said leads inevitably to the conclusion that certification should be based on knowledge and proficiency, *however acquired*. Fortunately, there is an increasing trend on the part of state departments of education to place on the teacher-training institution the responsibility for judging the total readiness of a candidate to teach. This is as it should be. Any other course of action reduces the function of the state department of education to that of bookkeeping instead of to that of supervising and safeguarding the *quality* of public education within its jurisdiction.

One matter is urgent: state departments of education cooperating nationally need to devise uniform certification procedures so that out-of-state teachers may be more easily recruited. Already eight states in the Northeast honor one another's certificates, a long step forward.

It remains to add a suggestion that relates more to our federal government than to our states, communities, and individual institutions. It has to do with the intensification of teacher exchanges. It has long been recognized that from the academic point of view the well-educated native speaker of a language is in some ways an ideal teacher. In many countries there are available qualified and experienced teachers who would appreciate the opportunity to spend a year or two teaching their language to American children. At the same time most countries show an increasing desire to learn English, which means that there are more openings for native speakers of English to teach abroad. Therefore, it would seem feasible for our government, under the leadership of the United States Office of Education and of the Department of State, to organize teacher exchanges on a more extensive basis than at present. Clearly, successful exchanges would involve careful screening of applicants, careful orientation programs in the summer preceding the school year, and careful guidance and supervision of the foreign teacher on the job. Such an experience would be invaluable, both for the foreign teacher, who would have an opportunity to improve his knowledge of English, and for the American teacher abroad, who would similarly be able to improve his command of the other language at the same time that he was enjoying the personal experience of life in a foreign culture. Both could profit from the increased perspective on the theory and practice of language education and could, after returning to their home posts, continue to correspond about professional matters.

Conclusion

Chief responsibility for improving the quality of teacher preparation and for supplying teachers in adequate numbers falls on our teacher-education institutions. Guidelines prepared by the Modern Language Association and the National Association of State Directors of Teacher Education and Certification provide a detailed plan for a teacher-education program. This plan includes a proposal for the certification of qualified teacher candidates on the basis of demonstrated proficiency, however acquired. Moreover, several suggestions have been advanced for tapping new sources of teacher supply. Hopefully these proposals will in time enable us to overcome the teacher shortage that is inhibiting the normal development of FLES.

9. Retrospect and Prospect

IN THE FOREGOING PAGES several aspects of the exciting educational movement, FLES, were examined. Its historical origins in this country and comparable though by no means identical practices in other countries were outlined. FLES has been justified in educational theory, and, because of an ingrained prejudice against foreign languages in American education, this justification has been extended to include foreign-language education in general. The values, objectives, materials, and methods of FLES teaching, and the role of the FLES teacher and related problems of recruitment, preparation, and certification were examined in detail. The analysis shows that, repeating the pattern of German FLES in the nineteenth century, the present movement, while still growing steadily and favored by a critical national need, is beset by certain weaknesses.

Perhaps the most conspicuous of these is the short supply of qualified teachers. This shortage, though occasioned by deeply rooted educational deficiencies and popular indifference, presents no insurmountable difficulty. We have a potential supply of teachers many times the actual supply. Our teacher-training institutions do not lack the resources and facilities—only the inclination—for converting promising recruits into highly qualified teachers. To be sure, the organization of effective training programs of sufficient flexibility to satisfy wide individual differences requires open-mindedness, a readiness to face the fact that traditional programs are not necessarily the best, and a willingness by both academic and professional educators to cooperate and to experiment.

A second weakness stems from a widespread misunderstanding— on the part of educators, including language teachers themselves, and of the public—of the nature of language and of the language-learning process. Because of this misunderstanding teachers have in the past taught language skills inadequately and in the wrong order and have achieved results that satisfied no one, least of all themselves. Our almost universal inability to conceive of another language except in terms of English rests on a kind of cultural myopia. Language as a vehicle and a reflection of behavior patterns and value systems is for many a relatively new concept, and the translation of this concept into a consistent teaching practice will require time. One of the most exacting responsibilities that the new generation of modern-language teachers has is to learn these basic concepts thoroughly and in turn to transmit to fellow educators and the general public a clear understanding of them. This is a demanding task but not an impossible one.

More alarming and more difficult to deal with is a widely shared willingness among those responsible for controlling our educational policies to accept mediocre standards. Reputable universities are willing to certify as ready to teach, and state departments of education are willing to license, candidates who can neither understand nor speak the language they propose to teach. School administrators are willing to assign teachers qualified in one subject to teach another subject for which they are not qualified. Communities are ready to launch a FLES program without understanding what is involved and without taking the steps necessary to prepare properly for it and to assure its continuity. Social studies teachers hail FLES as an enrichment of the social-studies program but fail to comprehend that learning to understand and speak another language under favorable conditions is a form of participation in another culture, not merely another way of talking *about* that culture.

Perhaps most insidious of all is the very widespread and unrealistic tendency to want quality in education but to vote against the tax increases needed to support it. It is obvious that education, like our national defense—and, indeed, as an important part of our national defense—must be supported and that, in an expanding economy, its cost will increase. It is our collective responsibility to hold this increased cost to a minimum. The all too commonly accepted way to do this is to resist all pressures to increase the budget. Only rarely are educational values considered carefully in relation to their cost. Thus, many school boards meet the pressure of FLES by organizing an out-of-school program and asking the parents to pay for it. Regular in-school programs are often started without sufficient financial support, which makes their survival precarious; and an occasional successful program is brought to a sudden halt by a coalition of "the opposition":[1] the economy-minded owners of property and those who see FLES as an educational frill or who regard it as a threat to other subjects in the school curriculum.

Many programs are launched without adequate provision for supervision, coordination, experimentation, and evaluation. A program of any size requires a supervisor or coordinator to assure continuity and particularly to achieve articulation between elementary- and secondary-school foreign-language instruction. FLES, not yet accepted as one of the "common learnings," is in particular need of experimentation, and carefully conducted experiments take time and money. An essential part of any good FLES program is evaluation. Are the objectives being achieved, and to what extent? Class visits, meetings, developing materials, designing experiments, and evaluating, all these require time, which of course adds to the cost. Some committees are not willing to assume these added costs, even though they may want a FLES program. The truth is that FLES is still condemned to play a defensive role. Many school administrators will humor parents who want FLES by reluctantly permitting a minimal program, preferably out of school, while welcoming a course in driver training, which should be handled by a state department of motor vehicles or of public safety. School boards and administrators

---

[1] For example, a newly elected school board in Montgomery County, Maryland, voted in 1963, without holding hearings or otherwise considering the educational value of an unusually successful program, to discontinue it despite protests of parents. Another case is described in "Special Report: FLES Abandoned in Arlington," *Bulletin of the Modern Foreign Language Association of Virginia,* Vol. XX, No. 2 (April, 1964). On the other hand there are cases in which FLES is dropped after having a fair trial because it has not achieved sufficient quality or success (see Mary M. Page, "We Dropped FLES," *The Modern Language Journal,* Vol. L, No. 3 [March, 1966], pp. 139–141). The difficulties in the way of achieving quality are explained by Ruth R. Cornfield ("The Other Side of FLES," *Hispania,* Vol. XLIX, No. 3 [September, 1966], pp. 495–497).

cite the various pressures for adding subjects to the curriculum and often seem to lack sure criteria for judging the relative values of the various subjects proposed. Not until a community decides the fundamental question of educational values can this problem be solved.

Lack of teachers; failure of teacher-training institutions to train FLES teachers; lack of funds or of willingness to meet legitimate educational costs; misunderstanding of what preparation and support a FLES program requires; unwillingness to think about, discuss, and reach a consensus on fundamental educational values—how can FLES possibly succeed in the face of so many obstacles?

Under more "normal," relaxed circumstances, FLES might very well not succeed. Our system of state and local educational autonomy, in contrast to the centralization of control in most countries of the world, exposes FLES and many other aspects of education to the winds of favor or disfavor. This is at once the weakness and the strength of our system. We cannot, as is done in other parts of the world, leave our public education altogether in the hands of professionals, however competent they may be. Control of education in the United States rests with lay boards that are in turn responsible to the community. When things work out well, popular responsibility means popular support, and a powerful educational system results, but we have a long way to go before reaching this goal everywhere. Sound professional theory is a factor but unfortunately not the decisive factor in our thinking about FLES. With our tendency to "get along" with what we have, not to "rock the boat," we may well prove those educators right who have said, "Oh, FLES is just a fad; it won't last long."

Fortunately the Russians, who have already, beginning with Sputnik, contributed so much to our education, and now the Chinese, leave us little choice. The Russians threaten us directly with their foreign-language instruction, which already permits them to talk to the underdeveloped peoples of the world in their own languages and to teach them needed techniques—and incidentally Communist ideology. They now *force* us to upgrade our language instruction as they have forced us to upgrade our teaching of mathematics and science. Better international communication is a condition of our survival, as Congress recognized in passing the National Defense Education Act of 1958. It would be ideal if we had a fervent belief in education and particularly in equality of educational opportunity

—to which we readily pay lip service—but since achievement of these ideals would require that we think hard and work hard and that we respect hard thought and work in others, we are not inclined to pay the price unless we are forced to. It is the purest chance that we are being forced by world events to make unusual efforts, to utilize a *part* of our capacity for hard work and rigorous thought.

There is little in the history of FLES to suggest that it will survive through a sense of good workmanship. Quality has been sporadic and exceptional. But here again we may be in luck, for just as FLES seems about to succumb to an all-enveloping mediocrity, a new trend in language education has appeared to point the way to a higher level of achievement. Bilingual education, beginning in the sixties, adds at least three new principles that are applicable to FLES. First, bilingual schooling begins in preschool classes, in kindergarten, or in the first grade—where FLES *should* have started in the first place. Secondly, two languages are used as media of instruction, thus suggesting that the second language is a real language and not just a school subject. And thirdly, the teachers in bilingual programs are usually native speakers and authentic representatives of their culture. FLES could well profit from the use of these three new educational factors.

FLES hangs precariously in the balance. On alternate days I think it will succeed—or fail. On the dark days I think of the thousands of guidance counselors in our high schools who steer our adolescents away from foreign languages—as from music, art, and literature—and I wonder what the products of a good FLES program can expect of them. Or I consider the rather poor workmanship of some teachers, modern-language teachers among them, and marvel that so many students surmount the obstacles these teachers put in their way. Or again I feel oppressed by the lack of motivation we provide children who are still capable of eagerness and inspiration. What trivialities we feed them when they are hungry for new knowledge and experience! And then on the bright days I am buoyed up by the thought of some FLES teachers I have seen whose affection for little children is overwhelming but not sentimental, whose resourcefulness in finding new ways and materials is inexhaustible, and whose respect for each individual child is but part and parcel of a respect for humanity itself.

The forces of light and of darkness, of distinction and of mediocrity are, in education as in all human activities, locked in uncertain combat. We have seen the hope-inspiring movement called FLES surrounded and all but overwhelmed by mediocrity. This ever-present and multiform power of mediocrity leaves the ultimate success of FLES very much in doubt. Nor will the irrepressible enthusiasm and magical skill of individual FLES teachers be enough to decide the outcome. What is required is unfortunately nothing less than the mobilization of the whole language-teaching profession for a no-nonsense kind of teaching and the vigorous support of FLES by the educational establishment and by fellow citizens. Anyone who thinks that this is asking too much for FLES or for any other legitimate segment of American education gives substance to the doubt that I feel on alternate days. But since FLES has at least maintained itself for the last fifteen years and since our international competitors are not likely to reduce their pressure, perhaps we may live to see its triumph and with it the competent teaching and learning of foreign languages in high school and college as well. Would that this might come to pass as a result of virtue rather than of necessity.

APPENDIX A

Values of Foreign Language Study[1]

The study of a foreign language, like that of most other basic disciplines, is both a progressive experience and a progressive acquisition of a skill. At no point can the experience be considered complete, or the skill perfect. Many pupils study a foreign language only two years; longer time is of course needed to approach mastery. At any point, however, the progress made in a language, when properly taught, will have positive value and lay a foundation upon which further progress can be built. It is evident therefore that the expectancy of values to be derived from language study must be relative to the amount of time and effort devoted to it.

The study of a foreign language, skillfully taught under proper conditions, provides a new experience, progressively enlarging the pupil's horizon through the introduction to a new medium of communication and a new culture pattern, and progressively adding to his sense of pleasurable achievement. This experience involves:

1. The acquisition of a set of skills, which can become real mastery for professional use when practiced long enough. The international contacts and responsibilities of the United States makes the possession of these skills by more and more Americans a matter of national urgency. These skills include:

a) The increasing ability to understand a foreign language when spoken, making possible greater profit and enjoyment in such steadily expanding activities as foreign travel, business abroad, foreign language movies and broadcasts.

b) The increasing ability to speak a foreign language in direct communication with people of another culture, either for business or for pleasure.

c) The ability to read the foreign language with progressively greater ease and enjoyment, making possible the broadening effects of direct acquaintance with the recorded thoughts of another people, or making possible study for vocational or professional (e.g. scientific or journalistic) purposes.

[1] Reprinted from *PMLA*, Vol. LXXI, No. 4, Part 2 (September, 1956), p. xiv.

2. A new understanding of language, progressively revealing to the pupil the structure of language and giving him a new perspective on English, as well as an increased vocabulary and greater effectiveness in expression.

3. A gradually expanding and deepening knowledge of a foreign country—its geography, history, social organization, literature, and culture—and, as a consequence, a better perspective on American culture and a more enlightened Americanism through adjustment to the concept of differences between cultures.

Progress in any one of these experiences is relative to the emphasis given it in the instructional program and to the interests and aptitude of the learner. Language skills, like all practical skills, may never be perfected, and may be later forgotten, yet the enlarging and enriching results of the cultural experience endure throughout life.

APPENDIX B

Foreign Languages in the Elementary Schools[1]

After more than three years of studying a variety of reports on the teaching of foreign languages in the public elementary schools, we express our approval of this popular movement in American education. In our judgment the movement deserves the support of parents and educational administrators because:

1. it recognizes the evidence concerning the process of language learning, introducing study of a second language to children at an age when they are naturally curious about language, when they have fewest inhibitions, and when they imitate most easily new sounds and sound patterns;

2. it recognizes the fact that the greatest natural barriers to international understanding are the unreasoning reactions to "foreign-ness" which are often acquired in childhood but which may be offset by experiences with foreign speech and behavior; and

3. it recognizes the fact that real proficiency in the use of a foreign language requires progressive learning over an extended period.

It is our further judgment that the public should be warned against faddish aspects of this movement. No new venture in American education can long prosper without the wholehearted support of parents, teachers, and educational administrators in a given community. Proponents of foreign language study in the elementary schools should not, therefore, initiate programs until:

1. a majority of the parents concerned approve at least an experimental program, and

2. local school boards and administrators are convinced that necessary preparations have been made.

Necessary preparations include:

1. recruitment of an adequate number of interested teachers who have both skill in guiding children and the necessary language qualifications,

2. availability of material appropriate to each age level, with new approaches and a carefully planned syllabus for each grade, and

[1] Reprinted from *PMLA*, Vol. LXXI, No. 4, Part 2 (September, 1956), p. xxi.

3. adequate provisions for appraisal.

The success of existing programs thus initiated, prepared for, and appraised convinces us of the urgent need of providing, for children who have the ability and desire, the opportunity for continuous progress in language study into and through junior and senior high school.

APPENDIX C

Foreign Languages in the Elementary School:
A Second Statement of Policy[1]

A. *Five Years Later.* Since the publication in 1956 of the first MLA statement on FLES there has been increasing awareness of the need for an early start to foreign-language learning. There is equal awareness of the dangers of inadequate attempts to meet this need. Hundreds of communities have ignored our warning against "faddish aspects of this movement" and our insistence upon "necessary preparations." Many of the resulting programs have been wasteful and disappointing, and they have misled many citizens about the nature and value of foreign-language learning.

B. *Redefinition.* We must sharpen our definition of FLES. It is not an end in itself but the elementary-school (K–6) part of a language-learning program that should extend unbroken through grade 12. It has 15- or 20-minute sessions at least three times a week as an integral part of the school day. It concerns itself primarily with learning the four language skills, beginning with listening and speaking. Other values (improved understanding of language in general, intercultural understanding, broadened horizons), though important, are secondary.

C. *FLES in Sequence.* We believe that FLES, as here defined, is an essential part of the long sequence, ten years or more, needed to approach mastery of a second language in school. There is good evidence that the learning of a second language considerably quickens and eases the learning of a third language, even when there is little or no relation between the languages learned. Since children imitate skillfully and with few inhibitions in the early school years, the primary grades (K–3) are the ideal place to begin language learning, and the experience is in itself exciting and rewarding.

D. *Priority.* If a school system cannot provide both a FLES program and a 6-year secondary-school FL sequence (grades 7–12), it should work *first* toward establishing the grade 7–12 sequence. Unless there is a solid junior- and senior-HS program of FL learning with due stress on the listen-

[1] Reprinted from *PMLA*, Vol. LXXVI, No. 2, Part 2B, (May, 1961), pp. vi-vii.

ing and speaking skills and fully articulated with the previous instruction, FLES learnings wither on the vine.

E. *Articulation.* It requires: 1) a FL program in grades 7 and 8 for graduates of FLES, who should never be placed with beginners at *any* grade level; 2) a carefully planned coordination of the FLES and secondary-school programs; 3) a frequent interchange of visits and information among the FL teachers at all levels; 4) an overall coordination by a single FL supervisor or by a committee of administrators. These cooperative efforts should result in a common core of language learning that will make articulation smooth and effective.

F. *Experimental Programs.* Experimentation is desirable in education, but we know enough about FLES methods and materials to obviate the need for "pilot" or "experimental" programs if these adjectives mean no more than "tentative" or "reluctant." If a shortage of teachers makes it impossible to offer instruction to all the pupils in a grade, a partial FLES program is an acceptable temporary expedient, but it will pose a special scheduling problem in grade 7. An "experimental" program should be a genuine experiment, not a desperate, inadequately planned program instituted by community pressure against the advice of authorities in the field.

G. *The Teacher.* Ideally he should be an expert in the FL he teaches, with near-native accent and fluency, and also skillful in teaching young children. Few teachers are currently expert in both areas. If a teacher's FL accent is not good, he should make every effort to improve it, and meanwhile he should rely on discs or tapes to supply authentic model voices for his pupils. But since language is communication, and a child cannot communicate with a phonograph or a tape recorder, no FLES learning can be wholly successful without the regular presence in the classroom of a live model who is also an expert teacher. The shortage of such doubly skilled teachers is the most serious obstacle to the success of FLES, and every institution that trains future elementary-school teachers should offer a major in one or more FLs.

H. *Cautions.* A FLES program should be instituted only if: 1) it is an integral and serious part of the school day; 2) it is an integral and serious part of the total FL program in the school system; 3) there is close articulation with later FL learning; 4) there are available FL specialists or elementary-school teachers with an adequate command of the FL; 5) there is a planned syllabus and a sequence of appropriate teaching materials; 6) the program has the support of the administration; 7) the HS teachers of the FL recognize the same long-range objectives and practice some of the same teaching techniques as the FLES teachers.

The need for a revised statement of FLES was the subject of a conference on 27 and 28 January 1961. Participants in this conference: Theodore Andersson, Emma Birkmaier, Nelson Brooks, Josephine Bruno, Dorothy Chamberlain, Austin E. Fife, Elton Hocking, Elizabeth Keesee, Margit W. MacRae, Kenneth W. Mildenberger, Ruth Mulhauser, William R. Parker, Filomena Peloro, Gordon R. Silber, G. Winchester Stone, Jr., Mary P. Thompson, W. Freeman Twaddell, Donald D. Walsh, Helen B. Yakobson.

The statement was developed and authorized by the Advisory and Liaison Committees of the Modern Language Association, whose members are Theodore Andersson, William B. Edgerton, Austin E. Fife, John G. Kunstmann, William R. Parker, Norman P. Sacks, Gordon R. Silber, Jack M. Stein, Louis Tenenbaum, W. Freeman Twaddell, and Helen B. Yakobson.

APPENDIX D

Qualifications for Teachers of Modern Foreign Languages[1]

Competence	Superior	Good	Minimal
Listening comprehension	Ability to follow closely and with ease all types of standard speech, such as rapid or group conversation and mechanically transmitted speech.	Ability to understand conversation of normal tempo, lectures, and news broadcasts.	Ability to get the sense of what an educated native says when he is making a special effort to be understood and when he is speaking on a general and familiar subject.
Speaking	Ability to speak fluently, approximating native speech in vocabulary, intonation, and pronunciation. Ability to exchange ideas and to be at ease in social situations.	Ability to talk with a native without making glaring mistakes, and with a command of vocabulary and syntax sufficient to express one's thoughts in conversation at normal speed with reasonably good pronunciation.	Ability to read aloud and to talk on prepared topics (e.g. for classroom situations) without obvious faltering, and to use the common expressions needed for getting around in the foreign country, speaking with a pronunciation understandable to a native.
Reading	Ability to read almost as easily as in English material of considerable difficulty.	Ability to read with immediate comprehension prose and verse of average difficulty and mature content.	Ability to grasp directly (i.e. without translating) the meaning of simple, nontechnical prose, except for an occasional word.

[1] Reprinted from *PMLA*, Vol. LXXVII, No. 4, Part 2 (September, 1962), p. 38.

Writing	Ability to write on a variety of subjects with idiomatic naturalness, ease of expression, and some feeling for the style of the language.	Ability to write simple "free composition" such as a letter, with clarity and correctness in vocabulary, idiom, and syntax.	Ability to write correctly sentences or paragraphs such as would be developed orally for classroom situations and to write a simple description or message without glaring errors.
Applied Linguistics	The "good" level of competency with additional knowledge of descriptive, comparative, and historical linguistics.	The "minimal" level of competency with additional knowledge of the development and present characteristics of the language.	Ability to apply to language teaching an understanding of the differences in the sound system, forms, and structures of the foreign language and English.
Culture and Civilization	An enlightened understanding of the foreign people and their culture, such as is achieved through personal contact, through travel and residence abroad, through study of literature and the arts.	The "minimal" level of competency with firsthand knowledge of some literary masterpieces and acquaintance with the geography, history, art, social customs, and contemporary civilization of the foreign people.	An awareness of language as an essential element of culture and an understanding of the principal ways in which the foreign culture differs from our own.
Professional Preparation	A mastery of recognized teaching methods, evidence of breadth and depth of professional outlook, and the ability to experiment with and evaluate new methods and techniques.	"Minimal" level of competency plus knowledge of the use of specialized techniques, such as audiovisual aids, and of the relation of language teaching to other areas of the curriculum. Ability to evaluate the professional literature of foreign-language teaching.	Knowledge of the present-day objectives of the teaching of foreign languages as communication and an understanding of the methods and techniques for attaining these objectives.

APPENDIX E

*Standards for Teacher-Education Programs
In Modern Foreign Languages*[1]

1. Prepared by a conference convened by the Modern Language Association in December 1963, this statement is addressed to state departments responsible for the certification of teachers and to institutions that prepare elementary- and secondary-school language teachers. Its purpose is to identify and clarify acceptable standards of preparation.

2. Only selected students should be admitted to a teacher-preparation program, and those selected should have qualities of intellect, character, and personality that will make them effective teachers.

3. The training of the future teacher[2] must make him a well-educated

person with a sound knowledge of United States culture, the foreign culture and literature, and the contrasts between the two cultures. It must also enable him to:

a) Understand the foreign language spoken at normal tempo.

b) Speak the language intelligibly and with an adequate command of vocabulary and syntax.

c) Read the language with immediate comprehension and without translation.

d) Write the language with clarity and reasonable correctness.

e) Understand the nature of language and of language learning.

f) Understand the learner and the psychology of learning.

g) Understand the evolving objectives of education in the United States and the place of foreign-language learning in this context.

4. In addition to his acquired knowledge and skills, the language teacher must be able to:

a) Develop in his students a control of the four skills (listening, speaking, reading, writing), that will eventually approach his own mastery of them.

[1] Reprinted from *PMLA,* Vol. LXXIX, No. 4D, Part 2 (September, 1964), pp. A-12, A-14.

[2] These specifications apply to the specialist in foreign languages at all levels. In the elementary school there is a clear need for specialists as well as for the classroom teachers who do the follow-up work on the specialist teacher's lesson.

b) Present the language as an essential element of the foreign culture and show how this culture differs from that of the United States.

c) Make judicious selection and use of methods, techniques, aids, and equipment for teaching modern foreign languages.

d) Correlate his teaching with that of other subjects.

e) Evaluate the progress and diagnose the deficiencies of student performance.

5. An approvable program to prepare such a teacher must include:

a) Intelligent evaluation and utilization of his pre-college language training through course placement according to results of proficiency tests.

b) An offering of language and literature courses advanced enough to enable him to teach the gifted student.

c) First-hand acquaintance with major works of literature, in courses and directed reading, tested by a comprehensive examination.

d) Use of the foreign language as the language of instruction in all language and literature courses.

e) Extensive exposure to several varieties of native speech, through teachers, lecturers, discs, tapes.

f) Instruction in the contemporary foreign culture.

g) Instruction in stylistics, phonetics, and linguistics.

h) Instruction in the psychology of language learning.

i) Instruction and practice in the use of the language laboratory and audio-visual aids.

j) Systematic observation of the foreign language being expertly taught, followed by the experience of teaching under expert direction.

k) Evaluation of the teacher candidate by (1) proficiency and other appropriate tests, (2) appraisal of his teaching skill by experts.

6. An approvable program *should* also make provision for:

a) Native speakers as teachers or informants.

b) Study abroad for at least one summer.

c) Organized extra-curricular foreign-language activities.

d) Development of interest in and ability to interpret research.

7. The institution must be able to demonstrate that its staff is of sufficient size and competence to give the desired instruction.

8. A candidate's readiness to teach (as attested by his foreign-language department, the education department, academic dean, and other college officials) must be certified not only by the department's directly concerned but in the name of the whole institution.

9. Teacher-preparing institutions should regularly evaluate the effectiveness of their programs by visiting their graduates on the job and by

inviting evaluations from administrators of the schools in which their graduates teach. In addition, institutions should plan formal research evaluations of these teachers' pupils to measure their achievement and interest in foreign languages and cultures. It is the responsibility of the institutions that prepare teachers of foreign languages—together with the state departments of education that certify them—to scrutinize constantly the effects of their programs upon foreign-language learning in the schools that employ their graduates.

A CALL TO ACTION
To Overcome the Critical Shortage of Teachers of Modern Foreign Languages

Recognizing the urgent need for greater numbers of qualified language teachers, a conference convened in December 1963 by the Modern Language Association addresses the following "call to action" to colleges and universities that prepare such teachers and to state departments of education. Close cooperation between these two agencies can result in new sources of supply and new, flexible, expeditious means of preparing and certifying language teachers for elementary and secondary schools.

The action proposed is to certify any teacher candidate who demonstrates that he possesses the requisite personal qualities, knowledge, and skills, *no matter how they have been acquired.*

The following steps are proposed:

1. Public announcement of certification requirements (statement of qualifications, course syllabi) and of ways of meeting these requirements expeditiously (recommended courses, summer institutes, reading lists, taped courses, and other audio-visual materials, qualifying exams).

2. Administration of the MLA Proficiency Tests for diagnostic purposes.

3. Interviews with teacher candidates by one or more experts to appraise their qualifications (including credentials from foreign universities) and to advise them how to overcome any deficiencies discovered.

4. Apprentice teaching, if needed, guided jointly by a demonstration teacher and a supervising teacher.

5. Final appraisal of the candidate's readiness to teach by a committee of three experts.

6. Administration of a second form of the MLA Proficiency Tests, if needed to determine proficiency.

7. Recommendation for certification by all those concerned with the candidate's preparation.

8. Granting of license by the state.

[The first drafts of these documents were written at a Conference at MLA headquarters in New York on 13 December 1963. Participants in the conference: Theodore Andersson, Chairman, Dept. of Romance Languages, University of Texas; Leonard Brisley, Indiana High School Program, Indiana University; Aaron Carton, School of Education, New York University; Jeremiah S. Finch, Dept. of English, Princeton University; John H. Fisher, Executive Secretary, MLA; Stephen A. Freeman, Vice-President and Dean of Language Schools, Middlebury College, Donald Herdman, Director of College Curricula in Teacher Education, New Jersey State Dept. of Education; Paul A. Irvine, Director of Guidance and Testing, Pennsylvania Dept. of Public Instruction; Frederick H. Jackson, The Carnegie Corporation of New York; Thomas W. Kelly, Instructor in Spanish, Somerville (N.J.) High School; Norman D. Kurland, Consultant, College Proficiency Exams, New York Dept. of Education; Archibald T. MacAllister, Professor of Italian, Princeton University; Howard Lee Nostrand, Chairman, Dept. of Romance Languages, University of Washington; Everett V. O'Rourke, Consultant, Secondary Education, California State Dept. of Education; F. André Paquette, New York State University at Plattsburg; Robert J. Solomon, Educational Testing Service, Princeton, N.J.; Wilmarth H. Starr, Director, MLA-NYU Testing Program, New York University; Donald D. Walsh, Associate Secretary, MLA, and Director, Foreign Language Program, *Chairman*. The documents were subsequently revised twice by correspondence before reaching their present form.]

APPENDIX F

*Guidelines for Teacher-Education
Programs in Modern Foreign Languages*[1]

Recommendations of the Modern Foreign Language Teacher Preparation
Study of the Modern Language Association in cooperation with the National Association of State Directors of Teacher Education and Certification with the support of the Carnegie Corporation of New York.

(The official statement below is addressed to college and university
personnel who are engaged in or are planning to engage in programs to
prepare teachers of modern foreign languages in American schools. The
statement was prepared in a special MLA project directed by F. André
Paquette. At various stages of development the statement has had the
benefit of review and comment by more than 500 members of the foreign
language profession, and it has been approved by the MLA Foreign Language Program Advisory Committee. Throughout the project, members
of the National Association of State Directors of Teacher Education and
Certification [NASDTEC] provided much helpful professional advice, and
the statement carries the formal endorsement of NASDTEC.)

A. *The Preparation of the American School Teacher*: The preparation
of a teacher in this country usually consists of: general education, courses
and experiences which help him become a well-educated person; academic specialization, courses and experiences which help him become
proficient in an area of concentration; and professional education, courses
and experiences which help him prepare himself as an educator.

The statement which follows is concerned only with academic specialization and professional education. It is intended to define the role of the
modern foreign language teacher, to state the minimal competence which
should be provided by a training program, and to characterize such a
program.

B. *The Modern Foreign Language Teacher in American Schools*: The
teacher of a modern foreign language in American schools is expected to:

1. Develop in students a progressive control of the four language
skills (listening, speaking, reading, writing).

[1] Reprinted from *PMLA*, Vol. LXXXI, No. 2 (May, 1966), pp. A-2, A-3.

2. Present the language as an essential element of the foreign culture and show how that culture is similar to and different from that of the United States.

3. Present the foreign literature in such a way as to bring the students to understand it and to appreciate its values.

4. Make judicious selection and use of approaches, methods, techniques, aids, material, and equipment for language teaching.

5. Correlate his teaching with that in other areas.

6. Evaluate the progress and diagnose the deficiencies of student performance.

C. *Minimal Objectives for a Teacher Education Program in Modern Foreign Languages:*[2] The program to prepare a beginning modern foreign language teacher must provide him with the opportunity to develop:

1. Ability to understand conversation at normal tempo, lectures, and news broadcasts.

2. Ability to talk with a native with a command of vocabulary and syntax sufficient to express his thoughts in conversation at normal speed with reasonably good pronunciation.

3. Ability to read with immediate comprehension prose and verse of average difficulty and mature content.

4. Ability to write a simple "free composition," such as a letter or message, with clarity and correctness in vocabularly, idiom, and syntax.

5. An understanding of the differences between the sound systems, forms, and structures of the foreign language and of English and ability to apply this understanding to modern foreign language teaching.

6. An awareness of language as an essential element of culture and an understanding of the principal ways in which the foreign culture differs from our own. First-hand knowledge of some literary masterpieces and acquaintance with the geography, history, art, social customs, and contemporary civilization of the foreign people.

7. Knowledge of the present-day objectives of modern foreign language teaching as communication, and an understanding of the methods and techniques for attaining these objectives. Knowledge of the use of specialized techniques, such as educational media, and of the relation of modern foreign language study to other areas of the curriculum. Ability to evaluate the professional literature of modern language teaching.

[2] Based on the "Good" level of the "Qualifications for Secondary School Teachers of Modern Foreign Languages," *The Bulletin of the National Association of Secondary School Principals*, Vol. XXXIX (November, 1955), as revised in Wilmarth H. Starr, "MLA Foreign Language Proficiency Tests for Teachers and Advanced Students," *PMLA*, Vol. LXXVII, Part 2 (September, 1962), p. 38.

D. *Features of a Teacher Education Program in Modern Foreign Languages*: An institution that seeks approval of its modern foreign language teacher education program accepts the responsibility for demonstrating that its program provides students with the opportunity to acquire the competences named above. It is characterized by the features listed below.

1. The institution has a clearly formulated policy concerning admission to, retention in, and completion of the program. The statement of this policy includes precise information about when and how to apply for admission to the program and what criteria are used in screening applicants; it states the minimal achievement required for successful completion of the program and it indicates when, how, and by what professional criteria students are eliminated from the program. A printed statement of this policy is available to all who request it.

2. The institution evaluates the previous language experiences of all applicants for admission to the institution as well as that of applicants to the modern foreign language teacher education program through the use of proficiency tests in the four language skills. It uses the results of such evaluation for student placement in modern foreign language instruction.

3. In order to provide candidates of varied backgrounds with the opportunity to achieve at least the level of "Good" in the seven areas of competence outlined in Section C above, the institution offers, or provides by special arrangement, instruction in:

a) The four language skills (listening, speaking, reading, writing). This instruction includes regular and extensive exposure to several varieties of native speech through teachers, lecturers, native informants, or mechanically reproduced speech, and exposure to several varieties of the written language through books, newspapers, magazines, documents, etc.

b) The major works of the literature. This instruction is largely or entirely in the foreign language.

c) Other aspects of the culture and civilization. The instruction includes the study of the geography, history, and contemporary civilization.

d) Language analysis, including a study of the phonology, morphology, and syntax of the modern foreign language and comparison of these elements with those of American English.

e) Professional education, including a study of the social foundations and the organization of public education in the United States, human growth and development, learning theory, and curriculum organization, including the place of foreign languages in the curriculum.

f) Methods of teaching modern foreign languages. A study of approaches to, methods of, and techniques to be used in teaching a modern foreign language. There is instruction in the use of the language laboratory and other educational media.

4. The institution provides an opportunity for systematic, supervised observation of a variety of modern foreign language teaching situations of differing quality in elementary and secondary schools, at beginning, intermediate, and advanced levels of instruction, in classroom and language laboratory.

5. The institution provides student-teaching experience under expert supervision in which the candidate can demonstrate his actual or potential ability to be a modern foreign language teacher.

6. The institution has a staff whose combined competences are superior to the level of instructional proficiencies which are the objectives of the program. The teachers of the methods courses and the classroom teachers (cooperating teachers) who supervise the student teaching are experienced foreign language teachers and are themselves proficient at least at the level of "Good" in the seven areas of competence. In addition, the cooperating teachers are interested in having student teachers work under their supervision.

7. The institution maintains a curriculum library containing the materials and equipment commonly used in teaching modern foreign languages in elementary and secondary schools.

8. The institution provides all students of modern foreign languages with such opportunities for reinforcement of their classroom learning as a language laboratory, foreign films, plays, and lectures; language reading and listening rooms with books, periodicals, records, and tapes; language houses and language tables.

9. The institution, if it does not have its own program outside the United States, calls to the attention of all foreign language majors specific foreign study programs which have been carefully selected.

10. A candidate's achievement in the seven areas of competence is evaluated through appropriate tests, his teaching skill is appraised by experts, and the results of the evaluation and appraisal are available for advising him in his continuing education and for recommending, licensing, and employing him. His readiness to teach is certified in the name of the whole institution. An official designated to make such certification is able to demonstrate that he has received information about the candidate from all units in the institution concerned with the candidate's preparation.

APPENDIX G

A RESOLUTION

Concerning the Education of Bilingual Children
El Paso, Texas, January 1966[1]

On November 13, 1965, over 500 foreign-language teachers, school administrators, and other educators met in El Paso at the Second Annual Conference of the Southwest Council of Foreign Language Teachers to consider educational problems faced by bilingual children. By an overwhelming majority they voted to approve the recommendations contained in the following resolution:

WHEREAS a disproportionately large number of families of Mexican or American Indian background are among the 35 million Americans who suffer the distress and waste of poverty,

[The per capita median income of 'Anglos' in Texas in 1959 was $4,137, that of Spanish-surname Texans $2,029, according to Harley L. Browning and S. Dale McLemore, "The Spanish-surname Population of Texas," *Public Affairs Comment*, Vol. X, No. 1 (January 1964), The University of Texas, Austin.]

AND WHEREAS the inadequate economic opportunity experienced by these bilinguals is directly related not to a lack of intellectual ability but rather to a school program which, judging by past results, does not develop their full potential,

[According to the Texas Education Agency's *Report of Pupils in Texas Public Schools Having Spanish Surnames*, 1955–1956, August 1957, the average Spanish-surname Texan was at that time spending three years in the first grade and was dropping out of school before reaching the fifth grade (4.7). This compares with 10.8 school years completed by "all whites" (which includes Spanish-surname Texans) and 8.1 by "non-whites" (primarily Negroes and Orientals)]

AND WHEREAS our present educational practices, hampered by widespread misunderstanding of the nature of language and language-learning

[1] Newsletter No. 1, Southwest Council of Foreign Language Teachers (name changed in 1968 to Southwest Council for Bilingual Education). Address inquiries to P. O. Box 47, University of Texas, El Paso, Texas 79999.

and of the relation of the mother tongue to a second language, produce bilingual persons who often fail to learn well either their mother tongue or English,

AND WHEREAS language deficiency, both in the mother tongue and in English, is one of the main causes of failure in school and of poverty afterward,

AND WHEREAS we know the importance of the mother tongue both as a medium for concept development and as a means of building confidence and security in children whose English is non-functional,

AND WHEREAS the early acquisition of literacy in the mother tongue is known to facilitate the learning of a second language.

AND WHEREAS our present educational policies, by preventing the full development of the bilingual child, squander language resources which are urgently needed by our Nation and which must be expensively replaced under the National Defense Education Act,

BE IT THEREFORE RESOLVED

THAT in the interest of our bilingual children and in the public interest a new policy regarding language education be widely adopted in bilingual areas, to wit:

1. That throughout the Southwest, wherever suitable conditions can be provided, schools plan a program of bilingual education in which non-English-speaking children can be given curriculum-wide instruction through the medium of their vernacular in the regular school day, especially in the pre-school and primary years,

2. That effectual instruction in and through the medium of English also be developed, based in the early stages on special techniques for teaching English as a second language,

3. That policies which prohibit the speaking of languages other than English on school premises be reviewed in light of new knowledge concerning the psychology of language and language learning,

4. That in order to relieve the present teacher shortage and to staff future bilingual programs, school districts be urged to make greater efforts to recruit strongly qualified teachers and teacher aides who speak with native fluency the languages of the pupils involved,

5. That schools, colleges, and universities be encouraged to conduct research in bilingual education, to prepare or retrain bilingual teachers, to create instructional materials, and in other ways to collaborate in building a tradition of strong bilingual education,

6. That, recognizing the importance of the mother tongue as a symbol of an inherited culture and as an enrichment of our total culture, all bi-

lingual citizens be encouraged to cultivate their ancestral language as well as the official language, English.

A NUMBER OF FEDERAL ASSISTANCE PROGRAMS COULD SUPPORT SCHOOL-BASED PROJECTS IN BILINGUAL EDUCATION, PARTICULARLY TITLES I AND III OF THE ELEMENTARY AND SECONDARY EDUCATION ACT OF 1965.

APPENDIX H

Excerpts from Reports concerning FLES Programs

Part 1: Report of Robert Nix[1]

"Section 1. All teachers of German in district schools shall be required to hold special teachers' licenses, in which the following subjects shall be named: 1. Certificate of Qualification in English. 2. Ability as a Teacher. 3. German Grammar. 4. German Composition. 5. General Knowledge of German. 6. General Knowledge of English. 7. Geography. 8. History. 9. Physiology. 10. Arithmetic. 11. German Literature.

"Section 2. In addition to the requirements in Section One, a teacher under contract must hold a diploma or a certificate of a reputable normal school, college or university, showing the completion of the following subjects:

1. Psychology and Principles of Education (not less than fourteen hours)
2. History of Education (not less than twenty hours)
3. School Hygiene (not less than twenty hours)
4. Methods of Teaching Modern Languages (not less than twenty hours)
5. Phonetics (not less than twelve hours)
6. Practice Teaching (not less than one year)

"Section 3. Graduates of commissioned high schools of Indiana, or of American educational institutions of equal or higher rank, in the estimation of the Superintendent of Schools, shall be exempt from examination in subjects 6–10, Section One. Graduates of National German-American Teachers' Seminary at Milwaukee shall be exempt from examinations in subjects 3–10, Section One.

"Section 4. A teacher meeting the requirements in Sections One and Two may be granted a license valid for five years.

"Section 5. For the renewal of the license, credit of at least nine hours in subject 11, Section One, is required. . . .

"The salary schedule range $500–$950.

"Four groups with top salaries in each group $825, $875, $925, $950.

"Automatic increases within each group until maximum has been reached.

---

[1] Quoted in Frances H. Ellis, "Historical Account of German Instruction in the Public Schools of Indianapolis, 1869–1919," *The Indiana Magazine of History*, Vol. L, No. 2 (June, 1954), pp. 366–367.

"Young women with diplomas from standard colleges who have had teaching experience receive two years credit. College graduates receive three years credit. Teaching service outside Indianapolis may be counted in determining salaries of teachers of German.

Part 2: Rules and Regulations concerning the German Department of the Public Schools of Indianapolis[2]

I. Instruction in the German language shall be given in the second, sixth, and ninth Districts [also Fourth and Eleventh] and in the High School.

II. Hereafter instruction in German shall be introduced in such schools as have an attendance of one hundred or more children that can speak [who wish to study] German, provided that the School be held in a building suitable for the purpose, and that the parents of the children attending the schools shall petition therefor.

III. There shall be appointed a teacher of German for the High School, who shall also be principal of German instruction in the District Schools. He shall devise such plans as may be expedient or necessary and report quarterly or semiannually to the Superintendent or the Board the condition of said classes. He shall furnish the different German teachers with instruction respecting the lessons and books, and is empowered to convene them, at some convenient time, to consult with them about the methods, and other matters pertaining to his department.

He shall visit at least one school each day without neglecting his classes, he shall examine the different schools and classes at the end of every scholastic year. . . .

IV. Female teachers shall be employed if they can be obtained. But no teacher shall be deemed competent to instruct in the German department, unless proficient also in English.

V. Instruction in German shall commence [with the German-speaking children] not before C Primary grade [i.e., grade two], and [with English-speaking children] in C Intermediate grade [grade six]. Children not able to speak German shall not be allowed to commence German before completing the D Intermediate grade [grade five].

VI. The instruction in the German language must adapt itself to the English classes.

The recitation of German classes is to be as follows: in the C Primary [grade two], two lessons per day, one in the forenoon of twenty minutes and one in the afternoon of fifteen minutes. In the B Primary [grade

[2] *Ibid.*, pp. 254–255.

three], one lesson in the forenoon and one in the afternoon, each twenty minutes in length. One lesson of thirty minutes each day in the A Primary [grade four], and upwards. In the High School one lesson of thirty minutes per day. The pupils from C Primary upward to be allowed one half of the time devoted to writing in school for the purpose of practicing German script, provided the German teachers can so arrange as to supervise the same.

The German language is to be used in giving instruction, except when the pupils do not speak German.

VII. Whenever it is practicable the instruction in English should be so regulated by the supervising principals of the different schools as not to overburden the scholars who wish to learn German.

VIII. It must be insisted, that no scholar who has once entered a German Class, can leave the same without the most urgent reasons, to be judged by the teacher and the German Principal. The classes are formed in the beginning of the scholastic year, and no pupils are admitted into them after they are started, except after due examination and approval by the German Principal.

IX. The boundaries of the respective schools in which the German is taught shall be no hinderance [*sic*] to a scholar who residing in another district wishes to join a German class.

Part 3: Excerpts from the Report of Peter Scherer, 1916[3]

"The aim of the German department is to acquaint the pupils with the history, customs, manners, and ideals of the German people through a knowledge of their language and literature.

"The 'direct method' with some modification is used in teaching the subject. That is to say, German is, as far as practical, the language of the classroom.

"Inasmuch as singing forms a vital part of German life, all the classes are taught the most familiar German songs and are permitted to sing them at intervals throughout the year.

"Another important feature of the German work is the programs arranged throughout the year for the benefit of the pupils and patrons. The most important of these are the 'Weihnachtsfeier' in which the idea of the German Christmas Celebration is carried out; the German play, which is given before the school annually as an auditorium exercise; and the 'Waldfest' which is given in one of the parks of the city each spring. . . .

". . . During the year 1915–1916, German was taught in forty-one dis-

[3] Quoted in *ibid.*, pp. 369–371.

trict schools and in the high schools. In February 1916, there were 476
German classes in the district schools and 85 in the high schools. The district school classes in German were taught by forty-four teachers and six
substitutes; in the high schools, German was taught by fifteen teachers. . . .

"In June 1916, 332 graduates from the elementary schools had completed the German course; 273 received high school credit; 288 will go
to high school; 271 enrolled in the advanced course of German in the high
schools. . . .

". . . In the district schools of Indianapolis, German is begun as an
optional study in the second year, and continued to the end of the eighth
year. It is a well known fact, that one who begins a modern language in
childhood will acquire a thorough knowledge. In childhood, the organs
of speech are in a plastic condition. Good habits are easily formed; bad
habits are easily corrected. Because the mind acts more naively and good
memory is more tenacious, forms of expression are readily mastered as
simple facts. Later, when the mind grows stronger and more rigid, when
the period of analyzing and reasoning begins, and speech habits in the
mother tongue have been fixed it is difficult to acquire even a fairly good
pronunciation, and thinking in the foreign language becomes a difficult
task. 'With the dawn of puberty, certain linguistic possibilities are lost
beyond the power of retrieval. This, I think, is the consensus on the con-
tinent and most here realize that we began too late.' The time allotted
to German in the district schools is from twenty-five to thirty minutes
daily. German is the language in the classroom. Books, objects, and pictures supply the material for oral and aural work, reading and writing. In
the primary grades the child's life and surroundings in school and home
furnish the principal subjects. . . .

"The systematic study of grammar is begun in the fifth grade. In this
grade the children become acquainted with little German stories and fairy
tales. . . . In all grades poems are memorized, stories dramatized, and
acted and the singing of German songs enlivens the classroom work and
enriches the lives of the children.

"All advanced German in the High Schools (3½ years). Pupils who
have completed the seven-year course in German in the district schools
with a high school credit are offered 3½ years of advanced German in
the high schools. This work is a continuation and extension of the work
in the grammar grades. In the application of the direct method, translation is the exception, and not the rule, because the 'Sprachgefühl' has
been developed to such a degree, and the vocabulary is of such wide
range, that the subject matter can be treated in the foreign vernacular.

"Each year a number of those who completed the advanced courses
and passed the written and oral examinations were licensed to teach Ger-

man in the Indianapolis district schools. Those who go to college will obtain advanced standing in the German department there."

Part 4: Excerpts from a Survey Conducted by the National Education Association and the American Association of School Administrators[4]

Languages Taught. In the fifty-three programs described, Spanish is the language most frequently taught . . . (thirty-seven school systems), with French running a close second (thirty-two school systems), ten teach German, two include Italian, one offers Polish, and one gives Latin in Grade VI. . . .

Grade Levels, Enrollment, and Time Allotted. . . . In seven of the larger school districts, foreign languages are introduced in kindergarten and carried on through Grade VI. Predominantly, however, foreign languages are given in Grades IV, V, and VI. Less than half of the fifty-three school systems include language offerings in the first three grades. . . . The number of minutes per week given to foreign-language instruction in 1954–1955 averaged between sixty and seventy-five. The least time reported was twenty minutes per week and the most was 175 minutes. . . .

Special Teachers. In the majority of the fifty-three school districts with elementary foreign-language programs, the instruction is given by regular classroom teachers. Less than one-third reported the use of special teachers.

Methods and Teaching Aids. It is apparent that the conversational or aural-oral methods of teaching foreign languages is used almost exclusively. . . . textbooks are seldom used. . . . games, songs, and dramatizations help build up the children's vocabulary. Slides, tape recordings, and puppets are some of the teaching aids used. Radio classes were reported by Cleveland, Ohio. . . ., and by Dade County, Florida. . . . Television instruction is included in the programs of Washington, D.C., . . . Pittsburgh, Pennsylvania, . . . Schenectady, New York. . . .

Costs and Financing. . . . The expenses of almost all the programs apparently are absorbed in the regular school budget and cannot be easily separated. . . . One . . . district estimated that the part of the budget allotted to the foreign-language program amounted to about $4,800. San Diego, California . . .—where the program is designated as an extra "en-

[4] National Education Association, American Association of School Administrators, and Research Division. *Foreign-Language Programs in Elementary Schools.* Educational Research Service Circular No. 6.

richment" offering, involving an assistant supervisor and three special teachers—reported that the additional cost is approximately $25,000.

Public Attitude Toward Programs. Nearly all of those who replied to the question regarding the reception of the foreign-language program by parents and general public used such terms as "enthusiastic" or "favorable." They also reported a rather general demand for expansion of the program, financing permitting. . . .

Pros and Cons. . . . Some respondents were convinced of the advantages and benefits of the program. Others, while admitting the possible value of such programs, pointed out certain difficulties involved. Still others were definitely opposed.

. . . Perhaps the most frequently mentioned advantages are:

1. Children learn foreign languages more easily in the early school years.

2. Knowledge of foreign languages helps to develop a constructive attitude toward international relations.

3. Foreign languages are particularly adapted for enrichment programs planned for children who are above average in foreign language learning ability.

Four points predominate in the statements of those who *do not* favor introducing foreign language in elementary grades:

1. The curriculum is already overcrowded, and the addition of foreign languages would mean neglecting the fundamentals or lengthening the school day. . . .

2. There is already a shortage of qualified regular classroom teachers, and to require language ability is not practical; in-service training courses would be expensive. . . .

3. Knowledge of foreign languages is unnecessary in some communities. . . .

4. The pressure for teaching foreign languages in the elementary grades is coming from teachers of languages in the high schools and colleges:

"Sources of requests for foreign languages at the elementary-school level should be examined. One group, the foreign language teachers facing decreasing enrollments in these secondary schools, could be, perhaps, seeking ways and means of perpetuating their positions."

BIBLIOGRAPHY

Abernethy, Thomas Perkins. *The South in the New Nation, 1789–1819.* A History of the South, edited by Wendell Holmes Stephenson and E. Merton Coulter, Vol. IV. [Baton Rouge, Louisiana:] Louisiana State University Press and the Littlefield Fund for Southern History of The University of Texas, 1961.

Alexander, Tom. "Those Amazing Cuban Emigrés." *Fortune,* Vol. LXXIX, No. 5 (October, 1966).

Alkonis, Nancy V., and Mary A. Brophy. "A Survey of FLES Practices." In *Reports of Surveys and Studies in the Teaching of Modern Foreign Languages, 1959–1961.* New York: The Modern Language Association of America, 1961.

Allen, Edith M. "Foreign Language Below the Ninth Grade: What Are We Doing?" *The Modern Language Journal,* Vol. L, No. 2 (February, 1966).

Allen, Harold B., ed. *Teaching English as a Second Language: A Book of Readings.* New York: McGraw-Hill Book Company, 1965.

The American Association of Colleges for Teacher Education. *Standards and Evaluative Criteria for the Accreditation of Teacher Education: A Draft of the Proposed New Standards, With Study Guide.* Washington, D. C.: The American Association of Colleges for Teacher Education, December, 1967.

―――. *A Summary of Revisions of Standards and Evaluative Criteria for the Accreditation of Teacher Education: April 1968 Revisions of the Draft of Proposed New Standards.* Washington, D. C.: The American Association of Colleges for Teacher Education, May, 1968.

The American Council of Learned Societies. Committee on the Language Program. "Language Study and American Education." Reprinted from *Language,* Vol. XXIX, No. 2 (April–June, 1953).

Andersson, Theodore. "The Bilingual in the Southwest." *The Florida FL [Foreign Language] Reporter,* Vol. V, No. 2 (Spring, 1967). Reprinted in *The TESOL [Teachers of English to Speakers of Other Languages] Newsletter,* Vol. 1, No. 1 (April, 1967).

―――. "Do We Want Certified Teachers or Qualified Ones?" *The Modern Language Journal,* Vol. XLVII, No. 6 (October, 1963).

―――. "The Faces of Language: Tool—Communication—Culture—

Style." *The Graduate Journal of the University of Texas,* Vol. VI, No. 2 (Fall, 1964).

————. "An FL Blueprint in Focus." *The Modern Language Journal,* Vol. XLVI, No. 3 (March, 1962).

————. "FLES: A Clarification." *The National Elementary Principal,* Vol. XLIII, No. 1 (September, 1963).

————. "FLES and the Conservation of Our Language Resources." *Hispania,* Vol. XLVII, No. 3 (September, 1964).

————. "FLES for Bilingualism." *The Florida FL [Foreign Language] Reporter,* Vol. IV, No. 1 (Fall, 1965).

————. "Foreign Language in the Elementary School in the United States of America: Retrospect and New Directions." In *International Conference: Modern Foreign Language Teaching: Papers and Reports of Groups and Committees—Preprints, Part 2.* Berlin: Paedagogische Arbeitsstelle and Sekr. Paedagogisches Zentrum, November, 1964.

————. "Languages and Education—A Criticism." *The Graduate Journal of the University of Texas,* Vol. IV, No. 2 (Fall, 1961).

————. "A Focus on the Bilingual Child." *The Modern Language Journal,* Vol. XLIX, No. 3 (March, 1965).

————. "The Optimum Age for Beginning the Study of Modern Languages." *International Review of Education,* Vol. VI, No. 3 (1960).

Angiolillo, Paul F. *Armed Forces' Foreign Language Teaching: Critical Evaluation and Implications.* New York: S. F. Vanni, Publishers & Booksellers, 1947.

————. "French for the Feeble-Minded: An Experiment." *The Modern Language Journal,* Vol. XXVI, No. 4 (April, 1942).

Armstrong, Earl. "The Teaching Profession: Retrospect and Prospect." *The Teacher's Role in American Society,* Lindley J. Stiles, ed. Fourteenth Yearbook of the John Dewey Society. New York: Harper and Brothers Publishers, 1957.

Arsenian, Seth. *Bilingualism and Mental Development: A Study of the Intelligence and the Social Background of Bilingual Children in New York City.* Contributions to Education, No. 712. New York: Columbia University, Teachers College, Bureau of Publications, 1937.

Australia, Commonwealth of. The Commonwealth Office of Education, for the Department of Immigration. *English for Newcomers to Australia.* Teacher's Book and Student's Books I and II. 4th ed. Canberra, Australia: The Commonwealth Office of Education, September, 1956.

Bagster-Collins, E. W. "History of Modern Language Teaching in the United States." In *Studies in Modern Language Teaching: Reports Prepared for the Modern Foreign Language Study and the Canadian Committee on Modern Languages.* Publications of the American and Canadian Committees on Modern Languages, Vol. XXVII. New York: The Macmillan Company, 1930.

Balakian, Anna. "Certification Requirements for Modern Language Teachers in American Public Schools (1959–1960)." *PMLA*, Vol. LXXVI, No. 2B (May, 1961).

Baltimore Public Schools. *Report of the Board of Commissioners of Public Schools of Baltimore*, 1899.

Bellugi, Ursula, and Roger William Brown, eds. *The Acquisition of Language*. Reports of the Fourth Conference Sponsored by the Committee on Intellectual Processes. Research of the Social Science Research Council. Monograph of the Society for Research in Child Development, Vol. XXIX, No. 1, Serial No. 92. Lafayette, Indiana: Child Development Publications of the Society for Research in Child Development, 1964.

Belyayev, B. V. *The Psychology of Teaching Foreign Languages*. Translated (from the Russian) by R. F. Hingley. Oxford, England: Pergamon Press Ltd., 1963; New York: The Macmillan Company, 1964.

Benedict, Ruth. *Patterns of Culture: An Analysis of Our Social Structure as Related to Primitive Civilizations*. A Mentor Book. Boston: Houghton Mifflin Company, 1934; New York: The New American Library, 1934.

Bird, Thomas E., ed. *Foreign Language Learning: Research and Development: An Assessment*. Reports of the Working Committees of the 1968 Northeast Conference on the Teaching of Foreign Languages. Menasha, Wisconsin: George Banta Company, Inc.

Bishop, G. Reginald, Jr., ed. *Culture in Language Learning*. Reports of the Working Committees of the 1960 Northeast Conference on the Teaching of Foreign Languages. Princeton, New Jersey: Princeton University Press, 1960.

Bloomfield, Leonard, and Clarence L. Barnhart. *Let's Read: A Linguistic Approach*. Detroit: Wayne State University Press, 1961.

Boyer, Mildred. "Texas Squanders Non-English Resources." *Texas Foreign Language Association Bulletin*, Vol. V., No. 3 (October, 1963).

Brega, Evelyn, and John M. Newell. "High School Performance of FLES and Non-FLES Students." *The Modern Language Journal*, Vol. LI, No. 7 (November, 1967).

Breunig, Marjorie. "Foreign Languages in the Elementary Schools of the United States, 1959–60." In *Reports of Surveys and Studies in the Teaching of Modern Foreign Languages, 1959–1961*. New York: The Modern Language Association of America, 1961.

Brooks, Nelson. "The Ideal Preparation of Foreign Language Teachers." *The Modern Language Journal*, Vol. L, No. 2 (February, 1966).

————. *Language and Language Learning: Theory and Practice.* 2nd ed. New York and Burlingame: Harcourt, Brace & World, Inc., 1964.

————. "Language Learning: A Multi-Discipline Approach." *The DFL Bulletin,* Publication of the Department of Foreign Languages of the NEA, Vol. IV, No. 2 (May, 1965).

————. Unpublished paper contributed to a Modern Language Association Conference on Foreign Language Teachers, December 6–7, 1958.

————. SEE ALSO Holt, Rinehart and Winston Series.

Busser, Alicia S. "Nursery Through Grade 4: An Experiment in the Teaching of French." *The Independent School Bulletin,* Vol. XXV, No. 3 (February, 1966).

California. State Department of Education. *A Field Test of Three Approaches to the Teaching of Spanish in Elementary Schools.* Cooperative Research Project No. D-177, Final Report. Sacramento: California State Department of Education, 1966.

————. *Looking Ahead in Foreign Languages.* A Report of the Production Seminar and Conference on the Improvement of Foreign Language Education in the Elementary School, January 11–16, 1960. Sacramento: California State Department of Education, 1961.

————. *Reports of Regional Conferences on Improving Modern Foreign Languages in the Elementary Schools.* Sacramento: California State Department of Education, 1962.

————. *Teacher's Guide to the Education of Spanish-Speaking Children.* Bulletin of the California State Department of Education, Vol. XXI, No. 14. Sacramento: California State Department of Education, October, 1962.

Carmichael, Leonard. *Manual of Child Psychology.* 2nd ed. New York: John Wiley & Sons, Inc.; London: Chapman & Hall, Limited, 1954.

Carnegie Corporation of New York. "The Best Years in Their Lives for Learning," and "Learning to Read: The Great Confusion." *Carnegie Quarterly,* Vol. XV, No. 3 (Summer, 1967).

Carroll, John B. "The Contribution of Psychological Theory and Educational Research to the Teaching of Foreign Languages." *The Modern Language Journal,* Vol. XLIX, No. 5 (May, 1965).

————. "Foreign Language Proficiency Levels Attained by Language Majors Near Graduation from College." *Foreign Language Annals,* Vol. I, No. 2 (December, 1967).

————. "Foreign Languages for Children: What Research Says." *The National Elementary Principal,* Vol. XXXIX, No. 6 (May, 1960).

————. *Language and Thought.* Prentice-Hall Foundations of Modern Psychology Series, edited by Richard S. Lazarus. Englewood Cliffs, New Jersey: Prentice-Hall, Inc., 1964.

————, ed. *Language, Thought, and Reality: Selected Writings of Benjamin Lee Whorf*. Foreword by Stuart Chase. New York: The Technology Press of the Massachusetts Institute of Technology and John Wiley & Sons, Inc., 1956.

————. "A Primer of Programmed Instruction in Foreign Language Teaching." *IRAL (International Review of Applied Linguistics in Language Teaching)*, Vol. I, No. 2 (1963).

Castillejo y Duarte, José. "Modern Languages in an International School." *New Era in Home and School*, January, 1933.

Chall, Jeanne. *Learning to Read: The Great Debate. An Inquiry into the Science, Art and Ideology of Old and New Methods of Teaching Children to Read, 1910–1965*. New York: McGraw-Hill Book Co., Inc., 1968.

Chamberlain, Jane Scott. *Source Materials for Teachers of Foreign Languages*. Washington, D.C.: National Education Association, Department of Foreign Languages, 1968.

Childers, J. Wesley. "Foreign Language Offerings and Enrollments in Public Secondary Schools, Fall 1959." In *Reports of Surveys and Studies in the Teaching of Modern Foreign Languages, 1959–1961*. New York: The Modern Language Association of America, 1961.

————. "Foreign Language Offerings and Enrollments in Public Secondary Schools, Fall 1960." *PMLA*, Vol. LXXVII, No. 4, Part 2 (September, 1962).

————, Barbara Bell, and Harry Margulis. "Teacher Education Curricula in Modern Foreign Languages." In *Reports of Surveys and Studies in the Teaching of Modern Foreign Languages, 1959–1961*. New York: The Modern Language Association of America, 1961.

Chomsky, Noam. "Language and the Mind." *Psychology Today*, Vol. I, No. 9 (February, 1968).

Cincinnati Public Schools. *Foreign Languages in the Elementary School*. Cincinnati: Cincinnati Public Schools, 1959.

————. *Twelfth Annual Report of the Condition of the Common Schools in Cincinnati*. [Cincinnati: Cincinnati Public Schools], 1841.

————. *85th Annual Report*. [Cincinnati: Cincinnati Public Schools], 1914.

Cleveland Public Schools. *Course of Study for French in the Elementary School (Grades 1–6)*. Rev. ed. Cleveland, Ohio: Board of Education, 1962.

College Entrance Examination Board. *Advanced Placement Programs: Course Descriptions, 1966–1968*. Princeton, New Jersey: College Entrance Examination Board, 1966.

————. *Curricular Change in the Foreign Languages: 1963 Colloquium* on *Curricular Change*. With an introduction by Theodore Andersson. Princeton, New Jersey: College Entrance Examination Board, 1963.

————. *A Guide to the Advanced Placement Program*. Princeton, New Jersey: College Entrance Examination Board, 1966.

Committee of Ten. SEE U.S. Bureau of Education.

Conant, James Bryant. *The Education of American Teachers*. New York: McGraw-Hill Book Company, Inc., 1963.

Cornfield, Ruth R. "The Other Side of FLES." *Hispania*, Vol. XLIX, No. 3 (September, 1966).

Couillard, Louis E. "The Role of Languages in the Development of National Consciousness: The Canadian Experience." *PMLA*, Vol. LXXII, No. 2 (April, 1957).

Debyser, Francis. "The Relation of Language to Culture and the Teaching of Culture to Beginning Language Students." *The CCD Language Quarterly: The Chilton-Didier Foreign Language Newsletter*, Vol. VI, No. 1 and No. 2 (Spring/Summer, 1968).

del Olmo, Filomena Peloro, and Guillermo del Olmo. "The Articulation of FLES: A Problem with Solution." *The Florida FL [Foreign Language] Reporter*, Vol. IV, No. 1 (Fall, 1965). Special FLES Issue.

————. "FLES: In Search of Discipline and Content." *The DFL Bulletin*, Publication of the National Education Association, Vol. VI, No. 3 (March, 1967).

Dodson, C. J. *Language Teaching and the Bilingual Method*. London: Sir Isaac Pitman & Sons, Ltd., 1967.

Donoghue, Mildred R., ed. *Foreign Languages and the Schools: A Book of Readings*. Dubuque, Iowa: Wm. C. Brown Company, Publishers, 1967.

————. "What Research Tells Us About the Effects of FLES." *Hispania*, Vol. XLVIII, No. 3 (September, 1965).

Dreier, Grace. "Developing and Introducing a Program of Conversational Spanish in the Elementary Schools of Los Angeles, California." Report submitted to the National Conference on the Role of Foreign Languages in American Schools, Washington, D.C., U.S. Department of Education, January 15–16, 1953.

Dunkel, Harold B., and Roger A. Pillet. *French in the Elementary School: Five Years' Experience*. Chicago: University of Chicago Press, 1962.

Eddy, Frederick D., ed. *The Language Learner*. Reports of the Working Committee of the 1959 Northeast Conference on the Teaching of Foreign Language. Washington, D.C.: Northeast Conference on the Teaching of Foreign Languages, Inc., 1959.

————. SEE ALSO Holt, Rinehart and Winston Series.

Edwards, Esther P. "Kindergarten Is Too Late." *Saturday Review,* June 15, 1968.

Ellis, Frances H. "Historical Account of German Instruction in the Public Schools of Indianapolis, 1869–1919." *The Indiana Magazine of History,* Vol. L, No. 2 (June, 1954).

Eriksson, Marguerite, Ilse Forest, and Ruth Mulhauser. *Foreign Languages in the Elementary School.* Englewood Cliffs, New Jersey: Prentice-Hall, Inc., 1964.

Estes, Dwain M., and David W. Darling, eds. *Improving Educational Opportunities of the Mexican-American: Proceedings of the First Texas Conference for the Mexican-American, April 13–15, 1967, San Antonio, Texas.* Austin, Texas: Southwest Educational Development Laboratory, Inter-American Education Center, Texas Education Agency, 1967.

Fairbanks, H. "Studies in Language Behavior: II, The Quantitative Differentiation of Samples of Spoken Language." *Psychological Monographs,* Vol. LVI, No. 2 (1944).

Finocchiaro, Mary. *Teaching Children Foreign Languages.* New York: McGraw-Hill Book Company, 1964.

Fishman, Joshua A. "Bilingualism, Intelligence, and Language Learning." *The Modern Language Journal,* Vol. XLIX, No. 4 (April, 1965).

————. *Language Loyalty in the United States: The Maintenance and Perpetuation of Non-English Mother Tongues by American Ethnic and Religious Groups.* London, The Hague, Paris: Mouton & Co., 1966.

Foley, Alice L., *et al. Impact of Elementary Foreign Languages on Secondary Programs: Final Report.* Rochester, New York: Brighton Schools, August 1, 1962.

Franklin, Judy. SEE Holt, Rinehart and Winston Series.

Fries, Charles Carpenter. *Linguistics and Reading.* 3rd ed. New York: Holt, Rinehart and Winston, Inc., 1966.

Gaarder, A. Bruce. "Conserving Our Linguistic Resources." *PMLA,* Vol. LXXX, No. 2B (May, 1965).

————. "Organization of the Bilingual School." *The Journal of Social Issues,* Vol. XXIII, No. 2 (April, 1967).

Garry, Ralph, and Edna Mauriello. *Evaluation of "Parlons Français" Program.* Boston: Modern Language Project of the Massachusetts Council for Public Schools, [1960].

Gaskell, William G. "They Dropped the Ball on FLES." *The Modern Language Journal,* Vol. LI, No. 2 (February, 1967).

Gatenby, E. V. "The Natural Process of Language Learning." *The New Delhi Sunday Statesman,* March–April, 1955. Reprinted in the Modern Language Association *FL [Foreign Language] Bulletin,* No. 44 (March, 1956).

————. "Popular Fallacies in the Teaching of Foreign Languages." *English Language Teaching*, Vol. VII, No. 1 (Autumn, 1952).

Geigle, Ralph C. "Foreign Language and Basic Learning." *Elementary School Journal*, Vol. LVII, No. 8 (May, 1957).

Geissinger, John B. "Foreign Languages in the Elementary Schools." *The American School Board Journal*, Vol. CXXXIII, No. 2 (August, 1956).

Gesell, Arnold, and Frances L. Ilg. "Developmental Trends in Language Behavior." *FL [Foreign Language] Bulletin*, No. 49 (August, 1956), pp. 6–9.

Ginsberg, V. S. "An Experiment in Teaching Pre-School Children a Foreign Language." *Soviet Education*, Vol. II, No. 11 (September, 1960). Translated from *Sovetskaia Pedagogika*, No. 5.

Goldschmidt, Walter, and Harry Hoijer. "A Word in Your Ear." *Ways of Mankind Series*. Urbana, Illinois: University of Illinois, The National Association of Educational Broadcasters [1960]. Tape recording.

Gorosch, Max, and Carl-Axel Axelsson. *English Without a Book: A Bilingual Experiment in Primary Schools by Audiovisual Methods*. Berlin: Cornelsen Verlag, 1964.

Gouin, François. *L'art d'enseigner et d'étudier les langues*. Paris: G. Fischbacher, 1880.

————. *The Art of Teaching and Studying Languages*. 9th English edition. Translated (from the French) by Howard Swan and Victor Betis. London: George Philip & Son, Ltd.; and Liverpool, England: Philip, Son, & Nephew, Ltd., 1912.

Gradisnik, Anthony. "A Survey of FLES Instruction in Cities Over 300,000." *Foreign Language Annals*, Vol. II, No. 1 (October, 1968), pp. 54–57.

Grew, James H. "An Experiment in Oral French in Grade III." *The Modern Language Journal*, Vol. XLII, No. 4 (April, 1958).

Haberman, Martin. "FLES: The Right Practice for Wrong Reasons." *The National Elementary Principal*, Vol. XLII, No. 6 (May, 1963).

Hadas, Moses. "Style in Education: Classics and the Classical." In *Curricular Change in the Foreign Languages: 1963 Colloquium on Curricular Change*. Princeton, New Jersey: College Entrance Examination Board, 1963.

Hakes, David T. "Psychological Aspects of Bilingualism." *The Modern Language Journal*, Vol. XLIX, No. 4 (April, 1965).

Hall, Edward T. *The Hidden Dimension*. Garden City, New York: Doubleday & Company, Inc., 1966.

————, and George L. Trager. *Human Nature at Home and Abroad: A Guide to the Understanding of Human Behavior*. U.S. Foreign Service

Institute. Washington, D.C.: U.S. Government Printing Office, 1953. Later elaborated by Hall as *The Silent Language*.

————. *The Silent Language*. A Premier Book. Greenwich, Connecticut: Fawcett Publications, Inc., 1961.

Hall, Theodore. *Gifted Children: The Cleveland Story*. Cleveland and New York: The World Publishing Company, 1956.

Handschin, Charles H. *The Teaching of Modern Languages in the United States*. U.S. Bureau of Education, Bulletin 1913, No. 3, Whole No. 510. Washington, D.C.: U.S. Government Printing Office, 1913.

Haugen, Einar. *Bilingualism in the Americas: A Bibliography and Research Guide*. University: The University of Alabama Press, 1964.

Hayden, Robert G. "Spanish-Americans of the Southwest: Life Style Patterns and Their Implications." *Welfare in Review*, April, 1966. Reprinted by the Department of Health, Education, and Welfare, Welfare Administration, n.d.

Hayes, Alfred S. *Plans for a Ph.D. in Language and Language Learning*. Washington, D.C.: The Modern Language Association of America, Center for Applied Linguistics, 1962.

Herslow, Nina Greer, and James F. Dershem. *Foreign Language Enrollments in Institutions of Higher Education, Fall 1965*. New York: The Modern Language Association of America, September, 1966.

Hocking, Elton. *Language Laboratory and Language Learning*. Monograph No. 2. Washington, D.C.: National Education Association of the United States, Department of Audio-Visual Instruction, 1964.

Holt, Rinehart and Winston Series. For grades 3 or 4 through 7. Components include a student's textbook, tapes, visual materials, and teacher's manual. (Published in New York by Holt, Rinehart and Winston.)

    Brooks, Robert, Frederick D. Eddy, Judy Franklin, Elizabeth Keesee, Elizabeth Michael, Patricia O'Connor, and Freeman Twaddell. *Introducing French*. 1964.

    ————. *Premier cours*. 1965.

    Holt Editorial Staff. *Deuxième cours*. 1967.

    ————. *Troisième cours*. 1968.

    Brooks, Robert, Frederick D. Eddy, Judy Franklin, Elizabeth Keesee, Elizabeth Michael, Patricia O'Connor, and Freeman Twaddell. *Introducing Spanish*. 1964.

    ————. *Primer curso*. 1964.

    ————. *Segundo curso*. 1965.

    Holt Editorial Staff. *Tercer curso*. 1965.

    Brooks, Robert, Frederick D. Eddy, Judy Franklin, Elizabeth Keesee,

Elizabeth Michael, Patricia O'Connor, and Freeman Twaddell. *Para empezar*. 1965.

Keesee, Elizabeth. *Para continuar*. 1966.

Howe, Harold, II. "Cowboys, Indians, and American Education." *The Texas Outlook*, Vol. LII, No. 6 (June, 1968).

Hutchison, Bruce. *Mr. Prime Minister, 1867–1964*. New York: Harcourt, Brace, & World, Inc., 1965.

Indiana State Department of Public Instruction. *Foreign Languages in the Elementary Schools: A Guide for Administrators, Teachers, and Parents*. Indianapolis: Indiana State Department of Public Instruction, 1964.

International Bureau of Education, Geneva. *Conférence internationale sur le bilinguisme: Le bilinguisme et l'éducation*. Luxembourg, 1928. *El bilingualismo y la educación*. Proceedings of the international conference held in Luxembourg from April 2–5, 1928, published with permission of the Grand Duke. Spanish Translation by Vicente Valls Anglés. "La Lectura" Edition. Bilboa, Madrid: Espasa-Calpe, 1932. Translation of *Le bilinguisme et l'éducation; Bilingualism and Education*, Brussels, 1928.

Jakobson, Roman. *Kindersprache, Aphasie und allgemeine Lautgesetze*. Uppsala, Sweden: Almqvist & Wiksells Boktryckeri, 1941.

————, ed., and Murray S. Miron. *Approaches to the Study of Aphasia: A Report of an Interdisciplinary Conference on Aphasia*. Urbana: University of Illinois Press, 1963.

JeKenta, Albert W. "FLES: Foreign Language in the Elementary Schools." Beverly Hills, California: Beverly Hills Unified School District, July, 1964. (Mimeographed.)

Jespersen, Otto. *How to Teach a Foreign Language*. Translated (from the Danish) by Sophia Yhlen-Olsen Bertelsen. London: G. Allen & Unwin, [1956].

————. *Language: Its Nature, Development and Origin*. London: George Allen & Unwin, Ltd., 1959.

Johnson, Charles E., Joseph S. Flores, Fred P. Ellison, and Miguel A. Riestra. *The Development and Evaluation of Methods and Materials to Facilitate Foreign Language Instruction in Elementary Schools*. Urbana: University of Illinois, Foreign Language Instruction Project, 1963; and Summary of the report (mimeographed).

————. "The Non-Specialist Teacher in FLES." *The Modern Language Journal*, Vol. LI, No. 2 (February, 1967).

Johnston, Marjorie C., ed. *Modern Foreign Languages in the High School*. U.S., Department of Health, Education, and Welfare, Office of Education, Bulletin 1958, No. 16, Publication No. OE–27005. Washington, D.C.: U.S. Government Printing Office, 1962.

————, and Elizabeth Keesee. *Modern Foreign Languages and Your*

Child. U.S., Department of Health, Education, and Welfare, Office of Education, Bulletin No. OE–27020. Washington, D.C.: U.S. Government Printing Office, 1964.

Joos, Martin. *The Five Clocks.* With an introduction by Albert H. Marckwardt. New York: Harcourt, Brace, & World, Inc., 1967.

Keesee, Elizabeth. *Modern Foreign Languages in the Elementary School: Teaching Techniques.* U.S., Department of Health, Education, and Welfare, Office of Education, Bulletin 1960, No. 29. Washington, D.C.: U.S. Government Printing Office, 1965.

―――. *References on Foreign Languages in the Elementary School.* U.S., Department of Health, Education, and Welfare, Office of Education, Publication No. OE–27008B. Washington, D.C.: U.S. Government Printing Office, 1963.

―――. SEE ALSO Holt, Rinehart and Winston Series.

King, Paul E. *Bilingual Readiness in Primary Grades: An Early Childhood Demonstration Project. Expanded Summary of Final Report.* U.S., Department of Health, Education, and Welfare, Office of Education, Bureau of Research, Project No. D-107, Contract No. OE–4–10–101. New York: Hunter College of the City University of New York, December, 1966.

Kluckhohn, Clyde. *Mirror for Man: The Relation of Anthropology to Modern Life.* New York: Fawcett World Library, April, 1959.

Kunkle, John F. "Two Years with the Saint-Cloud Materials." *The Modern Language Journal,* Vol. L, No. 3 (March, 1966).

Lado, Robert. *Language Teaching: A Scientific Approach.* New York: McGraw-Hill, Inc., 1964.

―――. *Language Testing: The Construction and Use of Foreign Language Tests. A Teacher's Book.* New York: McGraw-Hill Book Company, 1964.

―――. *Linguistics Across Culture: Applied Linguistics for Language Learners.* Foreword by Charles C. Fries. Ann Arbor: The University of Michigan Press, 1960.

Lagerlöf, Selma. *The Wonderful Adventures of Nils.* 6th ed. Translated (from the Swedish) by Velma Swanston Howard. Illustrations by H. Baumhauer. New York: Pantheon, 1961.

Lambert, Wallace E. "Psychological Approaches to the Study of Language." Part I: "On Learning, Thinking, and Human Abilities." *The Modern Language Journal,* Vol. XLVII, No. 2 (February, 1963). Part II: "On Second-Language Learning and Bilingualism." *The Modern Language Journal,* Vol. XLVII, No. 3 (March, 1963).

―――. "A Social Psychology of Bilingualism." *The Journal of Social Issues,* Vol. XXIII, No. 2 (April, 1967).

————, and J. Macnamara. "Some Intellectual Consequences of Following a First-Grade Curriculum in a Foreign Language." An unpublished paper, 1968.

Langer, Susanne K. *Philosophy in a New Key: A Study in the Symbolism of Reason, Rite, and Art.* 9th printing, rev. A Mentor Book. New York: The New American Library, 1958.

Leavitt, Sturgis E. "The Teaching of Spanish in the United States." In *Reports of Surveys and Studies in the Teaching of Modern Foreign Languages, 1959–1961.* New York: The Modern Language Association of America, 1961.

Leino, Walter B., and Louis A. Haak. *The Teaching of Spanish in the Elementary Schools and the Effects on Achievement in Other Selected Subject Areas.* U.S., Department of Health, Education, and Welfare, Office of Education, Contract SAE 9515. St. Paul, Minnesota: St. Paul Public Schools, November, 1963.

Lenneberg, Eric H. *Biological Foundations of Language.* With appendices by Noam Chomsky and Otto Marx. New York: John Wiley & Sons, Inc., 1967.

Leopold, Werner F. *Bibliography of Child Language.* Northwestern University Studies, Humanities Series, No. 28. Evanston, Illinois: Northwestern University Press, 1952.

————. "A Child's Learning of Two Languages." *Monograph Series on Languages and Linguistics,* No. 7 (September, 1954), pp. 19–30. (Institute of Language and Linguistics, School of Foreign Service, Georgetown University.)

————. *Speech Development of a Bilingual Child: A Linguist's Record.* 4 vols. Evanston, Illionis: Northwestern University Press, 1939–1949.

Levenson, Stanley, and William Kendrick. *Readings in Foreign Languages for the Elementary Schools.* Waltham, Massachusetts: Blaisdell Publishing Company, A Division of Ginn and Company, 1967.

Lind, Melva. "Modern Language Learning: The Intensive Course as Sponsored by the United States Army, and Implications for the Undergraduate Course of Study." *Genetic Psychology Monographs,* Vol. XXXVIII, First Half (August, 1948).

Los Angeles City Schools. *Instructional Guide for Spanish in the Elementary Schools.* Rev. ed. Publication No. 414. Los Angeles, California: Division of Instructional Services, 1957.

Macnamara, John. "The Bilingual's Linguistic Performance—A Psychological Overview." *The Journal of Social Issues,* Vol. XXIII, No. 2 (April, 1967).

————. "The Effects of Instruction in a Weaker Language." *The Journal of Social Issues,* Vol. XXIII, No. 2 (April, 1967).

————, ed. "Problems of Bilingualism." *The Journal of Social Issues,* Vol. XXIII, No. 2 (April, 1967).

MacRae, Margit W. *Mi cuaderno de español. Book I, II, III, IV.* Boston: Houghton Mifflin Company, 1959–1962.

————. *Spanish in the Grades. Book I, II, III, IV.* Pupil's edition and Teacher's edition. Boston: Houghton Mifflin Company, 1959–1962.

————. *Teaching Spanish in the Grades.* Boston: Houghton Mifflin Company, 1957.

Malherbe, Ernst Gedeon. *The Bilingual School: A Study of Bilingualism in South Africa.* 2nd ed. With an introduction by T. J. Haarhoff. London and New York: Longmans, Green and Company, 1946.

Manuel, Herschel T. *Spanish-Speaking Children of the Southwest: Their Education and the Public Welfare.* Austin: University of Texas Press, 1965.

McClain, William. "Twenty-five Years of the Cleveland Plan." *Education,* Vol. LXV, No. 9 (May, 1945).

McCormack, Margaret C. Report submitted to the National Conference on the Role of Foreign Languages in American Schools, Washington, D.C., January 15, 1953.

McGrath, Earl J. "Language Study and World Affairs." *The Modern Language Journal,* Vol. XXXVI, No. 5 (May, 1952).

McWilliams, Carey. *North from Mexico: The Spanish-Speaking People of the United States.* Edited by Louis Adamic. The People of America Series. Philadelphia and New York: J. B. Lippincott Company, 1949.

Mead, Margaret, ed. *Cultural Patterns and Technical Change: A Manual for the World Federation for Mental Health.* 2nd ed. A Mentor Book. New York: The New American Library, 1958.

Michael, Elizabeth. SEE Holt, Rinehart and Winston Series.

Mildenberger, Kenneth W. "Research Findings on Teaching a Second Language in the Elementary School." Work paper submitted to the Association for Supervision and Curriculum Development, National Education Association, for its annual meeting, March 18–21, 1957, in St. Louis, Missouri.

————. "Status of Foreign Language Study in American Elementary Schools, Fall Term 1953, 1954, 1955." Washington, D.C.: U.S. Department of Health, Education, and Welfare, Office of Education, Committee on Foreign Language Teaching, 1954, 1955, 1956. (Mimeographed.)

The Modern Language Association of America. "Childhood and Second Language Learning." *FL [Foreign Language] Bulletin,* No. 49 (August, 1956).

————. *FLES Packet: A Compilation of Materials on the Teaching of*

Foreign Languages in the Elementary Schools. New York: The Modern Language Association of America, Materials Center.

———. "FL Teacher Certification by Examination." Foreign Language Program Notes, *PMLA*, Vol. LXXVIII, No. 5 (December, 1963).

———. "Foreign Languages in the Elementary Schools." *PMLA*, Vol. LXXI, No. 4, Part 2 (September, 1956).

———. "Foreign Languages in the Elementary Schools: A Second Statement of Policy." *PMLA*, Vol. LXXVI, No. 2B (May, 1961).

———. "Guidelines for Teacher-Education Programs in Modern Foreign Languages." *PMLA*, Vol. LXXXI, No. 2 (May, 1966).

———. *MLA Teacher's Guides: Beginning French (German, Spanish) in Grade 3; French (German, Spanish) in Grade 4 (5, 6).* New York: The Modern Language Association of America, 1958–1962.

———. "Modern Foreign Languages in Teacher-Training Colleges." *PMLA*, Vol. LXX, No. 4, Part 2 (September, 1955).

———. "Proficiency Tests for Certification." Foreign Language Program Notes, *PMLA*, Vol. LXXIX, No. 2 (May, 1964).

———. *Publications of Interest to Teachers of Modern Foreign Languages.* New York: The Modern Language Association of America, Materials Center, 1966–1967.

———. *Reports of Surveys and Studies in the Teaching of Modern Foreign Languages, 1959–1961.* New York: The Modern Language Association of America, 1961.

———. "Qualifications for Teachers of Modern Foreign Languages." *PMLA*, Vol. LXXVII, No. 4, Part 2 (September, 1962).

———. "Standards for Teacher-Education Programs in Modern Foreign Languages." *PMLA*, Vol. LXXIX, No. 4, Part 2 (September, 1964).

———. *A Survey of Language Classes in the Army Specialized Training Program.* Report of a Special Committee Prepared for the Commission on Trends in Education of the Modern Language Association of America. Second printing, with the addition of recommendations. New York: The Modern Language Association of America, 1944.

———. "Values of Foreign Language Study." *PMLA*, Vol. LXXI, No. 4, Part 2 (September, 1956).

The Modern Language Journal. "Guidelines for Teacher Education Programs in Modern Foreign Languages—An Exposition." Compiled by F. André Paquette. Golden Anniversary Issue, Vol. L, No. 6 (October, 1966).

Modiano, Nancy. "National or Mother Language in Beginning Reading: A Comparative Study." *Research in the Teaching of English*, Vol. I, No. 2 (Spring, 1968).

National Association of State Directors of Teacher Education and Certification (in collaboration with the Modern Language Association of America). *Guidelines for the Preparation of Foreign Language Teachers.* Washington, D.C.: National Association of State Directors of Teacher Education and Certification, 1966.

National Center for School and College Television. "Television in Foreign Language Education." *NCSCT News*, Supplement No. 7, Bloomington, Indiana, 1967.

National Education Association. American Association of School Administrators, and Research Division. *Foreign-Language Programs in Elementary Schools.* Educational Research Service Circular No. 6. Washington, D.C.: National Education Association, 1955. Out of Print.

————. Department of Rural Education. *The Invisible Minority: Report of the NEA-Tucson Survey on the Teaching of Spanish to the Spanish-Speaking.* Washington, D.C.: National Education Association, 1966.

————. The Commission on Professional Rights and Responsibilities. *Las Voces Nuevas del Sudoeste/New Voices of the Southwest.* Symposium: "The Spanish-Speaking Child in the Schools of the Southwest." Conference on Civil and Human Rights in Education held in Tucson, Arizona, October 30–31, 1966. Washington, D.C.: National Education Association, 1966.

National Federation of Modern Language Teacher Associations. *The Modern Language Journal*, Golden Anniversary Issue, Vol. L, No. 6 (October, 1966).

New York City. Board of Education. Division of Elementary Schools. *Foreign Languages in the Elementary Schools.* New York: Board of Education, November, 1964.

————. *French in the Elementary Schools, Grades 4–5–6.* Curriculum Bulletin, 1961–1962 Series, No. 13. New York: Board of Education, 1963.

————. *Italian in the Elementary Schools.* Curriculum Bulletin, 1965–1966 Series, No. 9. New York: Board of Education, 1966.

————. *Spanish in the Elementary Schools, Grades 4–5–6.* Curriculum Bulletin, 1961–1962 Series, No. 14. New York: Board of Education, 1963.

New York Times, June 3, 1953; September 22, 1963.

Newmark, Gerald, Ray L. Sweigert, Jr., *et al. A Field Test of Three Approaches to the Teaching of Spanish in the Elementary Schools.* Sacramento: California State Department of Education, 1966.

Newmark, Maxim, ed. *Twentieth Century Modern Language Teaching: Sources and Readings.* With an introduction by Nicholas Murray Butler. New York: Philosophical Library, 1948.

Nostrand, Howard Lee. "A Second Culture: A New Imperative for American Education." In *Curricular Change in the Foreign Languages: 1963 Colloquium on Curricular Change.* Princeton, New Jersey: College Entrance Examination Board, 1963.

―――. *Understanding Complex Structures: A Language Teacher's Handbook.* Waltham, Massachusetts: Blaisdell Publishing Company, A Division of Ginn and Company. In press.

O'Connor, Patricia. SEE Holt, Rinehart and Winston Series.

―――, and W. F. Twaddell. "Intensive Training for an Oral Approach in Language Teaching." *The Modern Language Journal,* Vol. XLIV, No. 2, Part 2 (February, 1960).

Oil, Paint, and Drug Reporter, Vol. CLXXXV, No. 4 (January 27, 1964).

Osgood, Charles E. *Method and Theory in Experimental Psychology.* New York: Oxford University Press, 1953.

―――, ed. *Psycholinguistics: A Survey of Theory and Research Problems.* Indiana University Studies in the History and Theory of Linguistics. Bloomington: Indiana University Press, 1965.

Page, Mary M. "We Dropped FLES." *The Modern Language Journal,* Vol. L, No. 3 (March, 1966).

Parker, William Riley. "The Case for Latin." *PMLA,* Vol. LXXIX, No. 4, Part 2 (September, 1964).

―――. "Foreign Language in the Grades: A Caution." *The National Elementary Principal,* Vol. XXXVI, No. 5 (February, 1957).

―――. *The National Interest and Foreign Languages* (A Discussion Guide and Work Paper prepared by William Riley Parker, for the U.S. National Commission for UNESCO, Department of State). 3rd ed. Department of State Publication 7324, International Organization and Conference Series 26. Washington, D.C.: U.S. Government Printing Office, 1961.

―――. "Why a Foreign Language Requirement?" *PMLA,* Vol. LXXII, No. 2B (April, 1957).

Peal, Elizabeth, and Wallace E. Lambert. "The Relation of Bilingualism to Intelligence." *Psychological Monographs, General and Applied,* Vol. LXXVI, No. 27 (1962).

Penfield, Wilder G. "A Consideration of the Neurophysiological Mechanisms of Speech and Some Educational Consequences." *Proceedings of the American Academy of Arts and Sciences,* Vol. LXXXII, No. 5 (May, 1953).

―――. "The Uncommitted Cortex: The Child's Changing Brain." *The Atlantic Monthly,* Vol. CCXIV, No. 1 (July, 1964).

―――, and Lamar Roberts. *Speech and Brain-Mechanisms.* Princeton, New Jersey: Princeton University Press, 1959.

Philippine Center for Language Study. "Philippine Language-Teaching

Experiments." Preliminary edition. PCLS Monograph Series, No. 6. (Mimeographed.)

Philippines, Republic of the. *Teacher's Guide for English in Grade I, II, III, IV.* Manila, Philippines: Bureau of Public Schools and the Philippine Center for Language Study, 1960, 1961, 1962, 1963.

Phillips, Vanna. "War Brides 10 Years Later." *Ladies' Home Journal,* Vol. LXXII, No. 7 (July, 1955).

Piaget, Jean. *Le langage et la pensée chez l'enfant.* Etudes sur la logique de l'enfant, I. Preface by Professor Ed. Claparède. 3rd ed., rev. and augmented. Neuchâtel, Switzerland, Paris: Delachaux & Niestlé, 1948.

———. *The Language and Thought of the Child.* Translated (from the French) by Marjorie Gabain. Preface by Professor Ed. Claparède. New York: Meridian Books, Inc., 1959.

———. *Six Psychological Studies.* Translated (from the French) by Anita Tenzer and David Elkind. Edited, with an introduction and notes, by David Elkind. New York: Random House, 1967.

Pollack, Herman. Letter Sent to Cooperating Universities, January 18, 1963.

Pond, Sister Mary Lelia, S.S.N.D. "The Multiple Approach Method of Teaching French Versus the Grammar Method." *The French Review,* Vol. XIII, No. 6 (May, 1940).

Prator, Clifford H., Jr. *Language Teaching in the Philippines: A Report.* Manila, Philippines: U.S. Educational Foundation in the Philippines, 1956.

Pryor, Guy C. "An Evaluation of the Bilingual Instructional Project for Spanish-Speaking Children in the First Grade of the Stonewall Elementary School in the Harlandale Independent School District, San Antonio, Texas." June, 1966. (Mimeographed.)

Reid, J. Richard. "An Exploratory Survey of Foreign Language Teaching by Television in the United States." In *Reports of Surveys and Studies in the Teaching of Modern Foreign Languages, 1959–1961.* New York: The Modern Language Association of America, 1961.

Richardson, Mabel Wilson. "An Evaluation of Certain Aspects of the Academic Achievement of Elementary Pupils in a Bilingual Program. D.Ed. Dissertation, The University of Miami, January, 1968.

Rinsland, Henry D. *A Basic Vocabulary of Elementary School Children.* New York: The Macmillan Company, 1945.

Rivers, Wilga M. *The Psychologist and the Foreign Language Teacher.* Chicago & London: The University of Chicago Press, 1964.

Rojas, Pauline M. "Materials and Aids to Facilitate Teaching the Bilingual Child." *The Modern Language Journal,* Vol. XLIX, No. 4 (April, 1965).

Ronjat, Jules. *Le développement du langage observé chez un enfant bilingue.* Paris: Librairie Ancienne H. Champion, 1913.

Rosenzweig, Saul, Marion E. Bunch, and John A. Stern. "Operation Babel: A Survey of the Effectiveness of the Foreign Language Requirements for the Ph.D. Degree in Psychology." *American Psychologist,* Vol. XVII, No. 5 (May, 1962).

Ruiz, Ramón Eduardo. "Mexico: The Struggle for a National Language." *Social Research,* Vol. XXV, No. 3 (Autumn, 1958).

Salling, Aage. *Det Lille Sprog: En Sprogundervisningens Teori.* Copenhagen: Grafisk Forlag, 1952. Contains a summary in English, an edited version of which was published under the title "The Principle of Simplification" in *The French Review,* Vol. XXVIII, No. 2 (December, 1954).

Sapir, Edward. *Selected Writings in Language, Culture, and Personality.* Edited by David G. Mandelbaum. Berkeley and Los Angeles: The University of California Press, 1949.

Saporta, Sol, ed. *Psycholinguistics: A Book of Readings.* Prepared with the assistance of Jarvis R. Bastian. New York: Holt, Rinehart and Winston. 1961.

Saussure, Ferdinand de. *Cours de linguistique générale.* Published by Charles Bally and Albert Sechehaye with the collaboration of Albert Riedlinger. Paris: Payot, 1916. Translated by Wade Baskin under the title *Course in General Linguistics,* New York: Philosophical Library, 1959.

Sauzé, Emile Blais de. *The Cleveland Plan for the Teaching of Modern Languages, With Special Reference to French.* 5th ed. The Winston Modern Language Series. Philadelphia, Pennsylvania: The John C. Winston Company, 1959.

————. "Foreign Languages for the Gifted in the Cleveland Elementary Schools." Report presented to the National Conference on the Role of Foreign Languages in American Schools, Washington, D.C., U.S. Department of Education, January 15–16, 1953.

————. "An Oralist Looks at the Results." *Education,* Vol. LVII, No. 7 (March, 1947).

————. "Teaching French in the Elementary Schools of Cleveland." *The French Review,* Vol. XXVI, No. 5 (April, 1953). Based on a report submitted to the National Conference on the Role of Foreign Languages in American Schools, Washington, D.C., U.S. Department of Education, January 15–16, 1953.

Scherer, George A. "The Sine Qua Non in FLES." *The German Quarterly,* Vol. XXXVII, No. 4 (November, 1964).

Schmitt, Conrad J. "The Hackensack Story: A Long Sequence in Spanish." *The DFL Bulletin,* Vol. III, No. 1 (May, 1964). FLES No. 1.

Seashore, Robert H. "How Many Words Do Children Know?" *The Packet,* Vol. II, No. 2 (November, 1947).

Slama-Cazacu, Tatiana. *Langage et contexte: Le problème du langage dans la conception de l'expression et de l'interprétation par des organisations contextuelles.* The Hague: Mouton & Co., 1961.

Smith, George E. "What Can We Learn from the Peace Corps?" *Audiovisual Instruction,* Vol. VII, No. 9 (November, 1962).

Smith, Mary Katherine. "Measurement of the Size of General English Vocabulary Through the Elementary Grades and High School." *Genetic Psychology Monographs,* Vol. XXIV, Second Half (November, 1941).

Snygg, Donald. "Learning Theory as it Influences Instructional Materials and Resources." Unpublished report to the Association of Supervision and Curriculum Development Commission on New Media of Instruction, Oswego, New York, State University of New York, College of Education, 1960.

————. "The Tortuous Path of Learning Theory." *Audiovisual Instruction,* January, 1962.

————, and Arthur W. Combs. *Individual Behavior: A New Frame of Reference for Psychology.* New York: Harper & Brothers Publishers, 1949.

Social Science Research Council. Committee on Linguistics and Psychology. *Psycholinguistics: A Survey of Theory and Research Problems.* Report of the 1953 Summer Seminar Sponsored by the Committee on Linguistics and Psychology of the Social Science Research Council, by John B. Carroll, Charles E. Osgood, ed., and Thomas A. Sebeok, assoc. ed. With a foreword by John W. Gardner. Indiana University Publications in Anthropology and Linguistics, Memoir 10. Baltimore, Maryland: Waverly Press, 1954.

Society for the Psychological Study of Social Issues. *The Journal of Social Issues,* Special Issue on Problems of Bilingualism, Vol. XXIII, No. 2 (April, 1967).

Somerville (New Jersey) Public Schools. *Evaluation of the Effect of Foreign Language Study in the Elementary School Upon Achievement in the High School*: Final Report. Somerville, New Jersey: Somerville Public Schools, July 1962. NDEA Title VI Research Project No. SAE 9516, U.S., Department of Health, Education, and Welfare, U.S. Office of Education.

Southwest Council of Foreign Language Teachers. Second Annual Conference, November 13, 1965. *Reports: Our Bilingual: Social and Psychological Barriers, Linguistic and Pedagogical Barriers.* El Paso, Texas: Southwest Council of Foreign Language Teachers, 1965.

————. "A Resolution Concerning the Education of Bilingual Children," Newsletter, No. 1.

————. Third Annual Conference, November 4–5, 1966. *Reports: Bilin-*

gualism. Edited by Charles Stubing. El Paso, Texas: Southwest Council of Foreign Language Teachers, 1966.

————. Fourth Annual Conference, November 10–11, 1967. *Reports: Bilingual Education: Research and Teaching.* Edited by Chester Christian. El Paso, Texas: Southwest Council of Foreign Language Teachers, 1967.

Soviet Education, Vol. II, No. 11 (September, 1960).

Soviet Weekly, No. 1011, June 15, 1961.

Sparkman, Lee, ed. *Culture in the FLES Program.* No. 1769. Philadelphia and New York: Chilton Books, Educational Division, 1966.

"Special Report: FLES Abandoned in Arlington." *Bulletin of the Modern Foreign Language Association of Virginia,* Vol. XX, No. 2 (April, 1964).

Stabler, Ernest, ed. *The Education of the Secondary School Teacher.* Middletown, Connecticut: Wesleyan University Press. 1962.

Starr, Wilmarth H. "Foreign-Language Teaching and Intercultural Understanding." *School and Society,* March 19, 1955.

————. "MLA Foreign Language Proficiency Tests for Teachers and Advanced Students." *PMLA,* Vol. LXXII, No. 4, Part 2 (September, 1962).

Stern, H. H. "A Foreign Language in the Primary School." Paper read at the International Conference on Modern Foreign Language Teaching in West Berlin, September, 1964. Included in Modern Language Association *FLES Packet.*

————. *Foreign Languages in Primary Education: The Teaching of Foreign or Second Languages to Younger Children.* Report on an International Meeting of Experts, April 9–14, 1962. New rev. ed. Series International Studies in Education. London: Oxford University Press, 1967.

Strickland, Ruth Gertrude. *The Language Arts in the Elementary School.* 2nd ed. Boston: D. C. Heath and Company, 1957.

Tebbel, John. "Newest TV Boom: Spanish-Language Stations." *Saturday Review,* June 8, 1968.

Texas. Department of Education. *Tentative Course of Study for the Teaching of Spanish in Grades 3 to 8 Inclusive.* Bulletin No. 426. Austin: Texas Department of Education, 1943.

Texas Education Agency. Regional Educational Agencies Project in International Education. *Addresses and Reports Presented at the Conference on Development of Bilingualism in Children of Varying Linguistic and Cultural Heritages,* January 31–February 3, 1967. Austin: Texas Education Agency, 1967.

Texas Foreign Language Association. "Foreign Language Teacher Preparation in New Hampshire." *Texas Foreign Language Association Bulletin,* Vol. III, No. 4 (November, 1961).

————. "Proficiency Tests in Pennsylvania." *Texas Foreign Language Association Bulletin*, Vol. IV, No. 3 (October, 1962).

————. "Why I speack spanish." *Texas Foreign Language Association Bulletin*, Vol. V, No. 4 (December, 1963).

Thompson, Elizabeth Engle, and Arthur E. Hamalainen. *Foreign Language Teaching in Elementary Schools: An Examination of Current Practices*. Washington, D.C.: National Education Association, Association for Supervision and Curriculum Development, 1958.

Thonis, Eleanor Wall. *Bilingual Education for Mexican-American Children: An Experiment in the Marysville Joint Unified School District, October 1966–June 1967*. Marysville, California: Marysville Joint Unified School District, September 30, 1967.

Tomb, J. W. "On the Intuitive Capacity of Children to Understand Spoken Languages." *British Journal of Psychology*, Vol. XVI, Part I (July, 1925).

Torrenté, Henry de. "The Role of Language in the Development of Swiss National Consciousness." *PMLA*, Vol. LXXII, No. 2 (April, 1957).

Treviño, Bertha Alicia Gámez. "An Analysis of the Effectiveness of a Bilingual Program in the Teaching of Mathematics in the Primary Grades." Unpublished Ph.D. Dissertation, The University of Texas at Austin, January, 1968.

Twaddell, Freeman. SEE Holt, Rinehart and Winston Series.

United Kingdom. Ministry of Education. Central Advisory Council for Education (Wales). *The Place of Welsh and English in the Schools of Wales*. London: Her Majesty's Stationery Office, 1953.

United Kingdom. National Commission for UNESCO. *Bilingualism in Education*. Report on an International Seminar, Aberystwyth, Wales, August 20–September 2, 1960. London: Her Majesty's Stationery Office, 1965.

United Nations. Economic, Scientific, and Cultural Organization. "Second Language Teaching in Primary and Secondary Schools." *Education Abstracts*, Vol. XIII, No. 3 (1961).

————. *The Other Man's Language*. Tape recording prepared after the UNESCO Conference in Ceylon, August 1953. Paris: UNESCO, [1954].

————. *The Use of Vernacular Languages in Education*. Monographs on Fundamental Education, VIII. Paris: UNESCO, 1953.

United Nations. Statistical Office. *Monthly Bulletin of Statistics*, Vol. XX, No. 6 (June, 1966).

United States. Army. Headquarters, 45 Army Dependents' Education Group. *Statistical Report*, March 15, 1963.

United States. Bureau of Education. *Report of the Committee on Secondary School Studies* (Committee of Ten, appointed in 1892 by the National Education Association). Washington, D.C.: U.S. Government Printing Office, 1893.

United States. Congress. Senate. Committee on Labor and Public Welfare. *Bilingual Education. Hearings* before the Special Subcommittee on Bilingual Education of the Committee on Labor and Public Welfare, Senate, on S. 428 Parts 1 and 2. 90th Cong., 1st sess., 1967.

United States. Department of Commerce. "Investments in Latin America Foster Economic Progress." *Foreign Commerce Weekly,* October 17, 1960.

————. Bureau of the Census. *Historical Statistics of the United States, 1789–1945.* Washington, D.C.: U.S. Government Printing Office, 1949. A supplement to the *Statistical Abstract of the United States,* prepared with the cooperation of the Social Science Research Council.

————. *Historical Statistics of the United States, Colonial Time to 1957: A Statistical Abstract Supplement.* Washington, D.C.: U.S. Government Printing Office, 1960. Prepared with the cooperation of the Social Science Research Council.

————. *United States Census of Population, 1960,* Vol. I, *Characteristics of the Population,* pt. 34: New York, *Detailed Characteristics*; pt. 53: *Puerto Ricans in the United States.* Washington, D.C.: U.S. Government Printing Office, 1960.

————. *Statistical Abstracts of the United States.* Washington, D.C.: U.S. Government Printing Office, 1963, 1965, 1966.

————. *The Statistical History of the United States from Colonial Times to the Present.* Stamford, Connecticut: Fairfield Publishers, Inc., 1965. Prepared with the cooperation of the Social Science Research Council. A Companion Volume to *U.S. Deskbook of Facts and Statistics,* with Interrelating Statistical Series. Government Title: *Statistical Abstract of U.S.*

United States. Department of Health, Education, and Welfare. Office of Education. *Your Exchange Teacher from Abroad.* Publication No. OE–14028. Washington, D.C.: U.S. Government Printing Office, [1960].

United States. Department of State. Foreign Service Institute. *Human Nature at Home and Abroad: A Guide to the Understanding of Human Behavior.* Washington, D.C.: U.S. Government Printing Office, 1953.

United States Digest of Educational Statistics. Washington, D.C.: U.S. Government Printing Office, 1965.

University College of Wales. Faculty of Education. Llyfryddiaeth Dwyieitheg. *Bilingualism: A Bibliography with Special Reference to Wales.* Pamphlet No. 7. Aberystwyth: Faculty of Education of the University College of Wales, 1960.

The University of the State of New York. *French for Elementary Schools:*

A Teaching Guide. Albany, New York: The State Education Department, Bureau of Elementary Curriculum Development, 1966.

Valette, Rebecca M. *Modern Language Testing: A Handbook*. New York: Harcourt, Brace, & World, Inc., 1967.

Vamos, Mara, and John Harmon. *Modern Foreign Language Facilities in Colleges and Universities, 1959–1960*. New York: The Modern Language Association of America, 1960.

————, Harry Margulis, and Frank White. "Modern Foreign Language Enrollments in Four-Year Accredited Colleges and Universities, Fall 1958 and Fall 1959." In *Reports of Surveys and Studies in the Teaching of Modern Foreign Languages, 1959–1961*. New York: The Modern Language Association of America, 1961.

Vocolo, Joseph M. "The Effect of Foreign Language Study in the Elementary School Upon Achievement in the Same Foreign Language in the High School." *The Modern Language Journal*, Vol. LI, No. 8 (December, 1967).

Wall, W. D. *Education and Mental Health: A Report Based Upon the Work of a European Conference Called by UNESCO at the Musée Pédagogique in Paris, November–December, 1952*. Problems in Education Series, No. XI, Education and Mental Health. Paris: UNESCO, 1955.

Walsh, Donald D. *What's What: A List of Useful Terms for the Teacher of Modern Languages*. 2nd ed. New York: The Modern Language Association, February, 1964.

Watts, George B. "The Teaching of French in the United States: A History." *The French Review*, Vol. XXXVII, No. 1 (October, 1963).

Weinreich, Uriel. *Languages in Contact: Findings and Problems*. With a preface by André Martinet. New York: The Linguistic Circle of New York, 1953.

Weir, Ruth Hirsch. *Language in the Crib*. The Hague: Mouton & Co., 1962.

White, Emilie Margaret, Chairman, Marjorie Johnston, Ralph M. Perry, Josette E. Spink. "Report on Status of and Practices in the Teaching of Foreign Language in the Public Elementary Schools of the United States." *The Modern Language Journal*, Vol. XXXVII, No. 3 (March, 1953).

Whorf, Benjamin Lee. *Language, Thought, and Reality: Selected Writings*. Edited by John B. Carroll. Foreword by Stuart Chase. New York: The Technology Press of the Massachusetts Institute of Technology and John Wiley & Sons, Inc., 1956.

Wicker, James E. "Some Psychological Aspects of the Teaching and Learning of Languages." Unpublished paper for The University of Texas at Austin.

Willbern, Glen. "Foreign Language Enrollments in Public Secondary Schools, 1965." *Foreign Language Annals*, Vol. I, No. 3 (March, 1968).

Wisconsin. State Department of Public Instruction. *Voice of the Wisconsin Foreign Language Teacher, 1962 Curriculum Trends Edition*. Madison: Wisconsin State Department of Public Instruction, 1962.

Woman's Home Companion, May, 1945.

Woodworth, Robert S., and Harold Schlosberg. *Experimental Psychology*. 3rd rev. ed. New York: Holt, Rinehart and Winston, December, 1965.

The World Almanac. New York: *The New York World Telegram*, 1968.

Wylie, Laurence, Elsie M. Fleissner, Juan Marichal, Donald Pitkin, and Ernest J. Simmons. "Six Cultures (French, German, Hispanic, Italian, Luso-Brazilian, Russian): Selective and Annotated Bibliographies." In *Reports of Surveys and Studies in the Teaching of Modern Foreign Languages, 1959–1961*. New York: The Modern Language Association of America, 1961.

"Yankees Who Don't Go Home," *Business Week*, July 24, 1965, pp. 48–52.

York (Pennsylvania) Public Schools, "York Schools Pioneer in Elementary French." *Spotlight on Schools*, Vol. VII, No. 5 (May, 1964).

Zeydel, Edwin H. "The Teaching of German in the United States from Colonial Times to the Present." In *Reports of Surveys and Studies in the Teaching of Modern Foreign Languages, 1959–1961*. New York: The Modern Language Association of America, 1961.